Revitalizing Industrial Growth in Pakistan

**DIRECTIONS IN DEVELOPMENT**
Private Sector Development

# Revitalizing Industrial Growth in Pakistan

## Trade, Infrastructure, and Environmental Performance

Ernesto Sánchez-Triana, Dan Biller, Ijaz Nabi, Leonard Ortolano, Ghazal Dezfuli, Javaid Afzal, and Santiago Enriquez

**WORLD BANK GROUP**
Washington, D.C.

ISBN (paper): 978-1-4648-0028-3
ISBN (electronic): 978-1-4648-0029-0
DOI: 10.1596/978-1-4648-0028-3

*Cover photo:* © danishkhan / iStock. Used with permission. Further permission required for reuse.

**Library of Congress Cataloging-in-Publication Data has been requested.**

*In memory of Gajanand Pathmanathan*

# Contents

## Boxes

## Figures

## Maps

## Tables

# Foreword

How can Pakistan maintain steady medium-term economic growth? The answer to that question has eluded the country's policy makers for some time. Part of the answer lies in setting the right conditions for manufacturing to blossom and reach its full potential. This potential exists because of Pakistan's growing labor force and rising urbanization and connectivity. Yet, Pakistan's largely low-skilled labor force, poor commercial environment, lack of adequate infrastructure, and its failure to diversify production and climb up the technology ladder prevent this potential from becoming reality. Manufacturing remains heavily focused on low value-added consumer products, which do not attract investors. Though Pakistan's manufacturing sector is improving, it has room to expand its contribution to gross domestic product (GDP) while curtailing the public "bads" associated with an unemployed labor force, such as social conflict and the need for widespread social assistance. Likewise, negative impacts often associated with industrial expansion, such as pollution and congestion, need to be mitigated with a combination of economic instruments, public participation, industrial voluntary actions, infrastructure investments, and command and control regulations. This book addresses ways in which Pakistan can revitalize its manufacturing and promote agglomeration economies, thereby increasing manufacturing's contribution to medium-term growth and to job creation. Such revitalization is sorely needed to place the country on a sustained path of high economic growth by means of reducing the cost of doing business, improving the investment climate, and strengthening institutions.

As in other South Asian countries, Pakistan is experiencing a shift from an agriculture-based to a service-based economy. However, unlike East Asia—where manufacturing has had an increasing role in recent decades, moving East Asia further along the path to becoming largely middle income—South Asia has seen manufacturing's share of GDP stagnate since 1980 in all major economies except Bangladesh. For Pakistan, trends are complicated by declining growth since 1960 and overreliance on financial inflows (aid and worker's remittances). At the same time, a young and largely low-skilled unemployed labor force has also been rising. Part of the solution is for Pakistan to follow China's example by engaging in low-skilled labor-intensive manufacturing, filling the gap left behind as China moves up the value chain with its increasingly sophisticated labor force and amid pressure from increasing wages. Yet, it is equally important for Pakistan to join China in moving up the value chain.

This book examines the ways in which Pakistan can encourage and assist its private sector to fill the void in low-skilled labor-intensive manufacturing left by other economies—and do so without promoting domestic rent-seeking behavior. This report is organized as follows. An overview provides the context of manufacturing in the broad Pakistani economy. Chapter 1 introduces an industrial vision for Pakistan. Chapter 2 discusses the industrial sector's importance and its recent contributions to the country's economic development. Chapter 3 establishes the link between Pakistan's spatial transformation and manufacturing. The next two chapters focus on skills development (chapter 4) and on trade and competitiveness (chapter 5). Chapter 6 analyzes the importance of infrastructure modernization to boost manufacturing growth, and chapter 7 underscores the environmental issues related to industrial expansion. Chapter 8 concludes the report by looking at how existing institutions can foster a sustainable industrialization process in the country.

The importance of jolting Pakistan's manufacturing into increasing its share of GDP has been recognized early on by the country's new political administration. To increase the chances of success, appropriate actions will need to come from different actors in government, the private sector, and civil society. We hope this book stimulates dialogue on revitalizing manufacturing in Pakistan by stimulating green industrial growth in the country through appropriate reforms and investments.

John Henry Stein
*Sector Director*
*South Asia Sustainable Development*
*The World Bank*

# Acknowledgments

This book is a result of the fruitful collaboration between the Pakistan Ministry of Industries and Production (MoIP) and the World Bank.

A team led by Ernesto Sánchez-Triana prepared this report. The core team included Dan Biller, Ijaz Nabi, Leonard Ortolano, Ghazal Dezfuli, Javaid Afzal (co-TTL), Santiago Enriquez, Ashma Basnyat, Hammad Raza, Cecilia Belita, Marie Florence Elvie, Jeff Lewis, and Rahul Kanakia. The extended team included Kulsum Ahmad, Karin Kemper, Catalina Marulanda, Chaudhary Laiq Ali, Luis Miglino, Susan Rebellon, Mosuf Ali, Salman Shah, Azzer Uddin Khan, and the Lahore University of Management Sciences. Valuable guidance was provided by the peer reviewers: Doerte Doemeland, John Redwood, Yewande Aramide Awe, and Helena Naber. Several colleagues also provided helpful advice and detailed comments, particularly Luis Alberto Andres, Charles Joseph Cormier, Asif Faiz, Eric Manes, Ivan Rossignol, John Speakman, Jose R. Lopez-Calix, Sohail Malik, Mudassar Imran, and Javed Burki.

The authors are also thankful for the support of the World Bank management team and the Pakistan country office, including Rachid Benmessaoud (Country Director), John Henry Stein, Gajanand Pathmanathan, Eugenia Marinova, Karin Kemper, Herbert Acquay, and Maria Correia. The authors extend their sincere thanks and appreciation to Stan Wanat and Ashma Basnyat for their support preparing and editing the manuscript, and to Cecilia Belita, Afzal Mahmood, Sada Hussain, and Marie Florence Elvie for their administrative support. Jeff Lecksell amended the maps to conform to World Bank guidelines.

The Government of Pakistan, mainly through the MoIP, provided key feedback during the preparation of the study and participated actively in the production of diverse parts of the report. The task team is indebted to the Joint Secretary of MoIP, Ms. Shaista Sohail, for her leadership, passion, and perseverance. Particularly important was the contribution of the following government officials: Aziz Ahmed Bilour, Abdul Ghaffar Soomro, Shahab Anwar Khawaja, Niaz Ahmad Butt, and Samar Mobarak Mand. A multisectoral High Level Committee, including representatives from the private sector, academia, and nongovernmental organizations, provided crucial insights and critical feedback to key inputs to this report.

The team is particularly grateful to the governments of Australia, Finland, the Netherlands, Norway, and the United Kingdom for their support in funding some of the studies that underpin this report.

# About the Authors

**Ernesto Sánchez-Triana** is Lead Environmental Specialist for the World Bank. He has worked on projects in Afghanistan, Argentina, Bangladesh, Bhutan, Brazil, India, Mexico, Pakistan, and Peru. Prior to joining the Bank in 2002, he worked for the Inter-American Development Bank and served as director of environmental policy at Colombia's National Department of Planning. He has led numerous operations including analytical work on policy options for enhancing the sustainability of industrial development in Pakistan, which served as the basis for this book. Dr. Sánchez-Triana holds MS and PhD degrees from Stanford University and has authored numerous publications on clean production, environmental economics, energy efficiency, environmental policy, organizational learning, poverty assessment, and green growth.

**Dan Biller** is Sector Manager of the Economics Unit in the World Bank's Multilateral Investment Guarantee Agency. Previously, he was sustainable development lead economist for the Bank's South Asia Region, lead economist for the East Asia and Pacific Region, and environment and natural resources program leader at the World Bank Institute. He was also an Organisation for Economic Co-operation and Development senior economist, taught at various universities, and worked with the private sector and governments on infrastructure and mining/hydrocarbon regulatory issues at the Getulio Vargas Foundation, Brazil. His PhD and MS in economics are from the University of Illinois at Urbana-Champaign. He has published extensively on economic development, natural resource and environmental economics, sustainable consumption, urban/rural linkages, infrastructure, climate change, and social development.

**Ijaz Nabi** has worked on World Bank projects involving the Lao People's Democratic Republic, Malaysia, Mexico, Republic of the Union of Myanmar, the Republic of Korea, and Thailand (leading the Bank team during the East Asian financial crisis), and was Manager for Economic Policy, South Asia Region. Since 2009, he has served as Country Director of the Pakistan program at the International Growth Center, a London School of Economics and Oxford University policy research consortium. He is on the economics faculty at Lahore University of Management Sciences and serves as a member of the Prime Minister of Pakistan's Economic Advisory Council and as adviser on economic affairs to the

Chief Minister in Pakistan's Punjab province. Mr. Nabi studied at London School of Economics and Warwick University.

**Leonard Ortolano** is UPS Foundation Professor of Civil Engineering at Stanford University. He is a specialist in environmental and water resources planning, with a focus on the design and implementation of environmental policies and programs. He has also worked on aspects of corporate environmental management, including corporate responses to regulations on the management of hazardous chemicals. Independent of his Stanford University duties, Dr. Ortolano has worked on several projects related to linkages between environmental management and economic development in Bangladesh, India, and Pakistan. His most recent work has concerned the use and dissemination of cleaner production methods in Pakistan's industrial sector.

**Ghazal Dezfuli** holds a BA degree in economics and government from Bowdoin College, and a master of public policy degree from the University of Chicago. Since 2009, she has been working at the World Bank as a consultant in the South Asia Social, Environment, and Water Resources Unit in Washington, DC, conducting research on a variety of environmental and social issues.

**Javaid Afzal** is a Senior Environmental Specialist at the World Bank's Islamabad office. His responsibilities include moving the environment development agenda forward with client government agencies. He also task manages operations in water resources and the environment and provides environmental safeguards support for the Bank's South Asia Region. Previously, he worked at a leading consulting company in Pakistan. He holds a PhD in water resources management from Cranfield University, U.K., and master's and bachelor's degrees in agricultural engineering from the University of Agriculture, Faisalabad, Pakistan. Dr. Afzal has published in a number of peer-reviewed journals.

**Santiago Enriquez** is an international consultant with more than 15 years of experience in the design, implementation, and evaluation of policies relating to the environment, conservation, and climate change. He has developed analytical work for the World Bank, the United States Agency for International Development, and the Inter-American Development Bank. From 1998 to 2002, Mr. Enriquez worked at the International Affairs Unit of Mexico's Ministry of Environment and Natural Resources. Mr. Enriquez holds a master's degree in public policy from the Harvard Kennedy School.

# Abbreviations

| | |
|---|---|
| ADB | Asian Development Bank |
| BBSYDP | Benazir Bhutto Shaheed Youth Development Program |
| BISP | Benazir Income Support Programme |
| BLL | blood lead level |
| BOD | biochemical oxygen demand |
| BOI | Board of Investors |
| BOT | build-operate-transfer |
| BRAC | formerly known as Bangladesh Rehabilitation Assistance Committee, then as the Bangladesh Rural Advancement Committee |
| BXP | border crossing point |
| CAA | Civil Aviation Authority |
| CDR | central data repository |
| CETP | common effluent treatment plant |
| CP | cleaner production |
| CPC | cleaner production center |
| ECO | Economic Cooperation Organization |
| EG | Ellison and Glaeser |
| EIA | Environmental Impact Assessment |
| EMS | environmental management system |
| EPA | Environmental Protection Agency |
| ET | environmental tribunal |
| EU | European Union |
| FDI | foreign direct investment |
| GCI | Global Competitiveness Index |
| GDP | gross domestic product |
| GFCF | gross fixed capital formulation |
| GHG | greenhouse gas |
| GoP | Government of Pakistan |
| GT | Grand Trunk |

| | |
|---|---|
| HIV/AIDS | human immunodeficiency virus/acquired immune deficiency syndrome |
| HLC | High Level Committee |
| IEM | industrial environmental management |
| ILO | International Labour Organization |
| IPP | independent power producers |
| IRU | International Road Transport Union |
| ISO | International Organization for Standardization |
| IT | information technology |
| KDLB | Karachi Dock Labor Board |
| KP | Khyber Pakhtunkhwa |
| KPT | Karachi Port Trust |
| LPI | Logistics Performance Index |
| LUMS | Lahore University of Management Sciences |
| MCC | Ministry of Climate Change |
| MFN | most favored nation |
| MoE | Ministry of Environment |
| MoIP | Ministry of Industries and Production |
| MW | megawatt |
| NAVTTC | National Vocational and Technical Training Commission |
| NEC | National Economic Council |
| NEET | not in education, employment, or training |
| NEQS | National Environmental Quality Standards |
| NGO | nongovernmental organization |
| NHA | National Highway Authority |
| NLC | National Logistics Cell |
| NLTA | Non-Lending Technical Assistance |
| NTB | non-tariff barrier |
| NTC | National Trade Corridor |
| NTCTF | National Trade Corridor Task Force |
| PACCS | Pakistan Customs Computerized System |
| PAD | Product Appraisal Document |
| Pak-EPA | Pakistan Environmental Protection Agency |
| Pb | lead |
| PBTE | Punjab Board of Technical Education |
| PEPA | Pakistan Environmental Protection Act of 1997 |
| PEPC | Pakistan Environmental Protection Council |
| PIA | Pakistan International Airline Corporation |
| PM | particulate matter |

| | |
|---|---|
| PNC-ICC | Pakistan National Committee of the International Chamber of Commerce |
| ppm | parts per million |
| PPP | public-private partnership |
| PROPER | Indonesia's Program for Pollution Control, Evaluation, and Rating |
| PSDF | Punjab Skills Development Fund |
| PSQCA | Pakistan Standards and Quality Control Authority |
| RCA | revealed comparative advantage |
| RCT | randomized control trial |
| REACH | Regulation, Evaluation, Authorization, and Restriction of Chemicals |
| Rs | Pakistani rupees (also abbreviated as "PRs") |
| SD | standard deviation |
| SME | small and medium enterprise |
| SMEDA | Small and Medium Enterprises Development Authority |
| SPS | sanitary and phytosanitary |
| SRO | statutory regulatory order |
| TAP | Turkmenistan-Afghanistan-Pakistan |
| TBT | technical barriers to trade |
| TEU | 20-foot equivalent unit |
| TEVTA | Technical Education and Vocational Training Authority |
| TIR | international transport of goods |
| TVET | technical and vocational education training |
| WHO | World Health Organization |
| WTO | World Trade Organization |

# Overview

## Introduction

Like other countries in South Asia, Pakistan experienced a shift from an agriculture-based economy to a service-based one. As opposed to East Asia, where manufacturing has played a leading role at different stages of economic development, South Asia's manufacturing share of gross domestic product (GDP) has remained stagnant since 1980 in all major economies except Bangladesh. The fall of agriculture has been largely picked up by services. In countries like India, where the economy has been experiencing healthy rates of growth for the past quarter of a century, a lackluster manufacturing sector may not translate to a major concern. For Pakistan, the situation is different. The country's growth trend has been declining since 1960 and has largely been dependent on financial inflows via aid. Yet, a young and largely low-skilled labor force including women has been increasing. Following in the footsteps of China by engaging in low-skilled labor, intensive manufacturing is part of the solution to bring the country to the path of increasing medium-term growth and shared prosperity. As China moves up the value chain with an increasingly sophisticated labor force and increasing wages, the gap left behind could be filled by Pakistan, just as Bangladesh is moving towards this direction.

During the previous administration (2008–13), Pakistan's development efforts were guided by the 2011 *Framework for Economic Growth* (GoP 2011). The 2011 Framework lays out the growth strategy drafted by Pakistan's Planning Commission and identifies the strategic actions needed to create a prosperous, industrialized Pakistan through rapid and sustainable development. According to the Framework, industrialization has the potential to become a dynamic engine of economic growth and make significant contributions to meeting Pakistan's economic and human development goals. Pakistan's new administration is in its early stages, but it has already indicated the importance it places on sustained inclusive growth. In its Vision 2025, Pakistan's Planning Commission puts energy security, private sector led growth, the modernization of existing infrastructure and creation of state-of-the-art new infrastructure, and improving competitiveness in industry and trade, among a number of other themes, at the center of its development strategy (GoP 2013).

One of several items that the Government of Pakistan (GoP) considers critical for sustained economic growth is the "liberalization of Pakistan's trade and investment regime" (GoP 2011, 12). Indeed, the 2011 Framework emphasizes the centrality of industry in achieving economic and human development goals, and the current Vision 2025 and its approach paper continue to recognize this centrality. Both current and previous administrations recognize that accelerating industrialization will require reducing the cost of doing business and creating an incentive structure designed to achieve a competitive, dynamic, and export-driven industrial sector capable of providing employment to the growing labor force. The GoP also recognizes that competing in global markets requires a socially and environmentally sustainable industrialization strategy. To that end, the GoP requested inputs from the World Bank. The four main inputs for a sustainable industrial growth in Pakistan discussed in this book are

- macroeconomic stability and sectoral policies that support industrial competitiveness;
- upgraded trade facilitation and infrastructure (particularly transport and energy infrastructure) in order to address some of the spatial aspects of industrialization;
- greening of Pakistan's industrial sector to enhance international competitiveness; and
- strong institutions for effective industrialization initiatives, including those for small and medium enterprises.

These complementary areas were selected because they operate on the nexus of feedback between sustainability and competitiveness. Macroeconomic stability allows firms and governments to make long-term plans, including investments in cleaner production and in infrastructure, such as transport and energy infrastructure. Improved transport infrastructure will encourage more economically efficient transport modalities that will open access to Chinese and Iranian markets. Additionally, improved transport infrastructure will lower the environmental costs of production, thus making Pakistan a more attractive export partner for nations and firms that have made a commitment to green production. Improved transport infrastructure will also provide new opportunities to strengthen existing areas of high activity—industrial clusters—and thereby foster economies of scale. In these industrial clusters, clean production initiatives will result in lower production costs and increased international competitiveness. Finally, these growing industrial clusters will create a growing need for a strong set of institutions to implement industrialization initiatives, such as environmental management agencies to control pollution and cleaner production centers (CPCs) to increase domestic awareness of international environmental standards.

In 2009, a High Level Committee (HLC) was established by the Ministry of Industries and Production (MoIP) representing the federal government, the four provincial governments, academia, nongovernmental organizations, and industry. The HLC developed the Terms of Reference for Non-Lending Technical Assistance–(NLTA) supported analytical work, reviewed the recommendations, and held discussions with key chambers of commerce and industry in the major cities. The HLC then commissioned a series of reports by leading local and international experts on the four principal elements of the sustainable industrialization strategy. The findings of these reports were discussed as part of a broad nationwide consultation process that engaged multiple stakeholders and resulted in the elaboration of the draft National Industrial Development Policy aiming to modernize the country's industrial sector and strengthen productivity, industrial competitiveness, and environmental sustainability in an increasingly open and specialized trading regime. This overview summarizes the analytical work in the NLTA-supported reports. The chapters making up this book provide detail regarding that analytical work.

A review of recent industrial performance (chapter 1) shows that despite a promising start in the 1960s, Pakistan's industry has not been the engine of economic growth and high-productivity employment expected in government development visions. Boom-bust cycles of GDP growth have affected industrial outcomes. Fueled by remittances and a consumption boom, GDP grew at above 7 percent in 2002–06; it then fell to 4 percent in 2008 and 2 percent in 2009, in part because of the global economic crisis. In keeping with this trend, large-scale manufacturing surged to a growth rate of 20 percent in 2005, followed by a sharp contraction reflecting weakening aggregate demand as well as severe power shortages and deteriorating security.

Various measures of productivity underscore industry's weak international competitiveness. Total factor productivity growth in manufacturing was 1.64 percent during the 1990s and increased by only 0.9 percent in 1998–2007. Labor productivity growth in 1990–2006 was also sluggish at 1.29 percent compared to 9 percent in China and 3.4 percent in India. Globally, rapid growth in manufacturing exports in 1990–2008 allowed developing countries to gain a sizeable share of the world market. India, Malaysia, and Thailand more than doubled their share in world exports (increasing it by 185 percent on average). Pakistan's share, on the other hand, declined from 0.18 percent of world exports to 0.15 percent over this period. Nor have Pakistan's exports moved up the value chain even in textiles, where the country has a comparative advantage. Furthermore, Pakistan's exports are concentrated in products (textiles and clothing) whose share in world exports is declining, thus reflecting poor positioning for the future.

One consequence of the weak international competitiveness of Pakistan's industry is that its share in GDP has stagnated at about 25 percent. Accounting for over 50 percent of GDP, services now dominate the economy. A large part of the labor force (more than 40 percent) is still employed in agriculture; however, industry, which has the highest value added, has the lowest share of total employment (20 percent). This is a matter of concern, since the movement of labor from low productivity (agriculture) to relatively high productivity sectors (such as manufacturing) contributes to the surplus that spurs growth and improved living standards for workers.

## Implement Macroeconomic and Sectoral Policies for Strengthening Industrial Competitiveness

Industry's weaknesses have been accentuated by an economic management stance that favors consumption over both savings and investment in manufacturing, as exhibited in a host of policies regarding macro and sectoral pricing and public expenditures. Rapid growth of remittances and concessionary development assistance has allowed Pakistan to build up reserves while maintaining a large trade deficit. The exchange-rate management stance has fueled consumption-led growth, appreciated the equilibrium exchange rate, and may well be contributing to the "Dutch Disease" problem of declining international competiveness of manufactured exports (Acosta, Lartey, and Mandelman 2007a, 2007b; Montiel 2006). Consistent with the consumption-led growth-policy stance, personal loans in 2001–07 expanded most rapidly in the lending portfolios of financial institutions compared with loans to manufacturing establishments. The acute energy shortage also hits manufacturing firms the hardest. Residential households receive preference in both energy rationing and pricing. The manufacturing sector also bears a disproportionate burden of taxation, diverting investment to the more lightly taxed (or non-taxed) agriculture, service, and construction sectors. Poor education standards result in high costs for training workers needed by firms. Security incidents that disrupt commuting by workers and freight also affect manufacturing firms more than other sectors.

Recent modifications in trade policy have reversed the liberalization program that had virtually eliminated traditional quantitative restrictions and reduced and simplified import tariffs. Starting in 2006/07, there has also been an increase in the maximum level, dispersion, and complexity of customs duties. In 2008, regulatory duties were imposed on top of customs duties. Antidumping, which started in a small way in 2002, has expanded rapidly since 2008/09. Statutory regulatory orders (SROs), providing exemptions or partial exemptions, have made a strong comeback, with half the tariff lines subjected to SROs benefiting specific firms and inputs. Preferential trade agreements with China, Sri Lanka, and with seven other countries (Afghanistan, Bangladesh, Bhutan, India, Maldives, Nepal, and Sri Lanka) under the South Asia Free Trade Agreement have also added complexity to Pakistan's trade policy. Substantial distortions have thus crept back into trade policy, benefiting a few chosen enterprises while eroding the international competitiveness of the vast majority of firms.

Geography endows Pakistan with the potential to reap significant economic gains if it can become a hub for regional trade, which will have spillovers for industrialization and economic growth. To the northeast is China, the world's fastest growing economy and a population of over a billion. China is increasingly engaged in the development of its western frontier that lies close to Pakistan.

To the northwest and west are the resource-rich economies of Central Asia and the Islamic Republic of Iran, which are eager to combine their mineral wealth with skills to generate higher income for their citizens. To the east is India growing at 8 percent per annum (very different from the so-called Hindu rate of growth of 3 percent) with large pools of skilled labor and savings seeking gainful employment and investment avenues. In order to reap economic benefits in this context of growing opportunities, Pakistan needs to again play its historical role of a connector of markets that lie to the north (China) and west (Central Asia and the Islamic Republic of Iran), to those in the east (India). This requires liberalizing the highly restricted trade with India that has stunted cross-border legal commerce, encouraged smuggling, and prevented investment and technology exchange between the two countries. Rigorous analytical work, including a seminal report by Pakistan's Ministry of Commerce, supports such a move (Nabi and Nasim 2001; Naqvi and Nabi 2008).

In this context, the recent announcement granting most favored nation status (MFN) to India is a welcome development. However, this needs to be followed up with practical steps for an efficient payment system; a sensible policy that promotes trade but also avoids excessive (and unfair) injury to Pakistan's industry; trade-facilitating government services such as customs and quality-focused non-tariff barriers (NTBs); and transport networks. Most important of all, a sensible visa regime is needed so that all enterprises—and not just the largest—can share the benefits of granting MFN status to India. In addition, India will be looking to transit trade facilities, and Pakistan should seek to attract Indian investment and technology. Given current business practices, NTBs can creep in through any of these trade-facilitating measures and potentially nullify or reduce the benefits of the MFN announcement.

The upshot is that the broad policy stance has further accentuated the exchange-rate-driven Dutch Disease problem for manufacturing firms instead of correcting it. Accordingly, the first step towards a strategy for sustainable industrialization is to remove the bias against manufacturing in the broad policy stance. The other steps are modernizing trade facilitation and transportation, managing the environmental damage associated with industrial waste, and strengthening institutions for policy design and enforcement.

## Upgrade Trade Facilitation and Infrastructure

Investment climate surveys and competitiveness indexes consistently point to poor trade logistics and lack of adequate infrastructure, especially for transport and energy, as key bottlenecks to greater international competitiveness of Pakistani firms. A proactive trade and infrastructure policy, therefore, is an appropriate intervention to aid the efforts of Pakistan's industrial sector to move up the value chain and become a large-scale export-driven manufacturing economy that seeks to take on some of the mass-production niches that increasing wages in China are currently freeing up.

Key recommendations for improving trade and infrastructure, and for the reform program proposed for modernizing transport and logistics to strengthen competitiveness of the national economy, include the following:

- *Carrying out a comprehensive package of reforms to unleash the potential of Pakistan's freight transport sector,* which compares poorly with those of competing economies and whose inefficiencies represent 4–6 percent of GDP. Reforms to modernize the sector should prioritize
  - promoting the integration of different modes of transportation, giving preference to railways for long distances, where they are more efficient and sustainable than road transport;
  - redefining the government's role to focus on regulating and attracting private sector investments in the sector, and thereby gradually eliminate current biases that distort the market; and
  - fostering the adoption of new technologies and procedures that add value to the services provided by the trade and transport sectors, including those that help to move from the current focus on bulk cargo to containerized cargo.

- *Adopting a multimodal transport system and modernizing the trucking fleet will help reduce negative environmental and social externalities.* Above all, enhancing the economy-wide benefits of trade and transport reforms, and reducing the adverse impact, require strong environmental and social protection institutions that safeguard the well-being of groups that new investments and policy reforms may adversely affect.

- *Ensuring access, by breaking down trade barriers and improving suboptimal infrastructure,* to the major transport corridors and cross-border markets—especially in Khyber Pakhtunkhwa (KP) and Balochistan, and upper Sindh—in anticipation of greater trans-regional trade flows (with Afghanistan, Central Asia, China, India, and the Islamic Republic of Iran) through these regions following liberalization of trade with India.

- *Strengthening the institutional capacity of infrastructure and environmental agencies for environmental management.* Organizations in Pakistan's infrastructure sectors have limited capacity to address the environmental and social issues that arise during the construction and operation of transport infrastructure. Strengthening their capacity to incorporate environmental and social considerations at the earliest planning stages and address issues as they arise will generate significant benefits for Pakistan's population. Strengthening the capacity of environmental agencies (particularly after the devolution of environmental responsibilities to the provincial governments because of the Eighteenth Constitutional Amendment) should be the utmost priority, particularly as negative environmental externalities of the freight transport sector are already significant.

- *Identifying potential energy sources (both domestic and regional) that can be used to supply consistent power to the industrial sector.* Indeed, the shortages in energy have hit the industrial sector the hardest. The GoP should urgently develop new sources of energy supply to cater to industry, particularly developing cleaner sources of energy as an alternative to its limited gas sources, upgrading existing distribution networks, investing in thermal and hydel (hydroelectric) plants, utilizing coal as an alternative source of energy (as is done in India), and importing gas from neighboring countries.

The economic impact of modernizing the trade and transport sectors will generate a high payoff in terms of strengthening Pakistan's industry, thereby making it more internationally competitive. However, a sustainable industrialization strategy also requires that the potential negative effects of the program be evaluated and mitigation strategies adopted to minimize the impact. To that end, the present analytic work draws on the findings of the parallel *Greening Growth in Pakistan through Transport Sector Reforms: A Strategic Environmental, Poverty, and Social Assessment* (Sánchez-Triana et al. 2013).

## Greening Pakistan's Industrial Sector to Enhance International Competitiveness

The cost of environmental damage from air pollution, toxic waste, and other forms of water pollution can be substantial. Recent studies (Larsen and Strukova 2011; World Bank 2006, 2008) estimate the costs of such environmental degradation, including those associated with environment-related mortality and morbidity, to be as high as 9 percent of GDP. Industry is a major contributor to these costs. Thus, industrial growth that does not recognize costs to the environment and public health overestimates the real industrial contribution to GDP growth and, depending on the severity of the associated pollution, cannot be sustained.

Sustainable industrialization requires measures that promote cleaner production processes to reduce industry's contribution to air and water pollution, and the dumping of toxic solid waste. Furthermore, setting realistic and enforceable environment standards facilitates ISO 14001 certification and, thus, contributes directly to improved international competitiveness. Chapter 4 of this book focuses on the greening of Pakistan's industrial sector and reviews the evidence on industry's contribution to various types of environmental risks; chapter 4 also proposes measures for adopting cleaner production processes together with realistic and enforceable environment standards. Chapter 4 is based on studies completed under the NLTA on "Evaluation of Industrial Environmental Management (IEM) in Pakistan," "Evaluation of IEM in Developing Countries with Extensive IEM Experience," and "Evaluation of Cleaner Production Initiatives in Pakistan."

Industry contributes significantly to water pollution in the country. Thus, Pakistan cannot make significant improvements in ambient water quality without reducing waste from industry. This will require major changes for enterprises, since current treatment facilities are limited to a relatively few common effluent treatment plants (CETPs) that accept wastewater from firms in industrial clusters (for example, the Korangi and Kasur CETPs that treat discharges from tanneries).

Urban air pollution due to fine particulates ($PM_{2.5}$) is likewise a serious problem in Pakistan, as both stationary and mobile sources (many of which are part of the industrial supply chain) contribute to emissions of fine and ultrafine particulate matter. Indoor industrial air pollution is also quite common in tanneries, textile processing, pulp and paper mills, and sugar mills.

In spite of federal environmental regulation since 1983, a significant expansion of regulatory powers in 1997, and further clarification of regulatory powers in 2005, significant implementation gaps remain in the industrial environmental management system, particularly related to implementation of the National Environmental Quality Standards (NEQS). The revision of these standards is essential to make them more realistic and attainable under present conditions in Pakistan. For *water pollution*, the top priority should be given to imposing stringent concentration restrictions on releases of coliform bacteria, heavy metals, and other hazardous substances. A mechanism for enforcing pollution charges (such as the Shams Lakha committee's recommendation in the mid-1990s) is necessary. Clustering of small and medium enterprises (SMEs) to facilitate waste collection and treatment would also be an important measure. Regarding *air pollution*, the primary emphasis should be on reducing levels of $PM_{2.5}$. Rules governing *hazardous waste* have been developed, but need to be enforced. Regulations regarding Environment Impact Assessments (EIAs) also need to be restructured and enforced.

CPCs facilitate the application of an integrated environmental strategy to processes, products, and services to increase efficiency in resource use and to reduce risk to humans and the environment. Three CPCs have already been established (Lahore, Sialkot, and at the national level) and are operating with varying degrees of success. Currently funded by donor assistance, these centers need to be made commercially viable by charging fees for services and expanding their service to a broader range of firms.

Given the presently inadequate capacity of government environmental agencies with respect to enforcement, voluntary instruments such as ISO 14001 certification can play an essential role in improving the environmental performance of manufacturing companies.[1] This is important because many multinational corporations explicitly require their suppliers to be ISO 14001 certified; access to international markets is harder for firms that do not adhere to this standard. To be certified under ISO 14001, a firm must have an environmental management system (EMS) in place that conforms to the ISO 14001 standards, and the EMS must be implemented consistently. The experience with EMS and ISO 14001 certification in Pakistan to date, however, is mixed. In a recent survey, most tanneries, many textiles units, and nearly all sugar mills are not ISO 14001 certified although many have put in place EMS. Pulp and paper mills, and pharmaceutical and fertilizer companies, have EMS and are either ISO 14001 certified or rapidly progressing towards it. By extending clean production standards to the laggards, especially the highly polluting SMEs, progress towards ISO 14001 can be hastened for enhanced international competitiveness.

An NLTA-funded survey to assess firms' attitudes towards cleaner production revealed the unrealistic stringency of Pakistan's current NEQS, as well as the lack of skilled professional staff to be hired by both firms and enforcing authorities, and the absence of common treatment facilities as major reasons for noncompliance and slow progress towards ISO 14001 certification.

## Develop Strong Institutions for Effective Industrialization Initiatives, Including Those for Small and Medium Enterprises

The implementation of a strategy for sustainable industrialization requires institutions that function well. Recent literature (Rodrik 2004, 5) argues that there are significant market failures in the early stages of development due to, "information externalities entailed in discovering the cost structure of an economy, and coordination externalities in the presence of scale economies." These result in disincentives for entrepreneurs to search for profitable opportunities (Auerswald and Malik 2011) and retard industrial development. A possible solution is the East Asian model, specifically that of the Republic of Korea (Rodrik, Grossman, and Norman 1995), which requires a committed modern civil service and institutions that function well for policy formulation and implementation. An assessment of the quality of civil services is beyond the scope of this overview, but chapter 5 focuses on institutions that would aid the formulation and implementation of a strategy for sustainable industrialization in Pakistan.

Pakistan's MoIP, in its seminal 2005 report, *Towards a Prosperous Pakistan: A Strategy for Rapid Industrial Growth*, makes the best case for *effective policy coordination* at the level of the federal government. MoIP recognizes, as does this book, that many of the recommended policies for rapid industrial development do not fall directly under the purview of the MoIP. MoIP needs to enhance capacity (or augment it as needed by collaborating with local/international universities/research centers) to play its vital role as an advocate for industry at both the federal and provincial levels. The Cabinet and—given the Eighteenth Amendment to the Constitution that empowers the provinces—the National Economic Council (NEC) have to sanction this role. A critical capacity is the ability to engage with the private sector to identify crucial policy reforms (for example, exchange rate policy, credit allocation, energy pricing, tax rates, and tariff structure) needed to establish a level playing field for industry and lower the costs of doing business. Improved capacity to dialogue with the private sector is also necessary in order to prioritize public investment, especially in times of fiscal austerity, and leverage public-private partnership in infrastructure provision.

Recent developments have likewise made it imperative for MoIP to interact with provincial governments for successful implementation of the strategy for sustainable industrialization. Starting in 2004, provincial governments, in partnership with multilateral donors and especially the World Bank, have started to develop provincial "visions" for economic development. Industrial growth for high productivity employment is an important objective in all provincial visions. The other important recent development is the Eighteenth Amendment to the Constitution. Abolishing the concurrent list and increasing the provincial share taken together have empowered the provinces, which are now expected to take on the primary responsibility for delivering on the development objectives.

These developments will further strengthen the demand for regional balance in infrastructure provision for industry. While this is a welcome development, provincial industrialization has to be weighed against the economies of scale that come from the agglomeration of industrial activity in a few clusters. Striking the right balance to prioritize infrastructure investment in times of fiscal tightening is a major challenge and one that the MoIP will need to take up at the NEC, chaired by the Prime Minister, with provincial chief ministers as members, along with their respective economic teams. MoIP will have to set the agenda on spatial dimensions of sustainable industrialization at the NEC, in close coordination with provincial industries departments. MoIP will need to develop capacity to do this effectively.

The GoP views SMEs as major drivers of growth in Pakistan (GoP 2008, 8). They employ 80 percent of the non-agricultural labor force, and account for 40 percent of GDP and 25 percent of manufactured exports.[2] However, their small size—87 percent of manufacturing SMEs have five or fewer employees—poses problems of access to input and output markets. In addition, there is a lack of proper infrastructure for SMEs to operate with, and there is a lack of supply of skilled workers in Pakistan for them to employ. SMEs face market constraints in the form of lack of vendors, and limited access to foreign and many local markets. The Small and Medium Enterprises Development Authority (SMEDA) does not seem to have played its role in helping remove these constraints. Overall, its ratings in these areas have been low.

An assessment was conducted of SMEDA as part of the analytical work undertaken for this NLTA. A number of recommendations have been made to improve SMEDA's functioning. These include

- setting comprehensive goals and targets for SMEDA's board of directors to achieve over the next five years,
- authorizing and funding SMEDA to create a new organizational development plan in line with its goals and targets,
- restructuring SMEDA to enable it to develop a favorable policy environment for SMEs, and
- providing a budget that allows SMEDA to meet its goals and targets.

The Eighteenth Amendment to Pakistan's Constitution requires devolution of major responsibilities for environmental management to subnational governments, which will have significant implications for environmental quality management. In Pakistan, delegation of environmental functions from the federal to provincial governments is comprehensive, and it has empowered provincial environmental protection agencies (EPAs) to address most environmental issues in the provinces. Because of this decentralization, the sphere of operation of each provincial EPA increased considerably. However, many environmental issues cut across geographical boundaries, and systematized mechanisms for inter-sectoral coordination to address cross-cutting issues and harmonize common interventions are needed for effective decentralization. Without adequate coordination, decentralization can lead to substantial differences in environmental quality across regions.

On October 26, 2011, the Prime Minister announced creation of the Ministry of Disaster Management at the federal level, which became the Ministry of Climate Change (MCC) in early 2012. All functions relating to environmental management, which were under the purview of the Ministry of Environment before the Eighteenth Amendment to the Constitution, were recombined and assigned to this new ministry. Excepted from the Ministry of Environment's purview were the functions under the Pakistan Forest Institute and the National Energy Conservation Center. In June 2013, the MCC was downgraded from a ministry to a division and more than 60 percent of its budget was cut. The division has a clear mandate to carry out key environmental tasks, including coordination of international protocols, environmental protection/management across the country, and disaster management; however, its new status and limited resources raise questions about the organization's capacity to fulfill its mandate.

Pakistan might take advantage of international best practices to strengthen the new ministry. Most countries in the world currently have an apex central environmental ministry or agency with a number of technical and action-oriented agencies designating and implementing public policies and enforcing regulations. Specifically, the responsibilities that usually are maintained by the central government, regardless of the level of decentralization, include design and enactment of national environmental policies and standards; transboundary issues; coordination of regional agencies; and research related to climate change, biodiversity, or water issues, such as glacial melting. Other possible responsibilities that could be strengthened in Pakistan at the national level include the following: setting coordination incentives with subnational environmental units, establishing accountability mechanisms, promoting public disclosure, strengthening the demand side of accountability, and reducing vulnerability to natural disasters.

The NLTA's overall assessment of environment-related institutions is that, while Pakistan has in place an elaborate institutional framework for addressing environment issues, its impact on the ground is limited. This is because of insufficient capacity in terms of skilled personnel at the federal and provincial levels, unrealistically elevated environmental standards, and inconsistencies in legislation that put provincial governments at odds with the federal government. All of these factors contribute to poor enforcement and very limited progress towards certification of EMSs, which is critical for environmentally sound and internationally competitive industrialization.

The following tables (O.1–O.5) summarize this book's main recommendations regarding actions the GoP could take to mainstream sustainability considerations into its industrial sector. The recommendations center on

- improving the macroeconomic climate for long-term investment in green production and transport infrastructure;
- reforming Pakistan's cargo freight sector to provide better access to trading partners, lower the environmental costs of production, and aid the development of existing industrial estates;
- investing in green production in these burgeoning industrial estates; and
- improving the institutional environment for sustainable industrial policy.

**Table O.1  Key Potential Macroeconomic Policy Reforms to Encourage Industrial Growth**

| Policy reform | Time frame |
|---|---|
| Access to credit can be broadened by allowing manufacturing firms to leverage their real estate assets as collateral for loans. | Short term |
| Trade can be liberalized by ending tariffs, allowing a greater variety of imports from India and eliminating protectionist policies that favor a few firms at the expense of the general economy. | Medium term |
| The tax code can be reformed so that it apportions the tax burden in a non-distortionary manner that does not discriminate against manufacturing activities. | Medium term |

**Table O.2  Recommended Actions to Foster Sustainable Trade and Infrastructure in Pakistan**

| Action | Time frame |
|---|---|
| Foster the adoption of new technologies and procedures that add value to the services provided by the trade and transport sector. | Short term |
| Modernize the trucking fleet. | Short term |
| Strengthen the institutional capacity of infrastructure-sector agencies and environmental agencies for environmental management. | Short term |
| Develop a new energy policy that identifies both short-term and long-term energy sources to cater to the industrial sector. | Short term |
| Redefine the government's role to move away from direct operation and towards an impartial apparatus that fosters and regulates transport infrastructure. | Medium term |
| Improve transport infrastructure along trade corridors with Central Asia, China, and India. | Long term |

**Table O.3  Recommended Actions for Greening Pakistan's Industrial Sector**

| Recommended action | Responsible party | Time frame |
|---|---|---|
| *Revision of environmental regulations* | | |
| Develop both interim and revised permanent National Environmental Quality Standards. | New Standard-Setting Committee (includes representatives of enterprises, industry associations, NGOs, and public sector) | Short term |
| Revise and implement pollution charge system. | Government of Pakistan | Short term |
| Implement permanent National Environmental Quality Standards. | New Standard-Setting Committee/ Government of Pakistan | Long term |

*table continues next page*

**Table O.3 Recommended Actions for Greening Pakistan's Industrial Sector** *(continued)*

| Recommended action | Responsible party | Time frame |
|---|---|---|
| ***Construction of common effluent treatment plants*** | | |
| Create plans for funding and construction of common CETPs in industrial clusters. | Public body, industrial association, commercial venture, or public-private partnership | Short term |
| ***Strengthening cleaner production centers (CPCs)*** | | |
| Extend the work and scope of cleaner production (CP) centers to promote long-term integration of CP and environmental management systems (EMS) into firms' daily operations and management strategies, and establish additional CPCs. | CPCs, industry associations, CP working group | Short term |
| Create advisory board in CPCs to identify funding sources and develop business plans to ensure financial sustainability. | CPCs | Short term |
| Create "CP working group" within the Ministry of Industries and Production tasked with developing a national plan for CP and EMS and a strategy for financing construction of CETPs. | Ministry of Industries and Production | Short term |
| Create a national cleaner production center to promote information sharing among subnational CPCs and engage in international exchanges of information with other national CPCs. | CP working group | Short term |
| ***Public disclosure and information dissemination*** | | |
| Foster creation of informed citizenry through distribution of information regarding firms violating environmental regulations and data on health impacts of environmental degradation. | Pakistan Environmental Protection Agency and Provincial Environmental Protection Agencies | Short term |
| Collect, assemble, and release information to firms on foreign environmental standards, voluntary standards established by consortia and retailers, and requirements related to Pakistani products in potential export markets. | Pakistan Standards and Quality Control Authority and industry associations | Short term |
| Allow Pakistan's specific needs to be accounted for during the processes for formulating international standards in standard-setting bodies such as ISO. | Pakistan Standards and Quality Control Authority | Short term |

*Note:* CETP = combined effluent treatment plants, ISO = International Organization for Standardization, NGO = nongovernmental organization.

**Table O.4 Strengthening MoIP's Capacity for Sustainable Industrialization**

| Industrial strategy component | Ministry/line agency directly in charge | Needed MoIP capacity to fulfill the role |
|---|---|---|
| Reducing macroeconomic and financial risk (including inflation, interest rates, and crowding-out issues) | Ministry of Finance, State Bank of Pakistan | • Technical capacity to present industry perspectives on macroeconomic stability/competitive exchange rate/access to credit issues<br>• Regular dialogue with the private sector |
| Energy prices and energy availability | Ministry of Water and Power, PEPCO, OGRA | Technical capacity to represent industry energy needs and pricing issues |
| Non-discriminatory tax policy | Federal Board of Revenue | Capacity to ensure that the burden of taxation (via corporate, income, and sales tax) does not fall only on industry while other sectors escape the tax net |

*table continues next page*

**Table O.4  Strengthening MoIP's Capacity for Sustainable Industrialization** *(continued)*

| Industrial strategy component | Ministry/line agency directly in charge | Needed MoIP capacity to fulfill the role |
|---|---|---|
| Trade policy (including regional trade) and trade facilitation | Ministry of Commerce, Federal Board of Revenue, Ministry of Foreign Affairs | Capacity to maintain a liberalized trade regime (especially relative to the emerging large economies in the neighborhood) that is not injurious to local industry (appropriate antidumping stance), and capacity to promote modern customs procedures that strengthen internationally competitive supply chains |
| Efficient transportation and port handling | Ministry of Communications, Shipping and Ports, provincial governments, Ministry of Railways | Technical capacity to recommend cost-reducing public-private investment and management practices in roads, railways, ports, and shipping |
| Spatial location and regionally balanced industrialization | National Economic Council, Planning Division, provincial governments | Developing capacity to strike the right balance between the objectives of agglomeration for scale economies and helping strengthen investment climate to promote local industry |
| Managing industrial waste and environment pollution | Ministry of Environment and provincial environment departments | Promotion of realistic environment standards and facilitation of adoption of EMS to achieve eventual ISO 14001 certification |

*Note:* EMS = environmental management systems, ISO = International Organization for Standardization, MoIP = Ministry of Industries and Production.

**Table O.5  Recommended Actions for Improving Pakistan's Institutional Framework for Sustainable Industrialization**

| Recommended action | Responsible party | Time frame |
|---|---|---|
| Strengthen provincial EPAs so that they have the budgets and staffs needed to help provincial governments design new environmental regulations pursuant to the Eighteenth Amendment, and the capacity to monitor environmental pollution and enforce the new regulations. | Provincial environmental protection agencies | Short term |
| Create Cleaner Production Working Group within the Ministry of Industries and Production tasked with developing a national plan for CP and EMS, and a strategy for financing construction of CETPs. | Ministry of Industries and Production | Short term |
| Strengthen the Ministry of Climate Change with the following key responsibilities: coordinating environmental policy and priority setting; designing and enacting national environmental policies; handling trans-boundary issues; conducting research related to climate change, biodiversity, and water issues; establishing accountability mechanism; promoting public disclosure; and strengthening the demand side of accountability. | Government of Pakistan | Short term |

*Note:* CETP = combined effluent treatment plants, CP = cleaner production, EMS = environmental management systems, EPA = environmental protection agency.

## Notes

1. ISO (International Organization for Standardization), the world's largest developer of International Standards, is a network of the national standards institutes of 160 countries, one member per country; it has a Central Secretariat in Geneva, Switzerland, that coordinates the system. ISO 14001 is an international environmental standard created under the auspices of ISO and based on the work of committees composed of representatives of both public and private organizations.

2. See  www.sbp.org.pk/bpd/Conference/Day_One/SME_in_Pakistan.ppt.  Accessed May 6, 2011.

# References

Acosta, P. A., E. K. K. Lartey, and F. Mandelman. 2007a. "Remittances, Exchange Rate Regimes and the Dutch Disease." Working Paper 2008–08, Federal Reserve Bank of Atlanta, Atlanta, Georgia.

———. 2007b. "Remittances, Exchange Rate Regimes and the Dutch Disease: A Panel Data Analysis." Working Paper 2008–12, Federal Reserve Bank of Atlanta, Atlanta, Georgia.

Auerswald, P. E., and A. Malik. 2011. *Review of (LUMS) Industrial Policy: Its Spatial Aspects and Cluster Development*. Consultant report, Washington, DC: World Bank.

GoP (Government of Pakistan). 2008. *Pakistan Economic Survey 2007–2008*. Ministry of Finance. Islamabad. http://finance.gov.pk/survey_0708.html.

———. 2011. *Pakistan: Framework for Economic Growth*. Islamabad: GoP Planning Commission.

———. 2013. "Vision 2025 Approach Paper. Sustained and Inclusive Higher Growth." GoP Planning Commission, Islamabad. http://www.pc.gov.pk/?page_id=137.

Larsen, B., and E. Strukova. 2011. *Cost of Environmental Degradation*. Consultant report, Washington, DC: World Bank.

Montiel, P. J. 2006. "Workers' Remittances and the Long Run Equilibrium Exchange Rate: Analytical Issues." Mimeograph, Williams College, Williamstown, MA.

Nabi, I., and A. Nasim. 2001. "Trading with the Enemy: A Case for Liberalizing Pakistan-India Trade." In *Regionalism and Globalization: Theory and Practice*, edited by S. Lahiri, 170–97. London: Routledge.

Naqvi, Z. F., and I. Nabi. 2008. "Pakistan-India Trade: The Way Forward." In *Hard Sell: Attaining Pakistan's Competitiveness in Global Trade*, edited by M. Kugelman and R. Hathaway. Washington, DC: Woodrow Wilson Center.

Rodrik, D. 2004. "Industrial Policy in the 21st Century." CEPR (Center for Economic Policy Research) Discussion Paper 4767. http://www.hks.harvard.edu/fs/drodrik/Research%20papers/UNIDOSep.pdf.

Rodrik, D., G. Grossman, and V. Norman. 1995. "Getting Intervention Right: How Korea and Taiwan Grew Rich." *Economic Policy* 10 (20): 53–107.

Sánchez-Triana, E., J. Afzal, D. Biller, and S. Malik. 2013. *Greening Growth in Pakistan through Transport Sector Report: Strategic Environmental, Poverty, and Social Assessment of Trade and Transport Sector Reforms*. Washington, DC: World Bank.

World Bank. 2006. *Pakistan Strategic Country Environment Assessment*. Washington, DC: World Bank.

———. 2008. *Environmental Health and Child Survival*. Washington, DC: World Bank.

## CHAPTER 1

# Pakistan's Industrial Vision: A Summary

## Introduction

Pakistan faces multiple challenges; among them is a growing labor force seeking better employment opportunities. Lack of such opportunities presents an unacceptably low standard of living for those affected and has the potential to spark social unrest. Effective industrialization can help provide desirable employment opportunities and respond to Pakistan's ongoing spatial transformation. Pakistan also faces the challenge of improving its infrastructure in order to foster economic development and greater inclusion and equity for those at, or outside of, the margins of adequate economic means. Pakistan's transport infrastructure plays a key role in the country's internal and foreign commerce and, currently, multiple facets of that infrastructure are inefficient, and are impediments to socially and environmentally sustainable industrialization.

The competitiveness of global markets presents a continuing challenge for Pakistan, and many of those markets want export sources that are committed to green production. There is need for strong federal and provincial institutions to foster effective industrialization. However, government strategies that are insensitive to environmental and sustainability concerns will lead to increased mortality and morbidity, as well as prevent the industrial sector from having market access to countries and firms with import policies favoring "green" producers. Consequently, the nexus of sustainability and competitiveness is very important to the debate on Pakistan's green industrial growth.

An overarching question in this debate is "What steps can Pakistan take to foster effective industrialization in ways that are socially and environmentally sustainable?" This book addresses that question through consideration of four topic areas relating to federal and provincial policies and strategies: (1) improving macroeconomic stability to foster investment; (2) upgrading infrastructure (especially transport and energy); (3) greening industries to enhance export opportunities; and (4) developing strong supportive institutions to foster effective and sustainable industrialization.

## Chapter Synopses

### Chapter 2. The Importance of Manufacturing

Chapter 2 centers on the importance of Pakistan's manufacturing sector. With the decline of agriculture's share in gross domestic product (GDP), Pakistan is experiencing a large and rapid migration of people from rural to urban areas. The formation of urban clusters due to such migration has the potential to boost productivity and promote rapid economic growth. However, to realize the potential increase in productivity, also known as agglomeration economies, the urban clusters have to be governed well and provided social and infrastructure services. Furthermore, overall economic management, including the design of services delivered to the urban clusters, has to ensure that manufacturing grows rapidly. The attraction of manufacturing, especially if it is export oriented, is that it provides a range of jobs suited to the diversity of worker skills over a sustained span of time.

A review of recent industrial performance shows that, despite the promising start in the 1960s, industry has not been the engine of economic growth and high productivity employment expected in the Government of Pakistan's (GoP's) development visions. The boom-bust cycles of Pakistan's overall economic performance have affected industrial outcomes. Characterized by low labor productivity and weak international competitiveness, industry's share in GDP and total employment is declining. An economic management stance that favors consumption over savings and investment in manufacturing has accentuated these weaknesses. This is exhibited in a host of macro and sectoral pricing policies and public-expenditure priorities.

The identification of constraints faced by manufacturing is made more robust by focusing on the manufacturing of ready-made garments, which is highly labor intensive, moderately demanding of energy and capital, and generates high value addition in export markets. Consequently, this sector is ideally suited to Pakistan's comparative advantage in realizing the agglomeration economies associated with urbanization. Yet, garments manufacturing has performed well below potential. The policy and services constraints that have stunted garments manufacturing frame well the constraints faced by manufacturing as a whole.

Chapter 2 consists of five sections. The first section provides a brief introduction, preceding the second section, which summarizes the ongoing spatial transformation to provide a context for the third section's assessment of manufacturing performance, including its international competitiveness. The fourth section presents the case of garments manufacturing as a particularly suitable manufacturing activity that has the potential to create well-paid productive jobs over a sustained span of time. Section 5 draws generalizations from the constraints that hamper the growth of garments manufacturing, and discusses the policy and services impediments to manufacturing as a whole. That discussion frames the discussion in subsequent chapters.

### Chapter 3. Spatial Transformation

Chapter 3 discusses various aspects of the ongoing urbanization. With the highest population growth rate in South Asia, and the ongoing spatial transformation, Pakistan's population residing in cities is expected to increase from 36 percent in 2010 to nearly 50 percent in the decade starting in 2030. By 2020, Pakistan will have two megacities (over 10 million population), Karachi and Lahore, and several others with a population of one million or more (three in Punjab and one each in Sindh, Khyber Pakhtunkhwa, Balochistan, and the Islamabad Federal Territory). This migration trend will intensify, given the ongoing structural transformation of the economy by which agricultural modernization and mechanization displace a growing number of rural people.

The demographic dynamics will pose a serious social challenge if urban centers do not provide adequate employment opportunities. However, if appropriate policies are in place to promote agglomeration economies, the growing urban population has the potential to become an economic asset. Key to this is a vibrant industrial sector that is able to create a range of jobs requiring skills of different intensity. This book argues that skills development, trade reform, infrastructure modernization, environmental safeguards together with stronger implementation of those safeguards, and oversight institutions will be needed to realize the agglomeration economies and industrial vibrancy associated with rapid urbanization.

Section 1 of chapter 3 briefly introduces that chapter, followed by a review of the migration patterns in Pakistan in section 2. Section 3 discusses the spatial comparative advantage of urban centers, and the provision of infrastructure and social services. The fourth section highlights the agglomeration economies associated with urban centers that help promote industrialization. Section 5 concludes with remarks on managing the negative externalities of rapid urbanization that are further developed in subsequent chapters.

### Chapter 4. Skills Development

Chapter 4 discusses ongoing skills-development initiatives and what is necessary to strengthen them. Pakistan's two megacities and several million-plus cities emerging from the ongoing spatial transformation in Pakistan have the potential to become industrial hubs enjoying agglomeration economies. However, this will depend on how well the cities are governed and how judicious they are in investing in infrastructure to make them both livable and well connected. Importantly, this potential is more likely to be realized if the workers inhabiting the cities are appropriately skilled and can contribute to making industry internationally competitive and profitable.

The ongoing skills-development initiatives in Pakistan show two trends. One set of initiatives aims to improve the skills of the poorest segment of the society as a form of social protection. The Federal Benazir Income Support Program's Waseela-e-Rozgar (focused on the poorest 20 percent of the nationwide population) is an example. The other set does not specifically target the poor, but rather aims to enhance workers' general capabilities that make hiring firms more competitive—and therefore more profitable—so they are willing to pay higher wages to workers who acquire such skills. Typically, these initiatives require, as a prerequisite, many more years of school education than the poor can afford; consequently, the beneficiaries of such initiatives are generally from higher-income groups than the poorest 20 percent. All the provinces have such programs, as does the federal government. These may be called industrial competitiveness and growth-promoting skills initiatives.

A recently introduced program, the Punjab's Skills Development Fund (PSDF), on the other hand, provides skills to the vulnerable (young men and women in districts with few employment opportunities) who may lie well above the poverty line; PSDF is therefore a hybrid. While PSDF focuses on South Punjab's poorest districts, some of the courses offered require a level of education that poor households cannot afford and help to strengthen the competitiveness of hiring firms. Because of its interesting design features and initial success, PSDF is being scaled up to cover all of Punjab, and it is likely to become the premier initiative to upgrade worker skills to make firms more competitive and thus promote industrialization and economic growth.

After a brief introduction in section 1, the second section of chapter 4 summarizes the state of skills development in Pakistan. Section 3 introduces the key players in skills development in Pakistan at both the federal and the provincial levels. Section 4 reviews the main features of the Punjab Skills Development Fund and progress to date. Drawing insights from PSDF, section 5 recommends a reform agenda to improve other provincial and federal skills-development initiatives. Section 6 concludes with observations on the need to strengthen education, which constitutes the foundation for building sound skills-development programs to promote industrialization and economic growth.

### Chapter 5. Challenges in Trade

Chapter 5 brings together themes relating to international trade. Trade, industrial competitiveness, and urbanization are closely linked. Trade logistics are a large part of the costs of finished products and are often key to manufacturing firms' international competitiveness. How well urban clusters are connected to another is critical for taking advantage of openness to trade. Modern and supportive trade facilitation improves the response of urban clusters to trade opportunities. Trade policy influences costs via tariffs on inputs, and trade policy influences industrial efficiency and competitiveness via tariffs on outputs that provide protection. A supportive trade policy that does not tie up exporting firms' capital in refundable duties on imported inputs lowers costs, and promotes growth of urban clusters and the employment opportunities they create. Trade policy also affects access to markets, and allows comparative advantage and industrialization opportunities to emerge. Given Pakistan's geography and history, and rapid economic changes taking place in its immediate neighborhood, trade policy that promotes regional trade contributes to the growth of regionally diverse urban clusters and the agglomeration economies they generate.

Following a brief introduction, the second section of chapter 5 examines the principal challenges of trade logistics. Section 3 focuses on trade policy. It reviews recent developments in tariff policy and discusses regional trade in more detail, given its potential for sustained economic growth. Section 4 concludes with a discussion of some of the challenges that need to be surmounted for Pakistan to take advantage of the opportunities offered by regional trade.

### Chapter 6. Infrastructure Modernization

Chapter 6 focuses on what it will take for Pakistan to modernize its infrastructure. Given the manifold increase in the economy's size and the number of trade and logistics transactions in the last six decades, the infrastructure that helped create the Indus Basin market is now frayed and needs to be modernized. Well-functioning cities that enjoy agglomeration economies and become manufacturing hubs for employment generation and international competitiveness require modern services such as reliable and low-cost energy, well-maintained roads, and wastewater treatment that lower production costs. Upgraded and adequate infrastructure services that improve sanitation, access to clean drinking water, and public transport improve livability of cities and reduce congestion and other social costs of urbanization. Trade, especially the revival of regional trade, requires state-of-the-art infrastructure spanning inter-city and cross-border roads, railways, air transport, and telephones for regional connectivity. Efficient ports and shipping are integral to the national trade corridor. Cross-border standardization of freight transport regulations, improvements in the trucking fleet, and road safety standards are key to promoting regional trade. These themes, and the economic strategic objectives underpinning them, come together to provide the stimulus for upgrading Pakistan's infrastructure throughout the national economic corridor and provide a much-needed vibrancy to the Indus Basin market.

The chapter's first section introduces the chapter contents. Section 2 reviews the current state of Pakistan's infrastructure. Sections 3 and 4 discuss programs for infrastructure and trade facilitation reform, respectively. Section 5 addresses mitigation measures to address emerging externalities (social, environmental, and institutional capacity challenges) associated with rapid urbanization and infrastructure expansion.

### Chapter 7. Greening Pakistan's Industry

Chapter 7 discusses the environmental themes that affect urbanization and international competitiveness. Improved industrial environmental performance is essential if Pakistani firms are to be competitive in export markets like the European Union in which business customers demand high environmental compliance from their suppliers and often require certification to international standards, such as ISO 14001. Pakistan is behind its competitors in export markets with respect to environmental management. A significant number of Pakistani firms are not even aware that Pakistan has environmental regulations that they are supposed to meet. It will be impossible for Pakistani firms to remain competitive and for Pakistan to meet its goals for expanding exports unless the firms and the GoP become much more proactive about enhancing industrial environmental performance. Furthermore, clean production, crucial for internationally competitiveness, also helps make overall production more efficient, thus lowering costs and raising profitability even for those firms producing exclusively for the internal market.

Chapter 7's first section provides an introduction, followed by a summary, in section 2, of the state of the environment in Pakistan and industry's impact on it. Section 3 makes the business case for environmental compliance grounded in international competitiveness and overall production efficiency. Section 4 evaluates the response to the business case in terms of initiatives to abate industrial pollution. Section 5 discusses the importance of strengthening environmental infrastructure to improve compliance. Section 6 concludes with recommendations.

### Chapter 8. Institutions for Sustainable Industrialization

Chapter 8 focuses on institutions to advance sustainable industrialization in Pakistan. The implementation of a strategy for sustainable industrialization, as proposed in this book, requires institutions that function well. The justification for an industrial policy by which governments proactively promote industrial growth has been made by appealing to recent work by Rodrik (2007, 102). It is argued that in early stages of development there are significant market failures due to, "…information externalities entailed in discovering the cost structure of an economy, and coordination externalities in the presence of scale economies." These result in disincentives for entrepreneurs to search for profitable opportunities and retard industrial development. The way out is to follow the model of East Asia, specifically that of the Republic of Korea. As described by Rodrik, Grossman, and Norman (1995):

> What was required was a competent, honest and efficient bureaucracy to administer the interventions, and a clear-sighted political leadership that consistently placed high priority on economic performance….

Since an assessment of the quality of civil services is beyond the scope of this chapter, the focus here is on institutions that would aid the formulation and implementation of a strategy for sustainable industrialization in Pakistan. Our focus on such institutions stems from the hope that institutional strengthening can lead to an enabling environment having continuous processes for incorporating sustainability considerations into the design of Pakistan's industrial policy. This chapter's discussion centers on five dimensions of sustainability:

- The cost of doing business for industrial firms is kept low.
- Spatial location decisions are coordinated and are based on sound economic principles.

- Skills development is cost effective and responds to industry's needs.
- Specialized institutions such as the Small and Medium Enterprises Development Authority (SMEDA) for small enterprise development work well.
- Environmental concerns are addressed in a manner that reflects local realities and promotes the international competitiveness of firms.

Chapter 8 has the following structure: After a brief introduction in the first section, the second section discusses the role of the Ministry of Industries and Production as the coordinator of institutions that support sustainable industrialization in Pakistan. The third section focuses on the need to strengthen the National Economic Council and the Council of Common Interests as apex institutions for coordinating spatial transformation. The fourth section discusses the role of SMEDA in supporting industrialization. Institutional arrangements for environmental management are the focus of the fifth section.

## Bibliography

GoP (Government of Pakistan). 1988. *Pakistan Economic Survey 1987–88*. Ministry of Finance. Islamabad.

———. 1993. *Pakistan Economic Survey 1992–93*. Ministry of Finance. Islamabad.

———. 2000. *Pakistan Economic Survey 1999–2000*. Ministry of Finance. Islamabad.

———. 2004. *Pakistan Economic Survey 2003–04*. Ministry of Finance. Islamabad.

———. 2007. *Pakistan Economic Survey 2006–07*. Ministry of Finance. Islamabad.

———. 2010. Poverty Reduction Strategy Paper (PRSP)—II. Ministry of Finance. Islamabad. http://www.finance.gov.pk/poverty/PRSP-II.pdf

———. 2011. *Pakistan: Framework for Economic Growth*. Islamabad: Planning Commission. http://www.cprspd.org/Final%20Version%20-%20Pakistan%20Framework%20for%20Economic%20Growth%202011%20%28May%202.pdf.

Rodrik, D. 2007. *One Economics Many Recipes: Globalization, Institutions, and Economic Growth*. Princeton, NJ: Princeton University Press.

Rodrik, D., G. Grossman, and V. Norman. 1995. "Getting Intervention Right: How Korea and Taiwan Grew Rich." *Economic Policy* 10 (20): 53–107.

Sánchez-Triana, E., J. Afzal, D. Biller, and S. Malik. 2013. *Greening Growth in Pakistan through Transport Sector Reforms: A Strategic Environmental, Poverty, and Social Assessment*. Washington, DC: World Bank.

## CHAPTER 2

# The Importance of Manufacturing

## Introduction

With the decline of agriculture's share in gross domestic product (GDP), Pakistan is experiencing a large and rapid migration of people from rural to urban areas. The formation of urban clusters due to such migration has the potential to boost productivity and promote rapid economic growth. However, to realize the potential increase in productivity, also known as agglomeration economies, the urban clusters have to be governed well and provided social and infrastructure services. Furthermore, overall economic management, including the design of services delivered to the urban clusters, has to ensure that manufacturing grows rapidly. The attraction of manufacturing, especially if it is export oriented, is that it provides a range of jobs suited to the diversity of worker skills over a sustained span of time.

A review of recent industrial performance shows that despite a promising start in the 1960s, industry has not been the engine of economic growth and high productivity employment expected in the Government of Pakistan's (GoP's) development visions. Boom-bust cycles in Pakistan's overall economic performance have affected industrial outcomes. Characterized by low labor productivity and weak international competitiveness, industry's share in GDP and total employment is declining. An economic management stance that favors consumption over savings and investment in manufacturing has accentuated these weaknesses. This is exhibited in a host of macro and sectoral pricing policies and public expenditure priorities.

The identification of constraints faced by manufacturing is made more robust by focusing on the manufacture of ready-made garments, which is highly labor intensive, moderately demanding of energy and capital, and generates high value addition in export markets. Thus, the sector is ideally suited to Pakistan's comparative advantage in realizing the agglomeration economies associated with urbanization. Yet, garments manufacturing has performed well below potential. The policy and services constraints that have stunted garments manufacturing frame well the constraints faced by manufacturing as a whole.

The discussion in chapter 2 is organized as follows. This brief introduction precedes a summary, in the chapter's second section, of the ongoing spatial transformation. That summary provides a context for assessment, in the chapter's third section, of manufacturing performance, including its international competitiveness. Section 4 presents the case of garments manufacturing as a particularly suitable manufacturing activity that has the potential to create well-paid productive jobs, over a sustained span of time. Section 5 generalizes from the constraints that hamper the growth of garments manufacturing, discusses the policy and services impediments to manufacturing as a whole, and frames the discussion in the subsequent chapters.

## The Ongoing Spatial Transformation

Pakistan is in the midst of two key trends that can provide increased manufacturing potential: significant migration to urban areas and the development of "agglomeration" economies. The first trend is a physical concept, the second an economic one. Urbanization facilitates agglomeration, as face-to-face exchange of information is important in allowing labor and production to learn from each other and to apply technological advances. It can also reduce transport costs, as moving goods, people, and ideas become cheaper. People may take advantage of agglomeration when different ways to connect and exchange information are available (telecom, information technology [IT], and so forth). Agglomeration economies also help create internationally connected cities, concentrating production and further facilitating economic growth.[1] These trends combined can have a profound influence on how natural resources and infrastructure are used, which in turn may influence migration and agglomeration, and ultimately the prospects for high-productivity jobs and economic growth (box 2.1). However, if urbanization is unchecked, it may backfire due to the public "bads" associated with it—hence the importance of ensuring that such growth is "green" and inclusive (that is, it takes into account environmental and social issues).

As cities catalyze agglomeration, they are important engines of economic growth. Figures 2.1 and 2.2 provide snapshots of this relationship in 1960 and 2011. In 1960, Latin America was distant from South Asian and East Asian economies in not only urban population, but also GDP per capita. Half a century later, the Republic of Korea and Malaysia are not only as urbanized as Latin American countries, but are also richer. Pakistan, however, has not moved up the curve: although one of the most urbanized countries in South Asia, its urbanization and growth pale in comparison with those of other countries. It has been unable to use its urbanization and agglomeration to generate the growth and high-productivity jobs that should come with them. Equally, megacities like Karachi suffer from the public "bads" associated with urbanization, like congestion, pollution, and social conflict.

The failure to benefit from rapid urbanization is evident in the poor performance of industry that should have, but did not, create well-paid employment opportunities to those who moved to urban centers.

**Box 2.1  Infrastructure, Agglomeration, and Urbanization**

Rising shares of services and manufacturing in an economy are generally associated with urbanization as the economy increases its sophistication through stronger productivity and growth. Figure B2.1.1 presents a simple conceptual framework of various factors. All influence one another in a virtuous circle, and infrastructure services (connectivity) are inputs to the different quadrants and to the circle as a whole.

**Figure B2.1.1  The Goal of a Virtuous Circle**

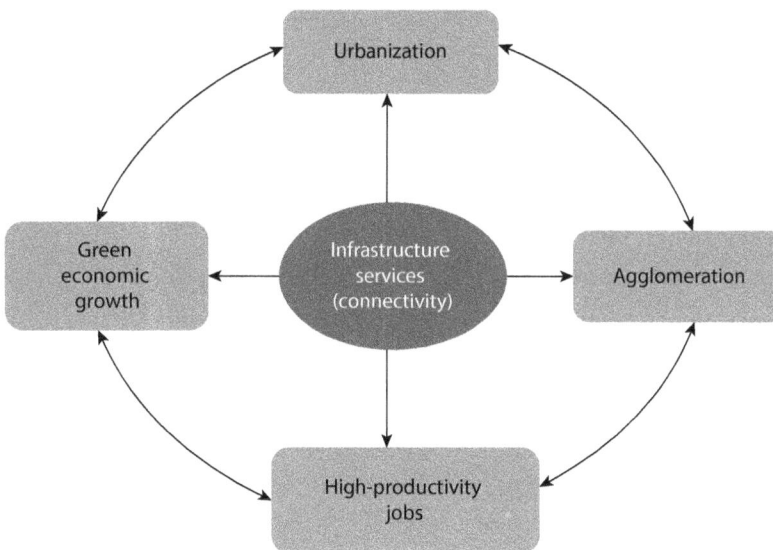

*Source:* Biller and Nabi 2013.

## Recent Economic Developments and the Industrial Sector
### *High Volatility of GDP Growth*

The stated economic policy for most of the last decade has emphasized trade-led growth and macroeconomic stability (GoP 2010). Recent performance of the economy, however, repeats the volatility that has characterized economic growth for several decades. Between 2001 and 2006, the growth rate rose dramatically following a surge in remittances and foreign aid that led to a consumption-fueled boom (figure 2.3). Growth exceeded all expectations, averaging over 7 percent per annum for almost four years; the capital market expanded rapidly, foreign exchange reserves increased to six months of imports, and there was a significant increase in per capita income. In 2007, however, the economy went into a sharp downturn. In 2008, growth fell to 4 percent and was further down to 2 percent in 2009.

**Figure 2.1  Snapshot of Urbanization, 1960**

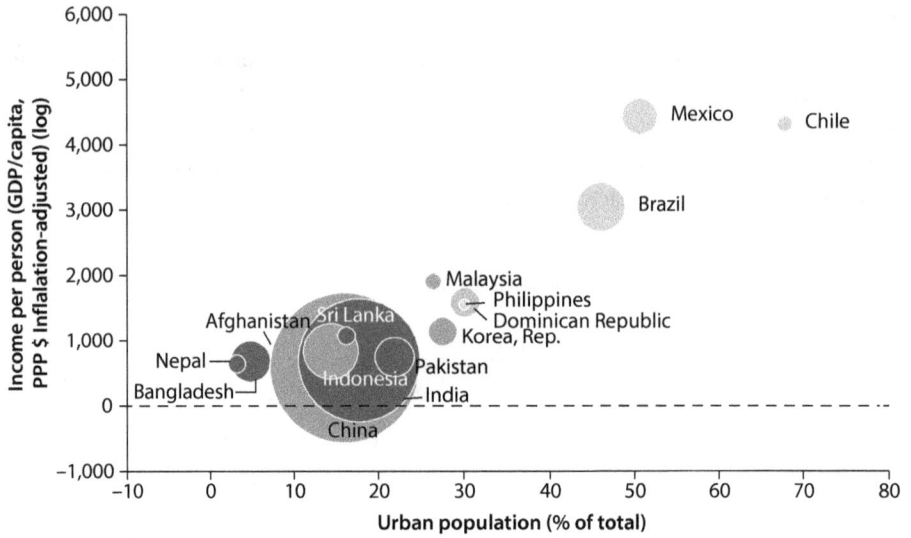

Source: Biller and Nabi 2013.
Note: GDP = gross domestic product, PPP = purchasing power parity. Regions are in different colors. The sizes of the bubbles represent country populations.

**Figure 2.2  Snapshot of Urbanization, 2011**

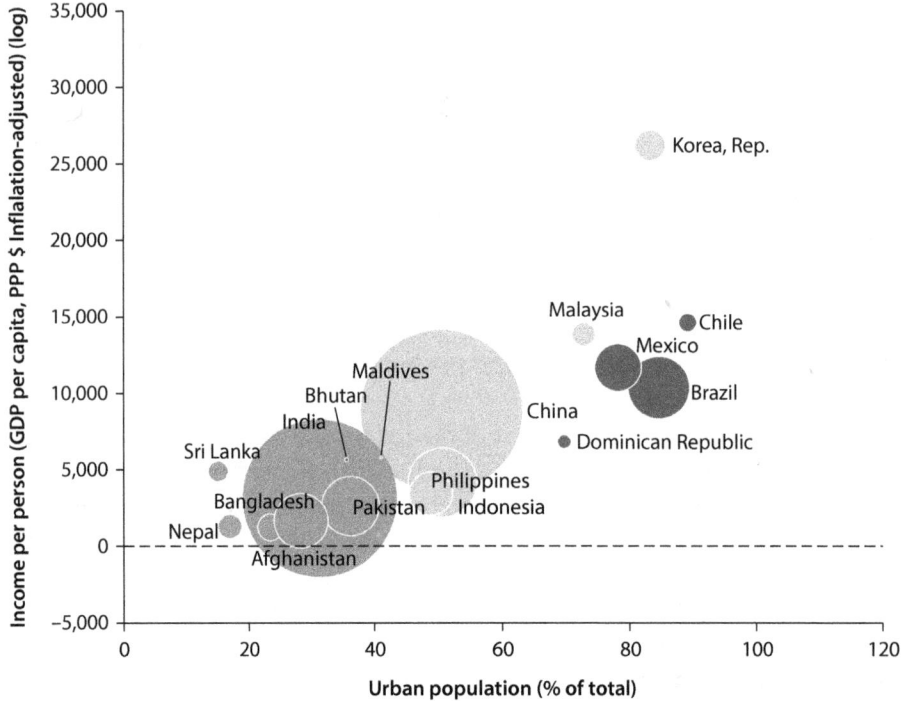

Source: Biller and Nabi 2013.
Note: GDP = gross domestic product, PPP = purchasing power parity. Regions are in different colors. The sizes of the bubbles represent country populations.

**Figure 2.3 GDP Growth Rate in Pakistan, 2001–09**
*Percent*

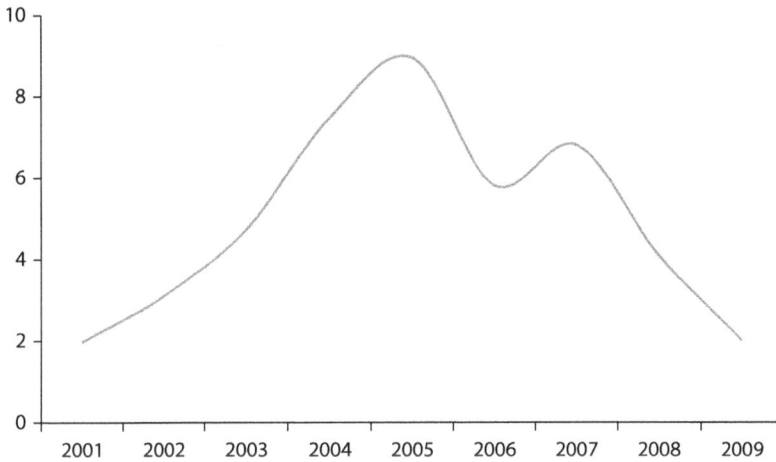

*Source:* GoP Federal Bureau of Statistics.
*Note:* GDP = gross domestic product.

The global recession was only partly responsible for the collapse of the growth rate.[2] The principal factor was the underlying structural weaknesses of the economy. Industrial vulnerability is signified by the fact that manufacturing growth had declined even during the consumption-led boom, falling eventually to −3.3 percent in 2009. This was mainly due to a slump in large-scale manufacturing; the growth rate of small firms has been steady since 2000 (figure 2.4). Large-scale manufacturing registered a sharp increase in its growth rate between 2002 (4 percent) and 2005 (20 percent), followed by a sharp contraction reflecting weakening aggregate demand, deteriorating security, and power shortages.

### Evolving Structure of the Economy

Structural change in the national economy has been a fundamental feature in the growth and development of both western economies and newly industrialized countries of the east (Timmer and Akkus 2008). As an economy develops, the share of agriculture in GDP inevitably declines, while that of manufacturing and services increases. This form of structural change represents a gradual shift from low-productivity to high-productivity activities. Along with this observable structural transformation, there is wide agreement in the empirical economics literature about the following stages in development (Klinger and Lederman 2004). At low-income levels, specialization is high and is primarily determined by resource-based comparative advantage. As a country becomes richer, the manufacturing base diversifies, with firms producing and exporting a wider range of relatively more sophisticated products. However, at higher levels of income, the process reverses: specialization again increases, but in high value added and technologically advanced products. Increased product diversification therefore

**Figure 2.4  Performance of the Large-Scale and Small-Scale Manufacturing Sector in Pakistan, 1950–2010**
*Percent*

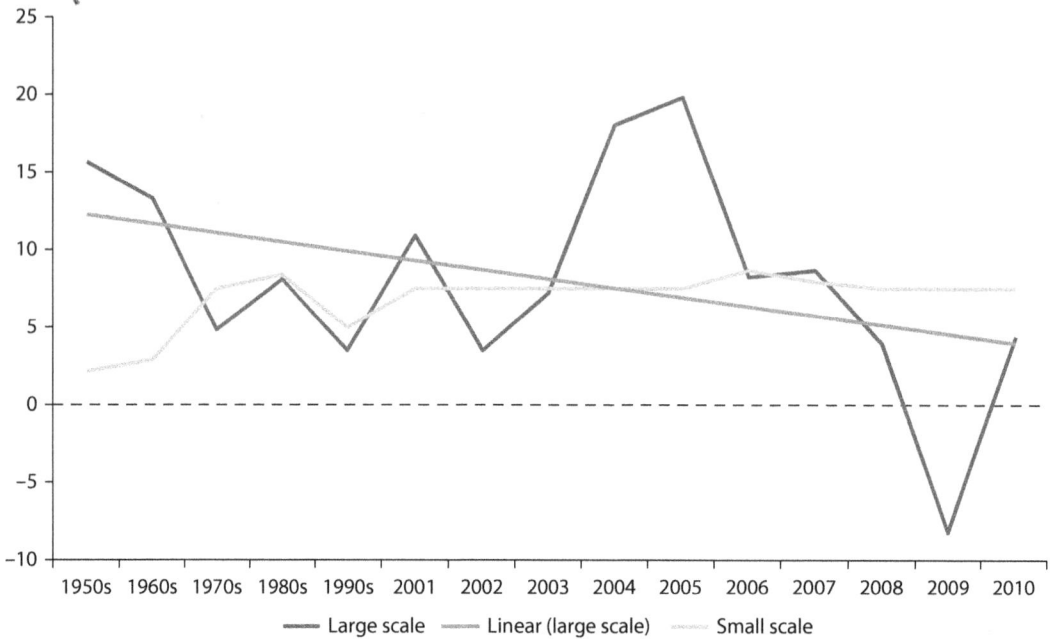

*Source:* GoP 2008.

represents an intermediate stage in the process of structural transformation during a country's economic development (Timmer and Akkus 2008).

Industrialization offers a range of potential benefits, including more job creation, higher economic growth, and tax revenues. However, in the context of Pakistan's economy, policies have been skewed in favor of the primary and tertiary sectors, depriving to a large extent the manufacturing sector. Services continue to increase their share in GDP, while agriculture's share is declining slowly and the manufacturing share is stagnant.

Figure 2.5 shows that services now dominate the economy and account for more than 50 percent of GDP. The manufacturing share, on the other hand, has remained constant at about 25 percent of GDP, whereas the contribution of agriculture has declined from more than 30 percent in the 1970s to less than 25 percent today. Meanwhile, a large part of the labor force (more than 40 percent) is still employed in agriculture and industry, with the former having the highest value addition, but the lowest share in employment (20 percent). This is a matter of concern, since movement of labor from low-productivity (agriculture) to relatively high-productivity sectors (such as manufacturing) generates the surplus that spurs growth and results in improved living standards for workers.

The evolving structure of the economy is indicative of the manufacturing sector's unsatisfactory performance. Manufacturing grew at an average rate of

**Figure 2.5  Sectoral Shares of GDP in Pakistan, 1970–2009**
*Percent*

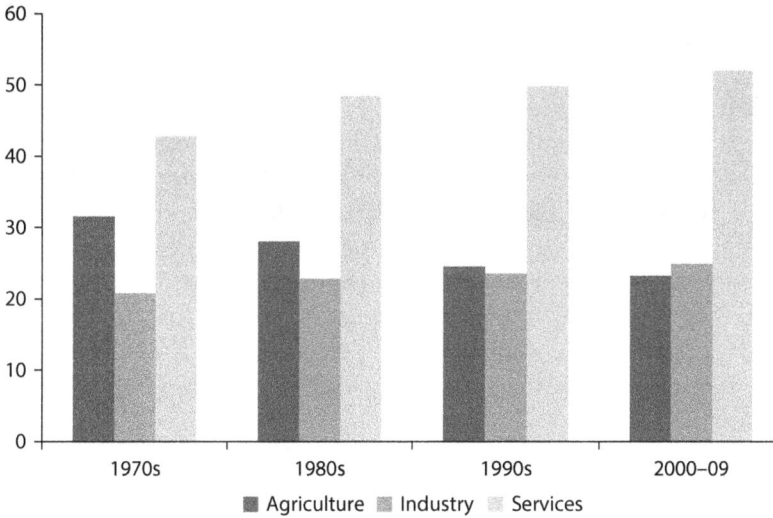

Sources: GoP 2004, 2009; Bureau of Statistics data on GDP up to 2009.
Note: GDP = gross domestic product.

**Table 2.1  Average Product Shares in the Manufacturing Sector of Pakistan, 1970–90**
*Percent*

| Product | 1970s | 1980s | 1990s |
|---|---|---|---|
| Food and beverage | 30.45 | 30.94 | 22.89 |
| Textiles | 27.78 | 18.14 | 25.06 |
| Apparel, leather, and textiles | 2.04 | 2.37 | 2.80 |
| Industrial chemicals | 11.20 | 14.29 | 15.50 |
| Petroleum and coal | 5.27 | 6.01 | 3.26 |
| Rubber and plastic | 1.80 | 1.80 | 1.42 |
| Metals and non-metals | 9.10 | 14.20 | 13.20 |
| Nonelectrical machinery | 1.84 | 2.14 | 2.09 |
| Electrical machinery | 3.31 | 3.26 | 5.43 |
| Transport equipment | 2.99 | 2.89 | 3.05 |

Source: GoP Pakistan Economic Survey (various issues).

10.6 percent in 1998–2007; however, on a yearly basis, the growth rate has fallen from 14 percent in 2004 to 5.4 percent in 2008 (ADB 2008).

A main reason for the industrial sector's poor performance continues to be that sector's heavy concentration on low value added consumer products, for example food, beverages, and textiles (table 2.1). Textiles, which account for more than 70 percent of Pakistan's total exports, are considered to be non-dynamic in nature, offer little possibility for technological improvements, and attract very little foreign direct investment (FDI). In general, the industrial sector has failed to move into capital goods that are more sophisticated and to develop upstream ancillary manufacturing, such as chemicals and engineering. Importantly, manufacturing is concentrated in items that are losing their share in the world market. In 2008, the share of textiles, garments, and footwear in Pakistan's exports was more than 60 percent, whereas these items constituted 5.8 percent of world exports.

### Investment and Savings Trends

Although GDP growth in Pakistan over the last three decades is comparable with other developing countries, investment has been sluggish. Total fixed investment as a percentage of GDP has remained in the range of 15 to 20 percent in the last three decades (figure 2.6). Due to improvements in the external environment, the share briefly rose from 15 to more than 20 percent between 2003 and 2006. However, in the last three years, worsening internal security and increased macroeconomic instability have brought about a sharp fall in private investment, pulling down the share of total investment in GDP by up to five percentage points.

Public investment has fallen sharply over the last three decades, from 9.2 percent of GDP in the 1980s, to below 5 percent in the mid-1990s. This was a result of fiscal consolidation in the 1980s.[3] The role of the government in the economy was further reduced through privatization of large public sector entities, and the share of the private sector increased to 84 percent of GDP (ADB 2008). The decline in public investment was offset by the private sector invigorated by financial sector reforms and later by major governance and economic reforms.[4] Private investment thus increased from 7.8 percent of GDP in the 1980s to 12.7 percent of GDP in the 2000s. FDI increased even more dramatically in the 2000s, from US$0.4 billion in 2001 to US$2.4 billion in 2008. This has changed since 2007, with both domestic private investment and FDI contracting sharply due to the uncertain economic environment and international liquidity constraints.

**Figure 2.6  Total, Private, and Public Gross Fixed Capital Formulation (GFCF) in Pakistan, 1980–2009**

*Percent*

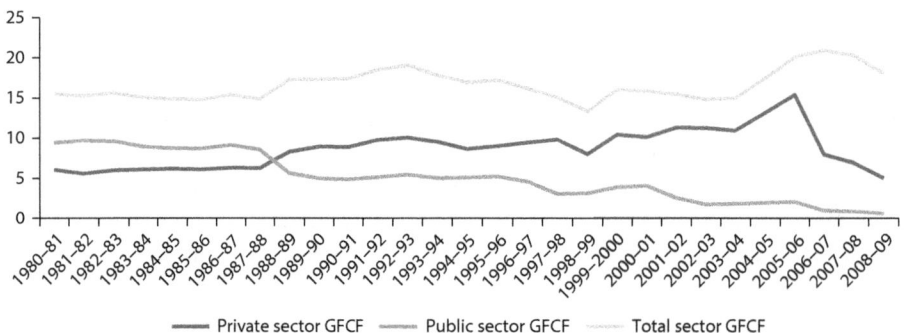

*Sources:* GoP 1988, 1993, 2000, 2004, 2007. *Pakistan Economic Survey 1987–88, 1992–93, 1999–2000, 2003–04,* and *2006–07.*
*Note:* Total GFCF includes private sector, public sector, and general government.

**Figure 2.7  Share of Manufacturing Investment in Total Fixed Investment, 2000–10**

*Percent*

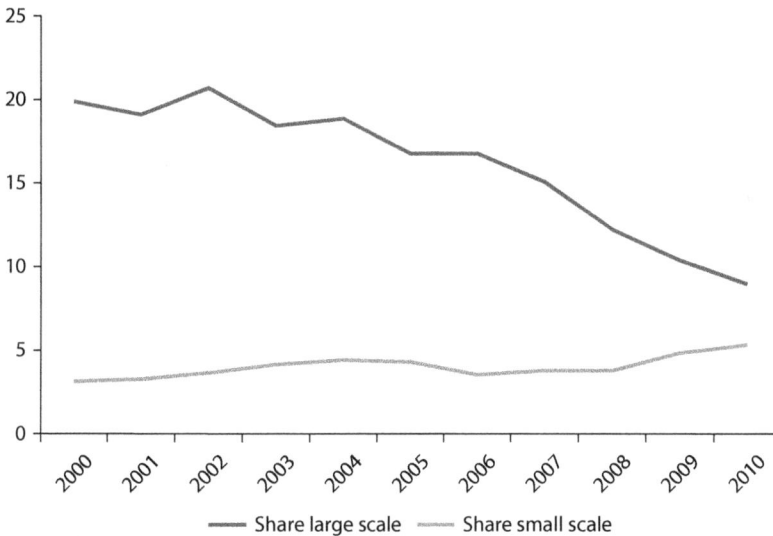

*Source:* GoP *Pakistan Economic Survey* (various issues).

The decline in investment is particularly problematic for the manufacturing sector, since Pakistan has recently experienced a sectoral shift of investment from the industrial sector (large-scale manufacturing, mining and quarrying, construction, and electricity) to services (finance, transport, and communications). In fact, the share of transport and communication investment in total investment rose from 12 to 24 percent between 2000 and 2010, while the share of industrial investment declined from 38 percent to 20 percent. A similar pattern can be observed in the share of total manufacturing, driven largely by a significant decline in investment in large firms (figure 2.7).

Similarly, the sectoral composition of FDI has shifted away from manufacturing. In the last two decades, FDI has come in the oil and gas sector, power, financial, and telecommunication sectors. Less than one-fifth of total FDI in 2008 went to manufacturing, reflecting a declining trend that started in 2004. Economic research reveals strong linkages between FDI in recipient countries and economic growth. For example, Wang (2009) finds that FDI in the manufacturing sector brings more benefits than in non-manufacturing sectors of the economy (Wang 2009). This is of concern for Pakistan because FDI, particularly in the manufacturing sector, is important in terms of realizing technological spillover effects and economies of scale.

### Low Productivity
Value added in industry (as a share of GDP) has ranged between 21 and 27 percent throughout the 1970s and 1980s (figure 2.8). From 1994 to 2003,

**Figure 2.8  Industry Value Added as Share of GDP, 1970–2012**
*Percent*

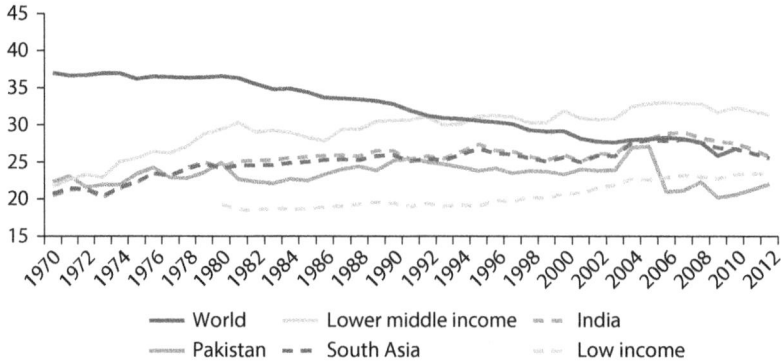

Source: World Bank 2009b.
Note: GDP = gross domestic product.

it was constant at about 23 percent, after which it rose to 27 percent, the level at which it has remained. Relative to other comparable countries, this is very low. For instance, India has had a higher value-added share since the early 1980s, and even low-income countries have recently overtaken Pakistan.

This poor performance is also reflected in Pakistan's deteriorating ranking of competitiveness as measured by the Global Competitiveness Index (GCI). Pakistan ranked 73rd out of 101 countries in 2003, and 101 out of 134 countries in 2010. In comparison with its regional competitors, Pakistan has ranked higher than Bangladesh, but far below India, which has outperformed Pakistan across all twelve pillars[5] on which the GCI is based.

### Poor Export Performance

Globally, rapid growth in manufacturing exports has allowed developing countries to gain a sizeable share of the world market. Pakistan, however, has not been part of this trend. For example, the global share of exports from India, Malaysia, and Thailand has increased significantly from 1974 to 2008, whereas Pakistan's share has remained stable for the period, actually declining between 1990 and 2008 (table 2.2).

Moreover, Pakistan exports a narrow range of manufactured products to which it has added little value. This can be captured by the PRODY index,[6] which associates a certain income level to each product, and the revealed comparative advantage (RCA),[7] which is a measure greater than one if the country has a comparative advantage in producing a given good. The results in table 2.3 suggest that despite being a major producer of raw cotton, Pakistan does not have a comparative advantage in the textile products that fetch the highest prices. Its exports are instead concentrated in those goods (raw cotton, cotton yarn, and cotton fabrics) that are produced by low-income countries. Pakistan's high RCA in these products is mainly due to government policies that favor

**Table 2.2 Country Export Shares Relative to Total World Exports, 1974–2008**
*Percent*

|  | 1974 | 1980 | 1990 | 2000 | 2008 |
|---|---|---|---|---|---|
| India | 0.56 | 0.43 | 0.57 | 0.70 | 1.32 |
| Malaysia | 0.55 | 0.74 | 0.94 | 1.61 | 1.43 |
| Pakistan | 0.14 | 0.15 | 0.18 | 0.15 | 0.15 |
| Thailand | 0.32 | 0.37 | 0.74 | 1.13 | 1.25 |

*Source:* UN Comtrade.

**Table 2.3 PRODY and RCA in Textiles, 2008–09**

| Product | PRODY (in US$) | RCA |
|---|---|---|
| Raw cotton | 2,036 | 5.9 |
| Cotton yarn | 5,631 | 86.5 |
| Cotton fabrics | 4,541 | 115.0 |
| Men's and boys' ready-made garments | 6,777 | 13.2 |
| Women's and girls' ready-made garments | 5,160 | 5.2 |
| Clothing accessories (knitwear) | 9,419 | 22.5 |
| Articles of felt (technical textile) | 22,486 | 0.1 |
| Bonded-fiber fabric | 31,250 | 0.2 |

*Source:* UN Comtrade.
*Note:* RCA = revealed comparative advantage.

low value added items over more sophisticated products, such as felt articles or bonded fiber.

As a consequence, Pakistan's export positioning in world markets is not very encouraging. This can be illustrated graphically by comparing the growth rate of a given good in world exports with the corresponding growth rate in Pakistan's exports. If the product is in the upper-right-hand quadrant (the "competitive quadrant"), then that product is considered internationally competitive. As is evident from figure 2.9 below, Pakistan has a minute proportion of its exports (only 2.6 percent) in the "competitive quadrant." Manufacturing exports are dominated by textiles (41.4 percent), whose world demand is falling. In comparison, India exports a great variety of manufactured products with several of its exports, namely pharmaceuticals, chemicals, iron and steel, and automotive parts, in the competitive quadrant (Nabi 2011).

The underlying reason for Pakistan's inability to achieve a dynamic competitive advantage is the persistent failure to diversify its production[8] and climb up the technology ladder (Lall 2000). In fact, in 2008, medium- and high-technology products accounted for merely 9.5 percent of Pakistan's exports, while they made up 57.6 percent in world exports (table 2.4). Moreover, the performance of medium-technology exports has not been encouraging; their growth rate was below both the corresponding world growth rate and Pakistan's total exports growth rate. The growth of high-technology exports, on the contrary, has been remarkable at 17.5 percent per year; however, their share in total exports is negligible and exceptionally low in comparison with other countries.

### Manufacturing of Ready-Made Garments as a Driver of Economic Growth and Job Creation

Pakistan, with its young and growing labor force and rapid urbanization, needs to give a fillip to manufacturing to create productive jobs and improve the prospects for transitioning to middle-income country status. The manufacturing activities best suited to achieving this objective include light engineering, especially the rapidly growing auto-parts sector, food processing, and ready-made garments, among others. This section focuses on ready-made garments because of its large potential in delivering productive jobs and export earnings. The discussion illustrates the supportive policy framework needed to promote rapid, labor-intensive, industrial growth.

**Figure 2.9  Competitiveness and Performance of India's and Pakistan's Exports, 2000–07**

*Percent*

a. Positioning of India's major manufactured exports in 2007

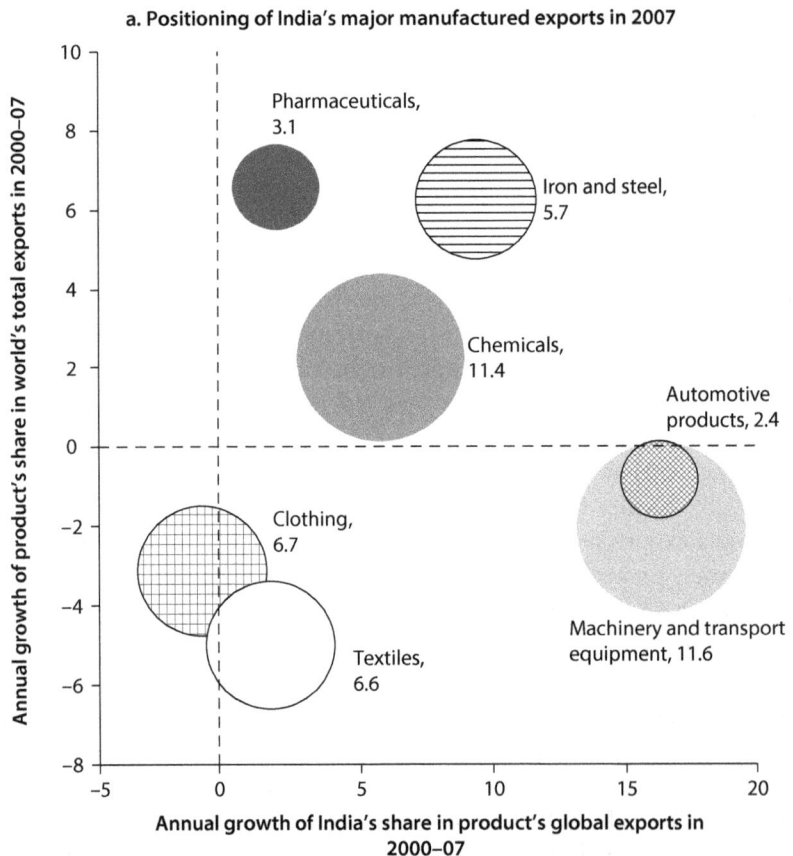

*figure continues next page*

**Figure 2.9 Competitiveness and Performance of India's and Pakistan's Exports, 2000–07** *(continued)*

**b. Positioning of Pakistan's major manufactured exports in 2007**

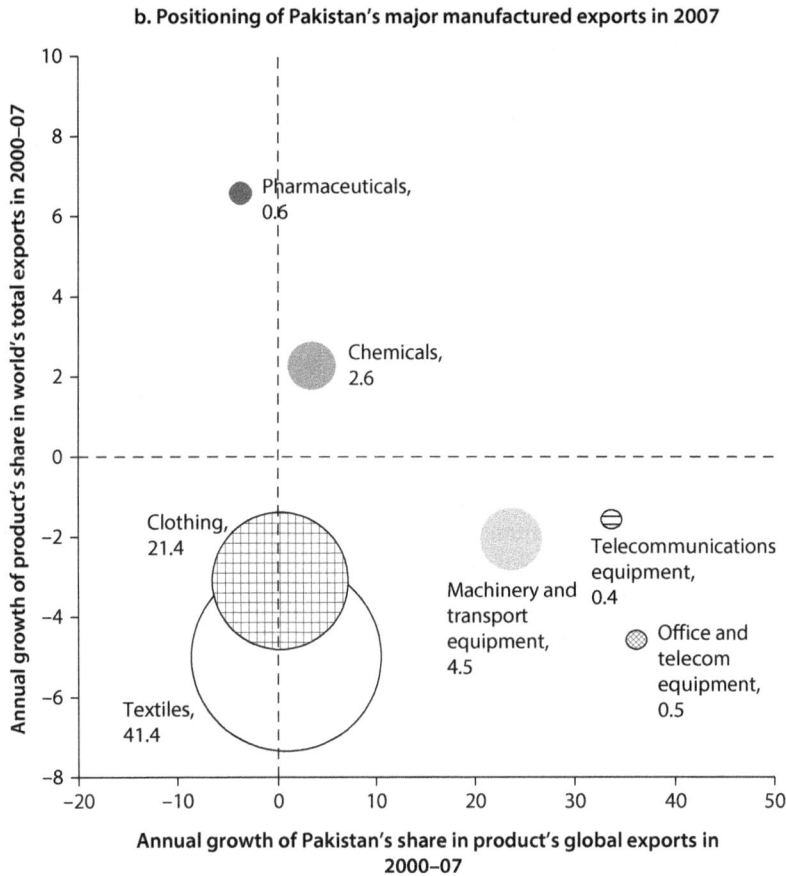

*Source:* Nabi 2011.

**Table 2.4 Technological Level of Pakistani and World Exports, 1998–2008**
*Percent*

| Sector | Pakistan exports | | | World exports[a] | |
|---|---|---|---|---|---|
| | Growth | Share | Share | Growth | Share |
| | 1998–2008 | 1998–2000 | 2006–08 | 1998–2008 | 2008 |
| Total | 9.6 | 100 | 100 | 10.1 | 100 |
| Primary | 10.1 | 12.3 | 12.7 | 11.2 | 11.4 |
| Resource based | 23.9 | 3.5 | 10.9 | 10.5 | 14.8 |
| Low technology | 8.2 | 74.7 | 66.7 | 9.2 | 16.2 |
| Medium technology | 8.7 | 8.6 | 8.1 | 10.1 | 35.5 |
| High technology | 17.5 | 0.8 | 1.4 | 9.3 | 22.1 |

*Source:* GoP *Pakistan Economic Survey* (various issues).
a. Exclusive of oil exports. Because of rounding, the total may not add up to 100 percent.

## Why Focus on Garments?

### A Growing Sector

Overall, textiles manufacturing remains central to Pakistan's economy. Pakistan is among the top five producers of cotton in the world, accounting for 9 percent of total world output of cotton. Putting this to its advantage, Pakistan has followed a proactive strategy of textiles-led industrialization. Textiles manufacturing accounts for 54 percent of exports (US$14 billion of total exports of US$24.5 billion), 46 percent of manufacturing, 38 percent of employment, and 8.5 percent of GDP (table 2.5).

Within textiles, garment manufacturing is a significant and growing component. The value of garment exports has sextupled from 1990 to 2010–11. Denim exports alone have grown at a rate of 27 percent per annum.

### Garment Manufacturing Responds to Pakistan's Resource Endowment

Expansion of the garments industry will provide a major boost to employment generation and export earnings. Fifty-thousand kilograms of cotton fiber creates 400 jobs in each spinning, weaving, and finishing stage of the textiles value chain but 1,600 jobs in garment manufacturing. Moreover, garment manufacturing is the least capital and energy intensive (energy costs are 2–3 percent of the total cost of production) of the textiles activities and generates the highest value addition in the export market. It is estimated that US$1 million invested in spinning and weaving results in US$0.27 million worth of exports, compared with US$3.2 million in exported garments. Garment manufacturing can thus help address Pakistan's recurrent balance of payments crisis.

### The International Opportunity in Garment Exports

The global garment industry is growing significantly. Between 2005 and 2010, world garment exports increased by 5 percent per annum, forming 2.4 percent (US$350 billion) of world merchandise trade (see figure 2.10). There is a consensus that, because of rising labor costs (a key determinant of international competitiveness in garments), it will be difficult for China to sustain its share in

**Table 2.5  Textiles Basic Facts**

*Percent*

| | |
|---|---|
| GDP | 8.5 |
| Large-scale manufacturing | 32.6 |
| Employment[a] | 38.0 |
| Manufacturing | 46.0 |
| Exports | 54.0 |
| Market capitalization | 3.2 |
| Foreign direct investment (FDI) | 1.6 |
| Private loans | 20.2 |
| Export finance scheme | 62.7 |

*Source:* Pakistan Economic Survey 2012; State Bank of Pakistan (Annual Report 2010–11).
*Note:* GDP = gross domestic product.
a. Percent of the manufacturing labor force.

**Figure 2.10  Trends in Textile Exports by Major Categories**
*Million US$*

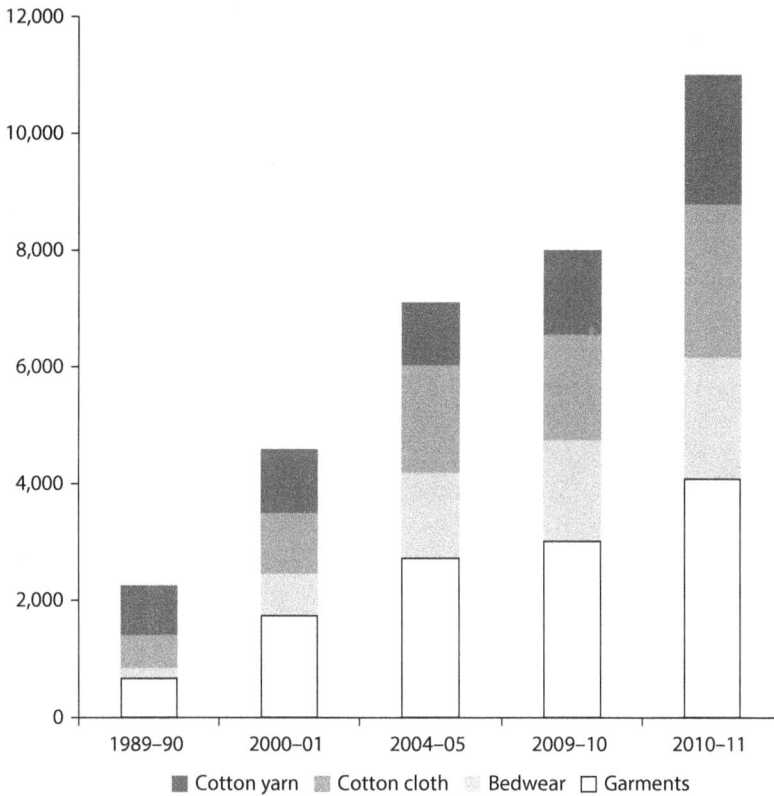

the world garment trade. It is estimated that the average labor cost of an operational hour is US$1.88 and US$1.44 in the coastal and inland regions of China, respectively, which is three times the cost in Vietnam and Pakistan, twice that of India, and six times that of Bangladesh. China's exit from the world garment trade, like Japan's and the Asian tigers' earlier exits, is inevitable. This leaves a world market of US$120 billion (and more as China becomes a net importer of garments) wide open. This is the opportunity on offer to Pakistan.

### Key Findings of Research

At the request of the Government of Pakistan, the International Growth Center has carried out several studies on garment manufacturing to contribute to the design of government policies that promote rapid expansion of the sector. One study (Husain et al. 2013) assesses the international competitiveness of Pakistan's garment manufacturers using United Nations data and the RCA approach. Data were also obtained from a survey of 234 garment firms across the major garment clusters in the country, and the Global Value Chain approach was used to explain the positioning of Pakistan's garment manufacturers. This enabled the identification of strengths to build upon and weaknesses that need to be addressed to make Pakistani exporters more competitive internationally. The second study (Nabi and Hamid 2013; see also Yusuf 2012) consists of detailed conversations with 33 garments manufacturing firms in the three major manufacturing centers: Lahore, Faisalabad, and Karachi, to assess firms' own perceptions of the growth potential and the hurdles that need to be crossed to realize that potential.

### A Modernizing Manufacturing Activity

Most garment-manufacturing entrepreneurs have a solid textiles or professional background. Most of the workforce is skilled and receives higher wages (Rs 15,000 to 20,000 per month) than unskilled workers (who earn around Rs 9,000 per month). The industry is part of intensely competitive international value chains that enforce high standards of quality and delivery. The more complex/differentiated a garment, the higher will be its value added, and hence there is a constant drive towards innovation in design and production. Most firms end up developing their own design capabilities to stay competitive. They do this by investing in research and development, hiring designers from abroad, and maintaining close links with the western fashion markets.

There is a constant drive to find niche markets and tap into new demand. For example, garment manufacturers in Pakistan are making uniforms for baseball and rugby football players during the peak seasons, heavy protective garments for bikers, school and army uniforms, and hoodies for Ivy League-type markets.

The industry also presents a great potential for the use of IT to improve its processes and quality of production. IT is used to monitor production (through closed-circuit television), to enable quality control and improve the efficiency of the internal value chain, and in accounting systems.

Contrary to the general view that garment factories are sweatshops that enable buyers to violate wealthy countries' safety and environmental standards, evidence reveals that being part of the global supply chain results in global standards for other (non-garment) manufacturers who are not directly subject to such standards. Many medium and large firms are Worldwide Responsible Accredited Production certified, which is a certification for social compliance.

## Main Challenges and Policy Interventions

The challenges and recommendations presented below are based on interviews with garment manufacturers.

### Import Policy and Market Access

Although the government allows duty exemption on re-exported items, the process is lengthy and cumbersome. It causes delays in production and restricts the diversification of product lines. These import items can be made duty free, since they do not generate sizeable revenue for the government.

The attainment of GSP-Plus status will provide a significant boost to the garment manufacturing industry and provide Pakistan with a level playing field relative to Bangladesh, which already has duty-free access to the European Union (EU).

Pakistan's total textile exports to the EU are approximately US$5.1 billion. Garment exports to the EU (excluding home textiles) currently stand at US$2.5 billion. The maximum expected increase per year for garments, after attaining the GSP-Plus status, is US$400 million. However, the EU's GSP-Plus regime will give Pakistan the potential to increase its export in Chapter 61 (clothing, knitted), Chapter 62 (clothing, woven), and Chapter 63 (textile made-ups) to the EU by US$280 million. The total potential in the current categories is approximately US$12 billion (resulting in 25,000 jobs per year).

GSP-Plus is not granted automatically; countries have to apply via a process. The GSP-Plus scheme is reviewed every three years for further extension, and is only applicable if the maximum market share per category is 6 percent or under. The Ministry of Commerce has taken the responsibility for filing the application, which has now been submitted. Voting takes place in the EU parliament.

Rising income and rising labor cost means that China will become an important export destination. Free Trade Agreement with China should include a liberalized import regime for garments. Joint ventures should be executed to take advantage of China's garments expertise (Masood Textiles' "bra" manufacturing joint venture is one example).

### Energy

Garment manufacturing is not energy intensive; nonetheless, it is severely hampered by the ongoing energy crisis. Captive power generation is not a viable option for the small and medium firms. Almost 95 percent of the industry cannot afford to set up captive power generation. One solution would be to take energy from large units from the grid and offer it to the smaller units in a manner that ensures uninterrupted supply. The benefit of solving the energy crisis is significant.

### Worker Skills

A skilled workforce is the principal driver of productivity in garment manufacturing. Also critical is middle management that supervises the workforce to ensure quality and timely delivery. The Punjab Skills Development Fund (discussed in chapter 4) should tie up with garment-manufacturing clusters as it scales up and becomes a fund for the development of growth-supporting skills. The fund will launch surveys to assess the skills needs of garment manufacturers and will design appropriate training programs; the fund will also conduct surveys in support of the cost-effective delivery of training programs.

### Garment-Manufacturing Clusters

Development of industrial clusters/economic zones is important to ensure better provision of infrastructure, and to provide connectivity and access to markets.

Since land near labor colony areas is expensive and labor's access to the firms is critical, clusters can be set up close to labor colonies, or both clusters and labor colonies can be set up simultaneously. Industrial clusters should be developed in or close to Lahore, because foreign investors would not be willing to travel to far-off locations. Cluster-agglomeration economies can be promoted by locating government worker housing projects nearby, providing public transport, opening centers for skills training, and providing facilities for the management of toxic waste.

### Logistics

Poor logistics greatly hampers the timely delivery of garment exports and thus affects manufacturers' ability to be part of the global supply chain. On-route safety and security for consignments on roads within Punjab and in Sindh need improvement. Improvement of highways and the trucking fleet are also critical for reducing inland transportation delays. There must also be strict implementation of National Highway Authority regulation on quality and carriage-load restrictions. Safety should be enhanced across the board. Local manufacturing of quality trucks of less-than-truckload (LTL) and half-truckload (HTL) must be encouraged along with training and development of the workforce.

Road connections should be improved for better connectivity among industrial clusters. As part of that, organized and secure trucking parks with the necessary support structure (fuel stations, maintenance, and resting areas) should be established near industrial clusters and near major cities. In the medium term, trucking routes via the Islamic Republic of Iran and Turkey need to be developed.

### Trade Facilitation

Customs procedures must be modernized, making them Internet related. Fast-track clearance for products and materials imported temporarily for garments will save time. Round-the-clock fast-track services for garment exports and imports at ports will also speed up delivery.

Good regional connectivity is also critical. Border crossing points (BXP) should be improved in participation with the stakeholders. The National Logistics Cell's role should be redefined, and the private sector should be encouraged to play a greater role. Investment-friendly environments in close proximity to border crossings will encourage private-sector participation. There must be a corruption identification and eradication platform.

### Industry Forum

There is a need to have a forum for knowledge exchange within industry (figure 2.11). The objective of collecting industry leaders and their affiliated supply-chain partners would be to promote information sharing and networking that triggers innovation and improvement in garment-manufacturing processes and products. Such a forum may also be used to define goals, celebrate success, and refine and align industry to a future vision.

A key element of this strategy would be a two- to three-day conference (annually or biannually) that brings together experts in garments manufacturing from around the world to have them interact with local manufacturers, government representatives, and academics. These conferences would organize visits by foreign consultants, and have them give seminars and lectures on new developments in the industry.

**Figure 2.11  Industry Forum Interactions**

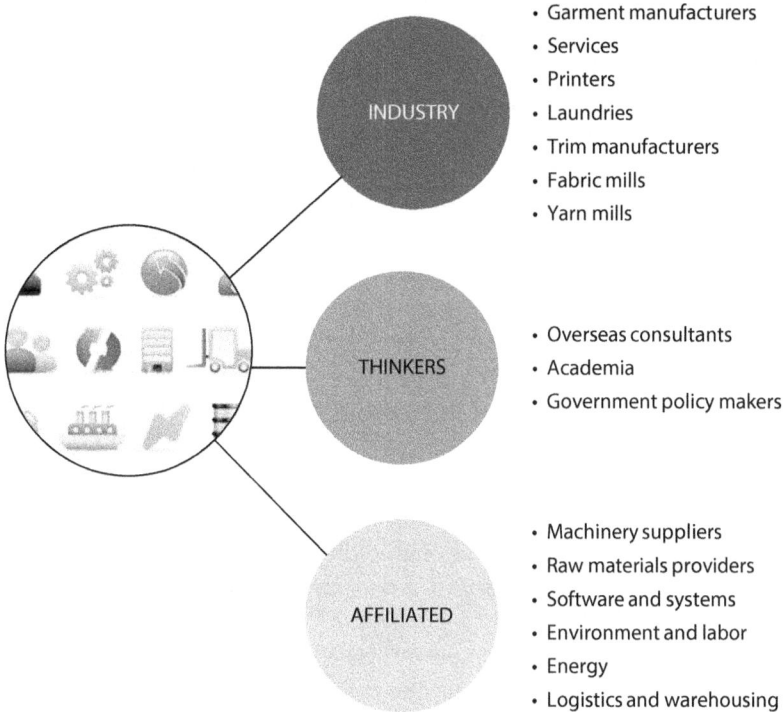

INDUSTRY

- Garment manufacturers
- Services
- Printers
- Laundries
- Trim manufacturers
- Fabric mills
- Yarn mills

THINKERS

- Overseas consultants
- Academia
- Government policy makers

AFFILIATED

- Machinery suppliers
- Raw materials providers
- Software and systems
- Environment and labor
- Energy
- Logistics and warehousing

## Generalizing to All Manufacturing Activity

The constraints faced by exporters of ready-made garments corroborate the findings of studies on the impediments that hamper industrial growth and job creation in other manufacturing activities. The discussion below sets the stage for subsequent chapters' analyses of the growth of urban clusters, skills development, trade-policy reform, and infrastructure upgrading—and related issues of environmental sustainability.

## Macroeconomic Management
### Remittances and International Competitiveness of Industry

Even though remittances and migration have been an important part of Pakistan's economy for a long time, their scale, and therefore their development impact, has taken on a new significance in the last three decades because of migration to much richer markets overseas. In 1995, total annual remittances were 1.7 percent of GDP. In 2007, they jumped to nearly 6 percent of GDP. Remittances spurred consumption-led growth in 2003–07, helped in reducing poverty, and allowed the large trade deficit to be financed without putting pressure on the exchange.

A review of economic literature on the relationship between remittances and competitiveness suggests there is considerable evidence that remittances result in appreciation of the equilibrium exchange rate (Acosta, Lartey, and Mandelman 2007a, 2007b; Montiel 2006). The high equilibrium exchange rate due to remittances can be deleterious to manufacturing that has the potential for generating employment and beneficial technological externalities. Considering that an appreciated equilibrium exchange rate erodes manufacturing firms' international competitiveness, compensatory elements may be built into other policies that affect the cost to firms of doing business. A quick review of salient policies shows that such elements have been absent in Pakistan.

The financial market in Pakistan is shallow. Firms largely rely on retained earnings to finance their working capital and investment needs, ranging from 78 percent in Sindh to 88 percent in Khyber-Pakhtunkhwa (Manes 2009). If firms draw on external finance, they mainly resort to banks and trust funds (67 percent), followed by the Central Directorate of National Savings (22 percent), non-bank financial institutions, such as development funds and venture capital (7 percent), and insurance (4 percent). A detailed breakdown of these lending categories clearly shows that personal loans have experienced the fastest growth in Pakistan over the 2001–07 period (figure 2.12).

Furthermore, access to finance is highly uneven across firms. Credit rationing largely affects small- and medium-sized enterprises (SMEs) that constitute a significant portion of the industry (figure 2.13). Consequently, it is difficult for them to grow in size and scale, and improve productivity. This is due to constraints on both the demand and supply sides. On the supply side, these comprise weak and poorly enforced creditor rights, as well as high unit costs of SME lending. In addition, SMEs are often perceived as risky borrowers. First, they face a more uncertain competitive environment than large firms, resulting in rates of return that are more variable, and thus higher rates of failure. Second, they have lower human and capital resources to withstand economic adversity. Third, their inadequate accounting systems and lack of financial controls undermine the accessibility and reliability of information on both profitability and repayment capacity. Last, they operate in a somewhat ambiguous governance environment, which reduces the security of transactions.

**Figure 2.12  Growth in Lending by Borrower Category, 2001–07 (Base Year 2001)**

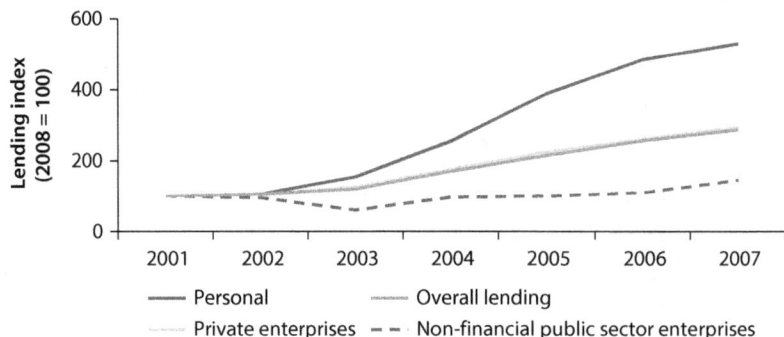

Source: Nabi 2011.

**Figure 2.13  Application for Loans/Lines of Credit by Firm Size**

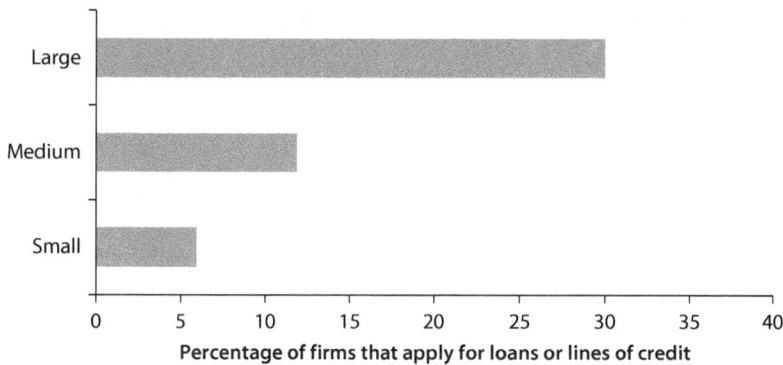

Percentage of firms that apply for loans or lines of credit

*Source:* Manes 2009.

On the demand side, the constraints consist of loan disbursement procedures, high interest rates, and significant collateral requirements (Bari, Cheema, and Haque 2005). The latter is particularly problematic, as banks often require collateral exceeding 100 percent of the loan in order to mitigate asymmetric information and adverse selection problems. However, the principal asset of manufacturing firms is land, which a highly inefficient land market effectively removes from the pool of acceptable collateral. The main problem is that land acquisition is a cumbersome process. It involves multiple agencies, complex record keeping, and sale transactions without valid conveyance documents. According to the World Bank, it takes 49 days to register a property and costs about 4.2 percent of its value. Consequently, formal titles often remain in place, preventing firms from accessing credit and land from being put to its most efficient use.

### Business Climate and Regulatory Performance

The business climate has implications for firm productivity, domestic and FDI, and overall competitiveness. Firms' experiences of the business climate tend to reveal that it has significant impacts on firm productivity and daily operations. In 2012, Pakistan ranked 105 out of 183 countries for overall ease of doing business, a decrease in rank of 9 points since 2011.[9] According to the 2011–2012 Global Competitiveness Report (World Economic Forum 2011), the biggest obstacles reported for doing business in Pakistan include government instability/coups, corruption, policy instability, inadequate supply of infrastructure, inefficient government bureaucracy, and poor access to funding. (See figure 2.14 for comparative data on regulatory performance.)

Roads and power generation are the number one infrastructure concern for businesses worldwide. However, Pakistan provides relatively low access to services that affect foreign investment. As examples, Pakistan has only 2 fixed telephone lines per 100 people compared with 70 in China, 2.9 in India, 15.8 in Indonesia, 16.1 in Malaysia, and 17.2 in Sri Lanka (World Economic Forum 2011–12). Road density stands at just 33 percent, compared with 113 percent in

**Figure 2.14  Regulatory Performance in Pakistan and Other Countries**

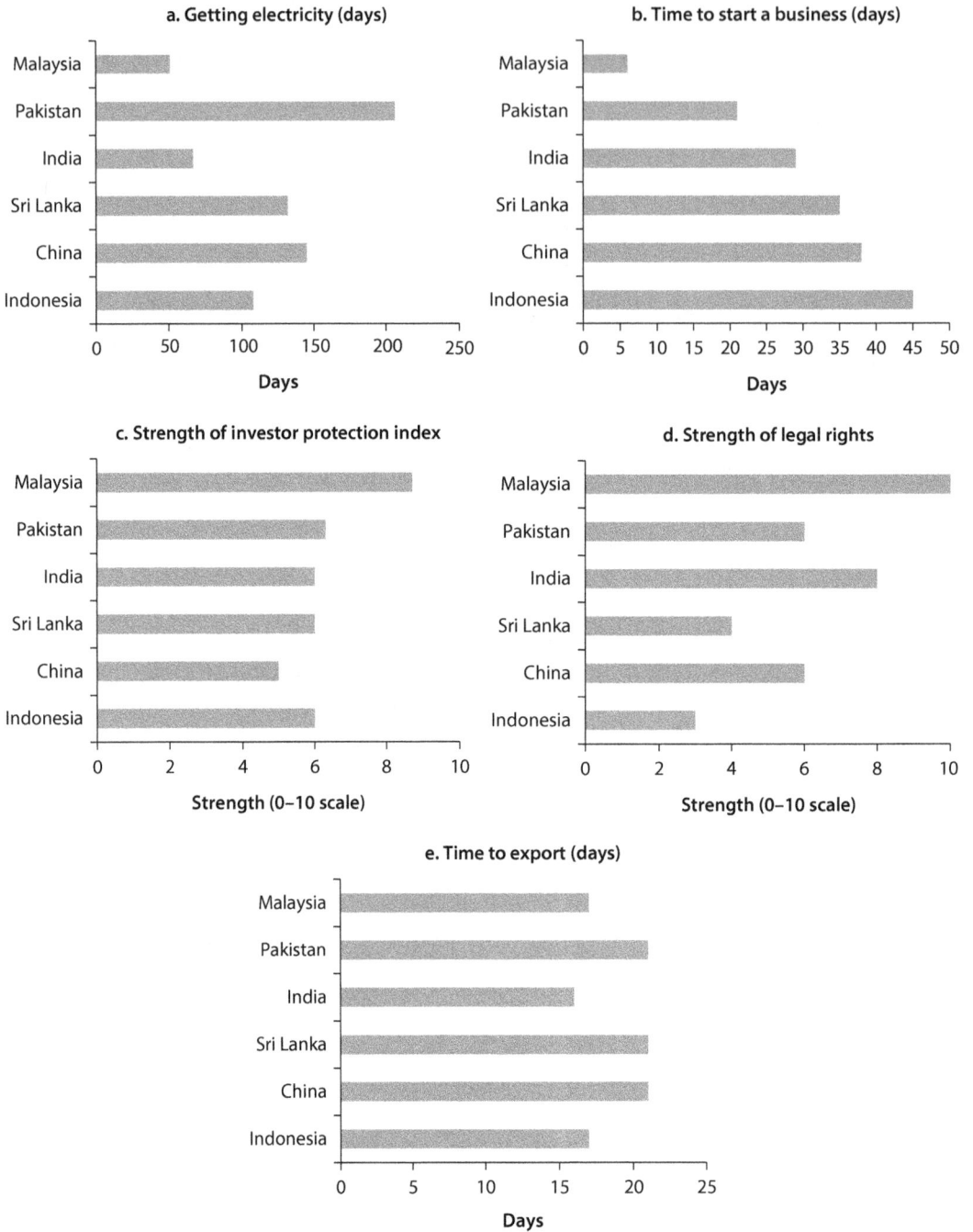

a. Getting electricity (days)

b. Time to start a business (days)

c. Strength of investor protection index

d. Strength of legal rights

e. Time to export (days)

*Source:* World Bank 2012.

India, and 150 percent in Sri Lanka. Only 54 percent of the population received electrical access, compared with 99 percent in China and 66 percent in Sri Lanka (World Bank 2009b). (See figure 2.15 for Pakistan's ranking on various infrastructure measures.)

Efficient trade and transport networks are critical determinants of competitiveness. Inadequate supply of infrastructure is one of the top problematic factors for doing business in Pakistan. The inefficient performance of the transport sector costs Pakistan's economy 4–6 percent of GDP every year.[10] The 2011–2012 Global Competitiveness Report ranks the quality of Pakistan's overall infrastructure as 115th out of 142 countries. Although Pakistan's transport sector is functional, its inefficiencies with high transport costs, long traveling and waiting times, and poor reliability are hampering the country's economic growth. These factors also reduce the competitiveness of the country's exports, limit Pakistan's ability to integrate into global supply chains, and increase the cost of doing business in Pakistan. (See table 2.6 for comparative data on access to services.)

**Figure 2.15  Ranking of Pakistan's Infrastructure Out of 142 Countries**

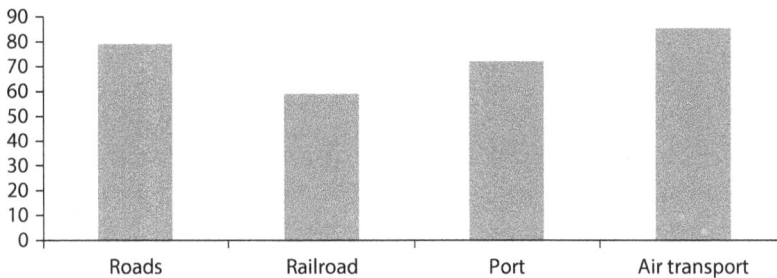

*Source:* World Economic Forum 2011–12.

**Table 2.6  Access to Services**

| Country | Avg GDP growth (2005–07) | Urbanization rate (2007) | Forecast urbanization rate (2030) | Telecom access (per 100 people) (2007) | Electricity access (% of pop.) (2005) | % Access to improved sanitation (2006) | % Access to improved water (2006) | % Paved roads | Road density (2000–06) |
|---|---|---|---|---|---|---|---|---|---|
| China | 11.67 | 42.0 | 60.3 | 27.7 | 99.4 | 65 | 88 | 70.7 | 20.7 |
| India | 9.36 | 29.0 | 40.6 | 3.5 | 55.5 | 28 | 89 | .. | 113.8 |
| Indonesia | 5.84 | 50.0 | 68.9 | 44.2 | 54.0 | 52 | 80 | 55.4 | 20.3 |
| Malaysia | 5.82 | 69.0 | 82.2 | 16.4 | 97.8 | 94 | 99 | 79.8 | 30.0 |
| Mexico | 3.74 | 77.0 | 83.3 | 18.8 | .. | 81 | 95 | 50.0 | 17.7 |
| Pakistan | 6.62 | 36.0 | 49.8 | 3.0 | 54.0 | 58 | 90 | 65.4 | 33.5 |
| Sri Lanka | 6.90 | 15.1 | 21.4 | 53.8 | 66.0 | 86 | 82 | 81.0 | 150.5 |

*Source:* World Bank 2009b.
*Note:* .. = negligible, GDP = gross domestic product.

*Other Salient Factors Eroding Manufacturing Competitiveness*[11]
*Scarcity of skilled workers:* Low overall education attainment implies that firms employ fewer trainable workers, and firms do not have a high regard for government programs for skill upgrading; this raises unit labor cost (wage divided by output per worker) and erodes competitiveness. The SME sector currently suffers from a lack of access to skilled labor. Pakistan today has the highest population growth rate in the South Asian region, with very large numbers of unskilled entrants into the labor force every year. These adverse demographics pose a serious challenge to effective policy making. If the industrial base of the country does not expand to absorb this surplus labor, the bourgeoning unemployment in both urban and rural areas is likely to have serious socioeconomic and political ramifications. On the other hand, a growing population has the potential to become a significant economic asset, if adequate policies are in place to facilitate the development of a large, healthy, and skilled labor force. By 2007, only 6.7 percent of firms offered formal training (World Bank 2007).

*Lack of Innovation and Technology:* Related to the scarcity of skilled workers, firms lag in conducting formal research and developing high-technology products and advanced production processes. Most SME sectors face issues relating to innovation and the development of original products and designs (LUMS 2011). In general, companies do not spend much on research and development activity, and business collaboration with local universities and product development centers is minimal at best. Local suppliers have little technological capabilities, and hence are not able to assist in developing new products and processes (Lopez-Claros, Porter, and Schwab 2005, 525). Only 9 percent of firms have an internationally recognized quality certification, and only 2.7 percent of firms use technology licensed from foreign companies (World Bank 2007). Suppliers operating in clusters stand to benefit from collaboration with their international counterparts that are knowledgeable about new product and process developments.

*Discriminatory Tax Regime:* Pakistan's tax system is one of the major obstacles to economic growth in the manufacturing sector. According to The Investment Climate Report by the World Bank (2009a), in 2009, 40 percent of firms in Pakistan stated taxes as being a barrier in doing business, even though this figure decreased from 47 percent in 2002. The bulk of the country's total tax revenue is collected from manufacturing firms (corporate income tax) and their output (sales tax and various excises), while agriculture and most services are out of the tax net; this makes it more attractive to invest in non-manufacturing activity. Overall, taxes increase the cost of doing business, reduce incentives to invest in the manufacturing sector, and create barriers for local producers to face competitive international markets, all of which are barriers to growth of the industrial sector (Manes 2009).

*Deteriorating Security:* Industrial activity with long supply chains and concentrated in vulnerable urban centers is relatively more adversely affected than agriculture and traditional services; this, in turn, affects the industrial investment climate. Furthermore, both remittances and official assistance increased sharply as security deteriorated, which may have exacerbated the Dutch Disease problem.

The poor law and security situation affects industrial production at two levels. First, lack of security creates a poor perception of Pakistan in international markets; buyers in these markets have become strongly skeptical about doing business with suppliers in Pakistan. Second, a perception of lack of security has implications for businesses' property and assets, since it results in the private sector reducing its economic activity in the country. Based on a World Bank survey, the percentage of firms considering law and order to be a major constraint on their business increased from 22 percent in 2002 to 35 percent in 2007.

## Notes

1. The literature on agglomerations is vast and relatively new. See, for example, Fujita and Thisse (2002) and World Bank (2009c).

2. The growth rates of other South Asian countries also dropped, but not to the same low levels as Pakistan's (ADB 2010). For example, India's GDP growth rate fell to 6.7 percent in 2008 but has risen since then to 7.2 percent in 2009. Similarly, Bangladesh has maintained its growth rates at an average of 6.2 percent.

3. Because of fiscal and external deficits, Pakistan sought help in the late 1980s from the World Bank and the International Monetary Fund on an emergency basis for the revival of its economy. The Structural Adjustment Program was introduced to address the twin deficits through reductions in expenditures and increases in tax revenue, along with conditions pertaining to the restructuring of the economy through liberalization, privatization, and deregulation.

4. The implementation of the Privatization Act 2000, and the creation of the Ministry of Privatization and Investment, Board of Investments (BOI), and the Insurance Act 2001 were important steps in this direction. A new legal structure was introduced to strengthen the financial system. This new system includes the introduction of recovery laws, a legal structure for non-bank financial institutions, a monetary and fiscal board for better coordination between monetary and fiscal policies, and the Fiscal Responsibility and Debt Limitation Act 2005, which was primarily aimed at reducing fiscal deficits.

5. Competitiveness is defined by 12 pillars (institutions, infrastructure, macroeconomic stability, health and primary education, higher education and training, goods market efficiency, labor market efficiency, financial market sophistication, technological readiness, market size, business sophistication, and innovation) and divided into three categories (basic requirement, efficiency enhancers, and innovation and sophistication).

6. The PRODY index is constructed as the weighted average of the per capita GDPs of the countries exporting a specific product, and thus represents the income (and productivity) level associated with that product. The weights are the revealed comparative advantage of each country in each product (normalized to one). If most high-income countries have revealed comparative advantage in the export of a product, PRODY would be high.

7. The RCA is the ratio of the share of product A in Pakistan's total exports to the share of product A in total world exports. If RCA is greater than 1, then it implies that the country has a comparative advantage in that product.

8. The product concentration level is measured using the index, $G_t=(\sum_k W_{it}^2)^{1/2}$, where $k$ is the number of products that account for more than 90 percent of Pakistan's exports,

and $Wi$ is the share of commodity $i$ in total export earnings. The index can take a value between 0 and 1; the closer it is to 1, the greater the degree of concentration. Pakistan's value is 0.40.

9. A World Bank report sheds light on how easy or difficult it is for a local entrepreneur to open and run a small to medium-size business when complying with relevant regulations. It measures and tracks changes in regulations affecting ten areas in the life cycle of a business: starting a business, dealing with construction permits, getting electricity, registering property, getting credit, protecting investors, paying taxes, trading across borders, enforcing contracts, and resolving insolvency (World Bank 2012).

10. GoP 2011, 2013. In many developed countries, transport contributes between 6 and 12 percent of national GDP (Rodrigue, Comtois, and Slack 2009). In India, the transport sector contributed between 5.7–6.4 percent of GDP between 1999 and 2005 (ADB 2007).

11. This summary is based on NLTA policy note "Increasing Pakistan's Competitiveness: Spatial Transformation, Industrial Development and Income Growth," and Nabi (2011).

## References

Acosta, P. A., E. K. K. Lartey, and F. Mandelman. 2007a. "Remittances, Exchange Rate Regimes and the Dutch Disease." Working Paper 2008–08, Federal Reserve Bank of Atlanta, Atlanta, Georgia.

———. 2007b. "Remittances, Exchange Rate Regimes and the Dutch Disease: A Panel Data Analysis." Working Paper 2008–12, Federal Reserve Bank of Atlanta, Atlanta, Georgia.

ADB (Asian Development Bank). 2007. *Profile of the Indian Transport Sector*. Manila: Asian Development Bank.

———. 2008. *Private Sector Assessment Pakistan*. Manila: Asian Development Bank.

———. 2010. *Asian Development Outlook 2010*. Manila: Asian Development Bank.

Bari, F., A. Cheema, and E. Haque. 2005. "SME Development in Pakistan: Analyzing the Constraints to Growth." Pakistan Resident Mission Working Paper 3, Asian Development Bank, Manila.

Biller, D., and I. Nabi. 2013. *Investing in Infrastructure: Harnessing its Potential for Growth in Sri Lanka*. Washington, DC: World Bank.

UN (United Nations) Comtrade (database). United Nations, New York. http://comtrade.un.org/.

Fujita, M., and J. F. Thisse. 2002. *Economics of Agglomeration. Cities, Industrial Location, and Regional Growth*. Cambridge, UK: Cambridge University Press.

Gapminder.org. 2012. "Data in Gapminder World." http://www.gapminder.org/data.

GoP (Government of Pakistan). 1988. *Pakistan Economic Survey 1987–88*. Ministry of Finance. Islamabad.

———. 1993. *Pakistan Economic Survey 1992–93*. Ministry of Finance. Islamabad.

———. 2000. *Pakistan Economic Survey 1999–2000*. Ministry of Finance. Islamabad.

———. 2003. *Pakistan Economic Survey 2002–03*. Ministry of Finance. Islamabad.

———. 2004. *Pakistan Economic Survey 2003–04*. Ministry of Finance. Islamabad.

———. 2007. *Pakistan Economic Survey 2006–07*. Ministry of Finance. Islamabad.

———. 2008. *Pakistan Economic Survey 2007–08*. Ministry of Finance. Islamabad. http://finance.gov.pk/survey_0708.html.

———. 2009. *Pakistan Economic Survey 2008–2009*. Ministry of Finance. Islamabad. http://finance.gov.pk/survey_0809.html.

———. 2010. Poverty Reduction Strategy Paper (PRSP) II. Ministry of Finance. Islamabad. http://www.finance.gov.pk/poverty/PRSP-II.pdf.

———. 2011. *Pakistan Economic Survey 2010–2011*. Ministry of Finance. Islamabad. http://www.finance.gov.pk/survey_1011.html.

———. 2013. Federal Bureau of Statistics. Islamabad.

Husain, T., K. Malik, U. Khan, A. Faheem, I. Nabi, and N. Hamid. 2013. "A Comparative Analysis of the Garments Sector of Pakistan." Draft report, Pakistan, International Growth Centre-Pakistan. London and Oxford, UK: London School of Economics and University of Oxford.

Klinger, B., and D. Lederman. 2004. "Diversification, Innovation, and Imitation off the Global Technological Frontier." Working Paper 3450, World Bank, Washington, DC.

Lall, S. 2000. "The Technological Structure and Performance of Developing Country Manufactured Exports, 1985–98." *Oxford Development Studies* 28 (3): 337–69.

Lopez-Claros, A., M. Porter, and K. Schwab, eds. 2005. *Global Competitiveness Report 2005–2006*. London: Palgrave Macmillan.

Lahore University of Management Sciences (LUMS). 2011. *Mainstreaming Environmental Sustainability in Pakistan's Industrial Growth*. Washington, DC: World Bank.

Manes, E. 2009. *Pakistan's Investment Climate Laying the Foundations for Growth. Volume 1: Main Report*. Washington, DC: Poverty Reduction and Economic Management Department Finance and Private Sector Unit, South Asia Department, World Bank.

Montiel, P. J. 2006. "Workers' Remittances and the Long Run Equilibrium Exchange Rate: Analytical Issues." Mimeograph, Williams College, Williamstown, MA.

Nabi, I. 2011. "Economic Growth and Structural Change in South Asia: Miracle and Mirage." Development Policy Research Center Monograph. Lahore University of Management Sciences, Lahore.

Nabi, I., and N. Hamid. 2013. "Garments as Driver of Economic Growth: Insights from Pakistan Case Studies." Draft report, International Growth Centre-Pakistan. London and Oxford, UK: London School of Economics and University of Oxford.

Rodrigue, J.-P, C. Comtois, and B. Slack. 2009. *The Geography of Transport Systems*. London and New York: Routledge. http://geonas.at.ua/_ld/0/34_The_Geography_o.pdf.

Timmer, P. C., and S. Akkus. 2008. "The Structural Transformation as a Pathway out of Poverty: Analytics, Empirics and Politics." Working Paper 150, Center for Global Development, Washington, DC. http://www.cgdev.org/content/publications/detail/16421.

Wang, M. 2009. "Manufacturing FDI and Economic Growth: Evidence from Asian Economies." *Applied Economics* 41 (8): 991–1002.

World Bank. 2007. Enterprise Survey Data for Pakistan, 2007. World Bank, Washington, DC. http://www.enterprisesurveys.org/Data/ExploreEconomies/2007/pakistan#infrastructure.

———. 2009a. *Pakistan's Investment Climate Laying the Foundations for Growth. Volume 1: The Main Report*. Poverty Reduction and Economic Management

Department Finance and Private Sector Unit, South Asia Department. Washington, DC: World Bank.

———. 2009b. World Development Indicators (database). World Bank, Washington, DC. http://data.worldbank.org/data-catalog/world-development-indicators.

———. 2009c. *World Development Report 2009: Reshaping Economic Geography*. Washington, DC: World Bank. http://wwwwds.worldbank.org/external/default /WDSContentServer/IW3P/IB/2008/12/03/000333038_20081203234958 /Rendered/PDF/437380REVISED01BLIC1097808213760720.pdf.

———. 2012. *Doing Business*. World Bank, Washington, DC. http://www.doingbusiness .org/.

World Economic Forum. 2011. *Global Competitiveness Report 2011–2012*. Geneva, Switzerland: World Economic Forum.

Yusuf, S. 2012. "Garment Suppliers Beware: The Global Garments Value Chain is Changing." International Growth Centre-Pakistan. London and Oxford, UK: London School of Economics and University of Oxford.

# CHAPTER 3

# Spatial Transformation

## Introduction

This chapter discusses various aspects of Pakistan's ongoing urbanization. With the highest population growth rate[1] in South Asia, and the ongoing spatial transformation, Pakistan's population residing in cities is expected to increase from 36 percent in 2010 to nearly 50 percent in the decade starting in 2030. By 2020, Pakistan will have two megacities (over 10 million population), Karachi and Lahore, and several others with populations of at least one million (three in Punjab, and one each in Sindh, Khyber Pakhtunkhwa, Balochistan, and the Islamabad Federal Territory). The ongoing structural transformation of the economy—by which agricultural modernization and mechanization displaces a growing number of rural people—will intensify this migration trend.[2]

The demographic dynamics will pose a serious social challenge[3] if urban centers do not provide adequate employment opportunities. However, if appropriate policies are in place to promote agglomeration economies, the growing urban population has the potential to become an economic asset. Key to this is a vibrant industrial sector that has the ability to create a range of jobs requiring skills of different intensity. This book argues that skills development, trade reform, infrastructure modernization, adoption and stronger implementation of environmental safeguards, and oversight institutions will be needed to realize the agglomeration economies and industrial vibrancy associated with rapid urbanization.

The next section reviews the migration patterns in Pakistan. The chapter's third section then discusses the spatial comparative advantage of urban centers, and the provision of infrastructure and social services. Section 4 highlights the agglomeration economies associated with urban centers that help promote industrialization. Section 5 concludes with remarks on managing the negative externalities of rapid urbanization that are further developed in subsequent chapters.

## Overview of Migration in Pakistan

Migration is ingrained in Pakistan's history, notably with the massive parti-
tion migration following the emergence of independent states in South Asia.
Migration remains a defining feature of the country's socioeconomic dynamics,
both internally and internationally. For one, Pakistan hosts the largest number
of refugees in the world, with 1.8 million refugees at the end of 2008, almost
all of whom are Afghans.[4] Furthermore, at the end of 2010, there were around
2 million internally displaced people, 1.4 million of them registered by the government (OCHA 2010). Second, migration is a key factor defining Pakistan's
society and labor markets. Migration operates at three levels: internationally,
regionally, and internally, all of which have strong socioeconomic implication for
Pakistan. These migrations are both vectors and outcomes of Pakistan's present
and future spatial transformation.

At the national level, internal migration is particularly strong; in Pakistan, the
share of rural-to-urban migration increased over time (1996–2006), while urban-
to-urban migration declined, yet remaining highest in internal migration (Hamid
2010). Such migrations are also likely to be facilitated by reforms in the freight
transport sector and have strong sociopolitical implication for Pakistan. Indeed,
the regional distribution of population also has key significance for provinces due
to its repercussions on their political representation and rights in the federation,
distribution of resources, and employment quotas as provisioned in the constitution. About 30 percent of total migration as of 2008–09 (or up to 3 million
people) has been from rural to urban areas.

Any analysis of urbanization trends that does not consider the inter- and intra-
provincial differences in migration trends in Pakistan would be incomplete (Arif
and Hamid 2009). According to the *Labor Force Survey 2008–09* (GoP 2009),
Punjab accounted for the bulk of migrant labor, both inter- and intra-provincial,
while the proportion of migrant labor in other provinces tapered down roughly
in consonance with their total population (GoP 2009). Intra-provincial migration has been particularly strong in Punjab with 71.7 percent of all those who
reported intra-provincial migration being based in Punjab (table 3.1). The
direction of inter-provincial migration seemed more towards Sindh, particularly
Karachi, Pakistan's largest city and commercial center, where 41.5 percent of all
workers who had migrated across provinces were found to be working. About
15 percent of the total workforce consists of internal migrants, and the proportion goes up to almost 20 percent for wage employment. Given that the total
civilian labor force in the country consists of 53.72 million people (GoP 2009),
this would mean that from 7 to 10 million people had migrated to join the labor
force outside their place of origin as of 2008–09. These migrants generally moved
towards wage employment (in larger cities) or self-employment in services (in
smaller towns).[5] This trend is accentuated by the structure of labor markets in
Pakistan, where almost a third of firms tend to rely on seasonal or temporary
labor, thus being able to add to, or shed from, the labor force as per trends in
market demand (GoP 2009).

**Table 3.1  Inter- and Intra-Migration in Pakistan, 2009**

| Provinces | Total | | | Inter-provincial | | | Intra-provincial | | |
|---|---|---|---|---|---|---|---|---|---|
| | Total | Male | Female | Total | Male | Female | Total | Male | Female |
| Pakistan | 100 | 100 | 100 | 100 | 100 | 100 | 100 | 100 | 100 |
| Punjab | 63.7 | 56.4 | 69.0 | 34.6 | 31.1 | 39.3 | 71.7 | 66.7 | 74.8 |
| Sindh | 25.1 | 28.3 | 22.7 | 41.5 | 37.9 | 46.0 | 20.6 | 24.4 | 18.2 |
| Khyber Pakhtunkhwa | 10.7 | 14.7 | 7.8 | 23.2 | 30.4 | 13.8 | 7.2 | 8.3 | 6.6 |
| Balochistan | 0.5 | 0.6 | 0.5 | 0.7 | 0.6 | 0.9 | 0.5 | 0.6 | 0.4 |

*Source:* GoP 2009.

**Table 3.2  International Migration**

| Year | Estimated number of international migrants at mid-year | International migrants as a percentage of the population |
|---|---|---|
| 1990 | 6,555,782 | 5.7 |
| 1995 | 4,076,599 | 3.1 |
| 2000 | 4,242,689 | 2.9 |
| 2005 | 3,554,009 | 2.1 |
| 2010 | 4,233,592 | 2.3 |

*Source:* UN 2011.

Internationally, migrants from Pakistan represent 2.3 percent of the country's population (table 3.2). Pakistani migrants are estimated to send back about US$8.6 billion in remittances (Ratha and Mohapatra 2009). At the regional level, Pakistan hosts 2.8 million intra-regional migrants. In facilitating connectivity, reforms of the freight transport sector could also contribute to the international migration of workers from Pakistan, an option that may particularly appeal to younger migrants. It will also likely increase the attractiveness of Pakistan's major cities—notably Karachi—to migrants from the region.

## Spatial Comparative Advantage of Urban Centers: Provision of Infrastructure and Social Services

The considerable variation in the provision of services in urban versus rural areas is a major "pull factor" for spatial transformation. The evaluation conducted by LUMS (2011) under the Non-Lending Technical Assistance clearly shows this. Highly agglomerated areas have both more hospitals and more post-primary education (map 3.1 and figures 3.1 and 3.2).

Map 3.1 shows the mapping of districts based on their development index[6] for 2005–06. The map confirms the above findings that investment in social infrastructure is highly concentrated in cities and their surrounding districts, whereas districts located away from these urban demand centers (for example, southern Punjab, the interior of Sindh, and remotely located districts in Khyber Pakhtunkhwa and Balochistan) are lagging behind. As new literature on economic geography predicts, better-ranked districts with pools of skilled workers

**Map 3.1  Location of Districts by Hospital and Education Index**

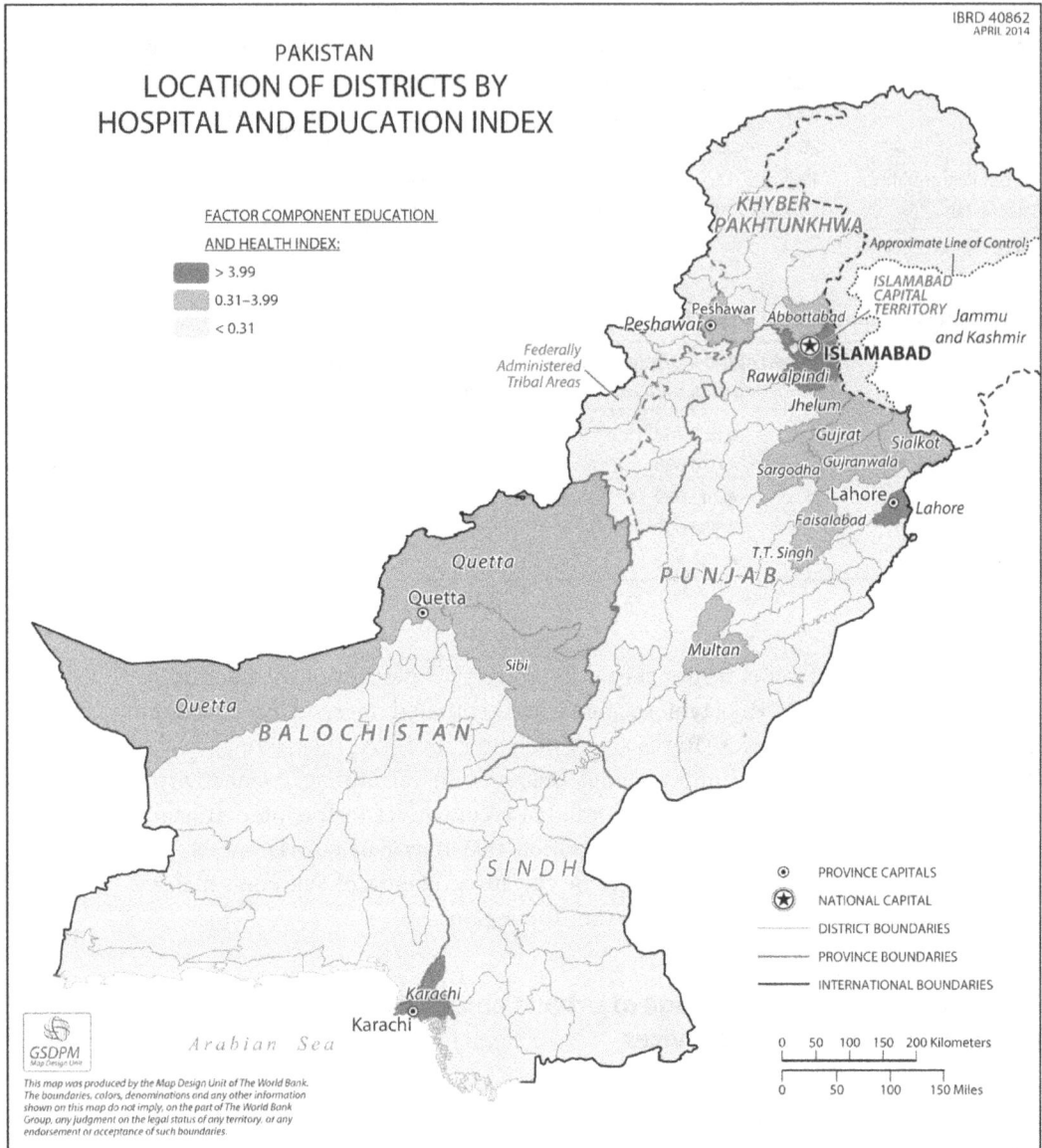

IBRD 40862
APRIL 2014

PAKISTAN
LOCATION OF DISTRICTS BY
HOSPITAL AND EDUCATION INDEX

FACTOR COMPONENT EDUCATION
AND HEALTH INDEX:

> 3.99
0.31–3.99
< 0.31

KHYBER
PAKHTUNKHWA

Approximate Line of Control

ISLAMABAD
CAPITAL
TERRITORY   Jammu
and Kashmir

Peshawar   Abbottabad
Peshawar

ISLAMABAD

Federally
Administered
Tribal Areas

Rawalpindi

Jhelum

Gujrat   Sialkot
Sargodha Gujranwala

Lahore
Faisalabad   Lahore

Quetta
Quetta

T.T. Singh

PUNJAB

Sibi

Multan

Quetta

BALOCHISTAN

SINDH

PROVINCE CAPITALS
NATIONAL CAPITAL
DISTRICT BOUNDARIES
PROVINCE BOUNDARIES
INTERNATIONAL BOUNDARIES

Karachi
Karachi

Arabian Sea

0    50   100  150  200 Kilometers

0      50       100       150 Miles

GSDPM
Map Design Unit

This map was produced by the Map Design Unit of The World Bank.
The boundaries, colors, denominations and any other information
shown on this map do not imply, on the part of The World Bank
Group, any judgment on the legal status of any territory, or any
endorsement or acceptance of such boundaries.

*Source:* LUMS 2011.

have a higher concentration of large-scale manufacturing clusters than lower-ranked districts (figure 3.3).

Districts with higher levels of agglomeration also have a greater proportion of large-scale manufacturing production (map 3.2). Figure 3.3 shows that the value of manufacturing production is positively correlated with district-level population growth from 1981 to 2005. Overall, districts in Pakistan with a population density of more than 600 persons per km$^2$ are characterized by industrial

**Figure 3.1  Post-Primary School System and Current Population, 2005–06**

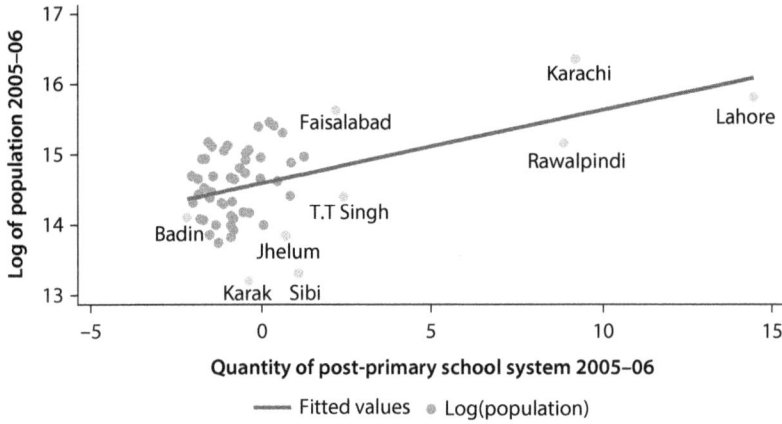

*Source:* LUMS 2011.
*Note:* Names and green dots are used to highlight the district with the most extreme values.

**Figure 3.2  Hospital Size and Current Population, 2005–06**

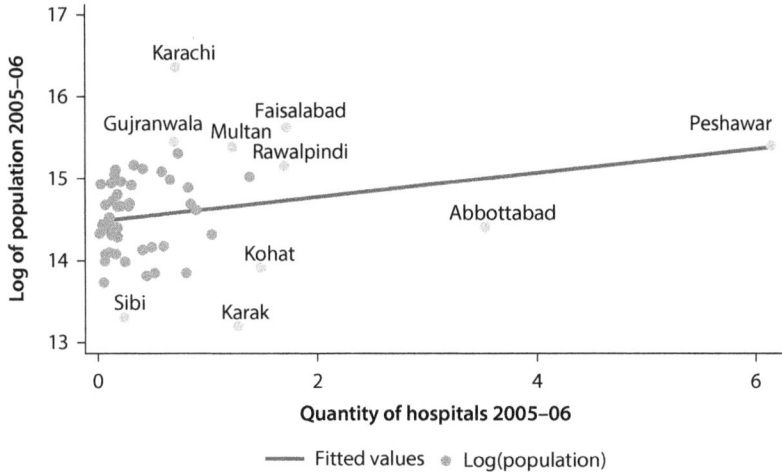

*Source:* LUMS 2011.
*Note:* Names and green dots are used to highlight the district with the most extreme values.

development, better education and health infrastructure, and better sanitation facilities than those in rural areas (LUMS 2011). These districts include Karachi, Lahore, Peshawar, Faisalabad, Sialkot, Islamabad, Multan, Swabi, Gujrat, Rawalpindi, Charsadda, and Gujranwala (LUMS 2011).

In addition, districts with medium-level population densities—that is, between 300 and 600 persons per km²—have some industrial development and are endowed with agricultural resources. In contrast, districts with low population densities—that is, below 30 persons per km²—are characterized by limited job opportunities, little to no industrial presence, and poor agricultural endowments (LUMS 2011).

**Figure 3.3  Value of Large-Scale Manufacturing Production and Population Growth**

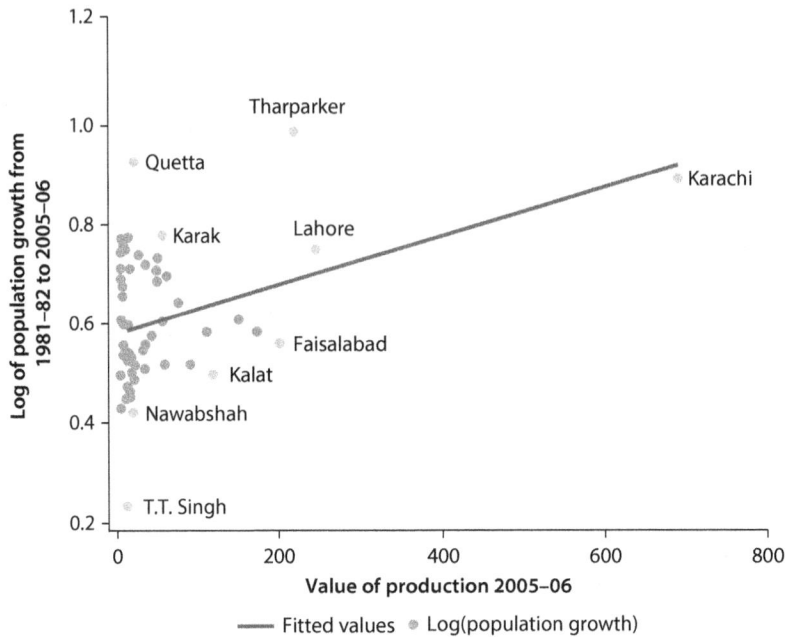

Source: LUMS 2011.
Note: Names and green dots are used to highlight the district with the most extreme values.

## Urban Centers as Agglomeration Economies

Recent work in economic geography and urban economics highlights the significance of agglomeration economies as the defining factor for both industrial firms' and people's location decisions. A pronounced feature of industrial economic activity in Pakistan is the highly geographic concentration (clustering) of firms around the metropolitan cities of Lahore and Karachi (map 3.2). Even medium-concentrated districts are clustered in proximity to these two big cities. Statistical results based on the Ellison and Glaeser[7] (EG) Index indicate that 35 percent of the industries in Pakistan are highly agglomerated, 38 percent are moderately agglomerated, and 27 percent are not agglomerated. This finding is further supported in figure 3.4, which plots the frequency distribution of the EG index across industries, and in figure 3.5, which shows the overall level of agglomeration in the country. In Pakistan, the most highly concentrated industries are ship breaking, followed by sports and athletic goods. The other highly concentrated industries are those sectors for which it is critical to be in proximity to consumers and suppliers, such as furniture and fixtures, scientific instruments, pharmaceutical industry, wearing apparel, handicrafts and office supplies, printing and publishing, pottery and china products, and paper and paper products (LUMS 2011).

**Map 3.2 Industry Clusters and Development Ranking of Districts, 2005–06**

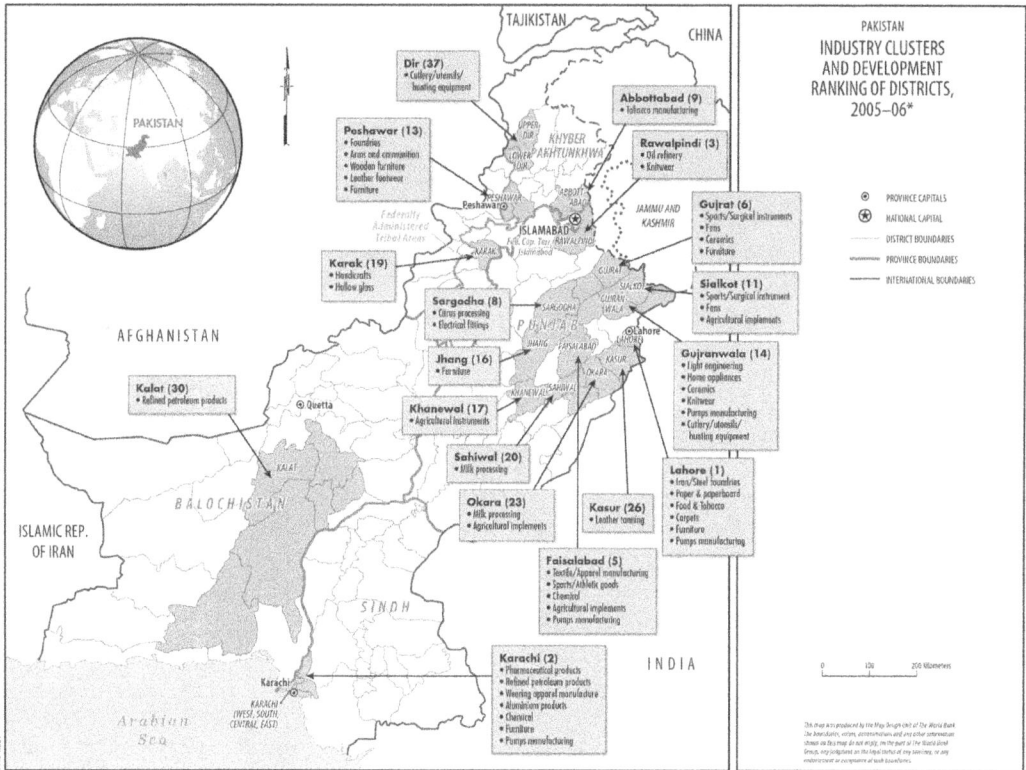

TAJIKISTAN

CHINA

PAKISTAN
INDUSTRY CLUSTERS
AND DEVELOPMENT
RANKING OF DISTRICTS,
2005–06*

PAKISTAN

Dir (37)
• Cutlery/utensils/
  boating equipment

Abbottabad (9)
• Tobacco manufacturing

Peshawar (13)
• Foundries
• Iron and ammunition
• Wooden furniture
• Leather footwear
• Furniture

KHYBER
PAKHTUNKHWA

Rawalpindi (3)
• Oil refinery
• Knitwear

⊕ PROVINCE CAPITALS
⊛ NATIONAL CAPITAL
------ DISTRICT BOUNDARIES
▬▬▬ PROVINCE BOUNDARIES
▬▬▬ INTERNATIONAL BOUNDARIES

Federally
Administered
Tribal Areas

ISLAMABAD

JAMMU AND
KASHMIR

Gujrat (6)
• Sports/Surgical instruments
• Fans
• Ceramics
• Furniture

Karak (19)
• Handicrafts
• Hollow glass

Sargodha (8)
• Citrus processing
• Electrical fittings

P U N J A B

Sialkot (11)
• Sports/Surgical instrument
• Fans
• Agricultural implements

AFGHANISTAN

Lahore

Jhang (16)
• Furniture

Gujranwala (14)
• Light engineering
• Home appliances
• Ceramics
• Knitwear
• Pumps manufacturing
• Cutlery/utensils/
  boating equipment

Kalat (30)
• Refined petroleum products

Quetta

Khanewal (17)
• Agricultural instruments

Sahiwal (20)
• Milk processing

Lahore (1)
• Iron/Steel foundries
• Paper & paperboard
• Food & Tobacco
• Carpets
• Furniture
• Pumps manufacturing

B A L O C H I S T A N

Okara (23)
• Milk processing
• Agricultural implements

Kasur (26)
• Leather tanning

ISLAMIC REP.
OF IRAN

Faisalabad (5)
• Textiles/Apparel manufacturing
• Sports/Athletic goods
• Chemical
• Agricultural implements
• Pumps manufacturing

S I N D H

Karachi (2)
• Pharmaceutical products
• Refined petroleum products
• Wearing apparel manufacture
• Aluminium products
• Chemical
• Furniture
• Pumps manufacturing

INDIA

Karachi

KARACHI
(WEST, SOUTH,
CENTRAL, EAST)

Arabian
Sea

0　　100　　200 Kilometers

*Source:* CMI 2005–06.

Evidence in Pakistan suggests that firms tend to locate in areas where there are "location economies," which are areas that minimize procurement costs (transport costs associated with the transportation of raw materials to the firm) and distribution costs (transport costs associated with distributing the products to customers). These areas have available specialized labor, inter-industry spillovers, local transfers of knowledge, and access to export markets. However, from 2000–01 to 2005–06, industry concentration decreased dramatically by about 33 percent (LUMS 2011).

The benefits of agglomeration of industries are often associated with the reduction of three types of transport costs: "moving goods," "moving people," and "moving ideas" (knowledge spillovers and sharing). Agglomeration is fundamental to industrial competitiveness because it promotes (a) knowledge and information spillovers and innovative ideas among firms, (b) labor-market pooling, and (c) input-output linkages. Spatial proximity of firms attracts suppliers and consumers to the region. Proximity also promotes the exchange of ideas between firms in clusters (Breschi and Lissoni 2003). A high concentration of firms can also attract and sustain a large labor force with the skills demanded

**Figure 3.4  Distribution of 3-Digit Ellison-Glaeser (EG) Index**

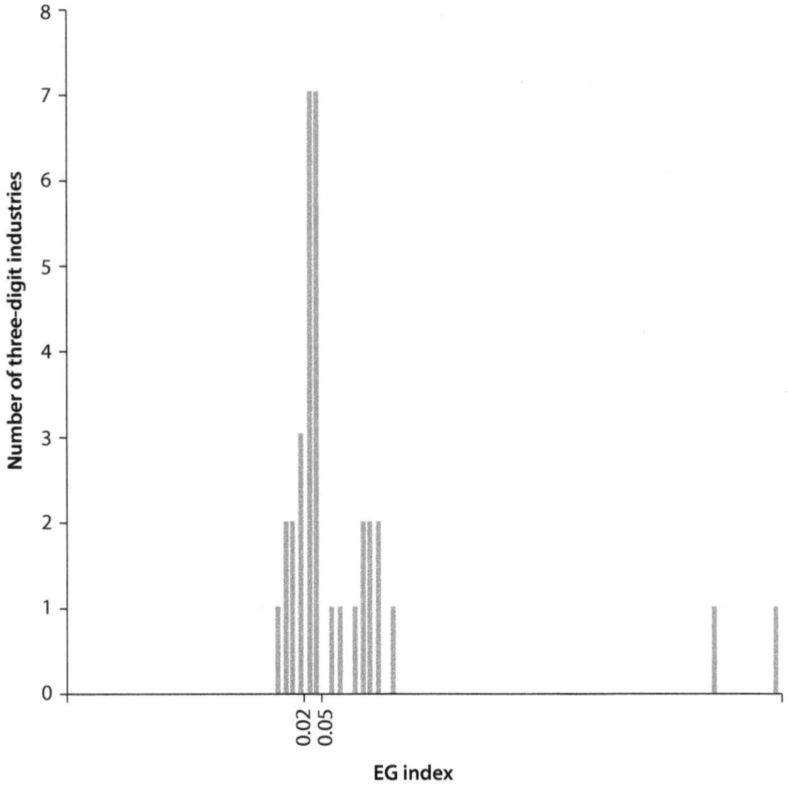

Source: LUMS 2011.

by that industry. Hence, location economies help create competitive advantage by improving firms' access to resources.

The LUMS 2011 study finds that the size of district-level population and road density help promote the agglomerating of industrial firms. Moreover, there are positive correlations between industrial locations and employment (map 3.3). Indeed, as stated in *World Development Report 2009: Reshaping Economic Geography*, "The pull of agglomeration forces in prosperous places is simply too strong for any opposing measure to be sustained."[8] According to the *Labor Force Survey 2008–09* (GoP 2009), 41.5 percent of all workers who had migrated across provinces were found to be working in Sindh, particularly Karachi, Pakistan's largest city and commercial center.

A recent study found that the majority of males (61 percent) cited economic reasons as main factors for migration (Arif and Hamid 2009). For females, marriage and reuniting with family are the most important reasons for migration between different regions. Average income of working men and women improves considerably after migration to cities. In a separate study,[9] males reported an average difference of 1,192 rupees in their monthly income after migration, which is 1.84

**Figure 3.5   Agglomeration Level in Pakistani Manufacturing Industries**
*Percent*

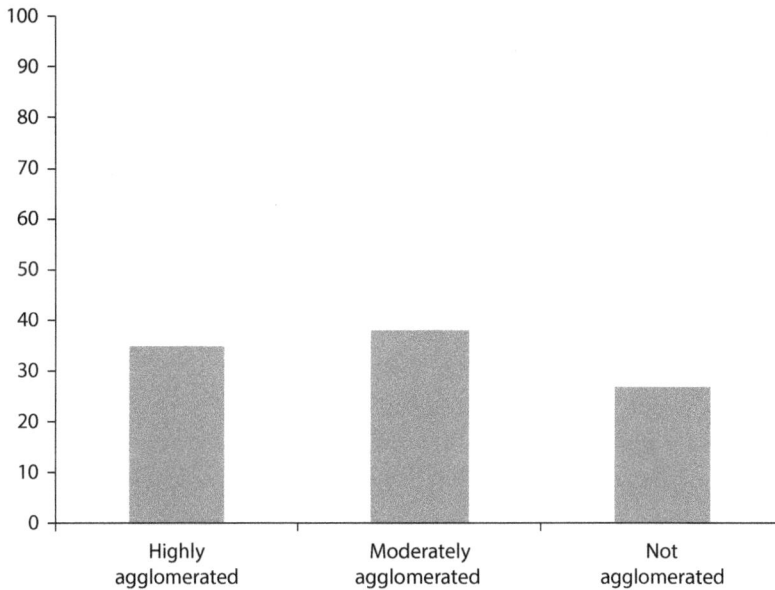

Source: LUMS 2011.

times higher than their pre-migration average income. Women were also able to augment their incomes after migration; their income was 2.4 times more than their earning in rural areas. However, women's average income remained lower than men's before and after migration, even though the income gap decreased. Before migration, women's monthly income was 62 percent of men's income, and after migration, this ratio increased to 85 percent. Income data reveal two important findings: (a) migration contributes to improved earnings for both sexes; and (b) gender differentials in incomes for urban areas are lower than in rural areas.

By 2025, Pakistan is expected to have two megacities (over 10 million), Karachi and Lahore, and eight additional cities over one million (table 3.3) (UN HABITAT 2011). With economic motivations dominating rural to urban migration, it is not surprising to find Lahore and Karachi, the two most highly concentrated districts in large-scale manufacturing employment, among those attracting a larger number of migrants.

Given the importance of urban centers and their linkages with employment, urbanization, and industrial development, the reforms proposed in this book would contribute to agglomeration economies in urban areas, thereby increasing job opportunities in those places, while also increasing mobility. The structural and spatial transformations can be facilitated by investments to improve Pakistan's spatial connectivity between industrial clusters and investments to provide clusters with key infrastructure and services, including energy, to allow them to benefit from agglomeration economies.

**Map 3.3 District-Level Employment Shares in Pakistan's Manufacturing Sector, 2005–06**

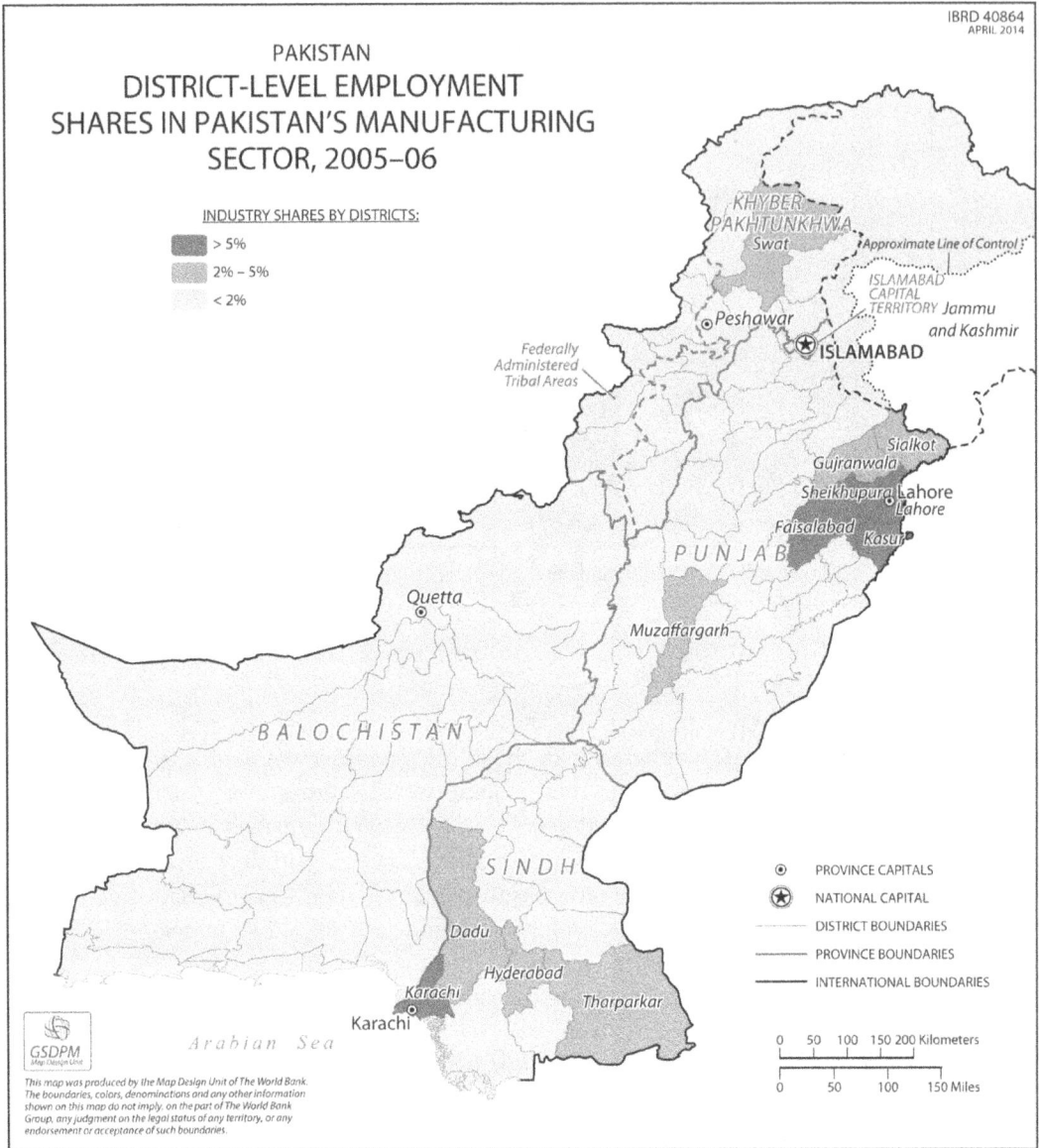

PAKISTAN
DISTRICT-LEVEL EMPLOYMENT
SHARES IN PAKISTAN'S MANUFACTURING
SECTOR, 2005–06

INDUSTRY SHARES BY DISTRICTS:
> 5%
2% – 5%
< 2%

IBRD 40864
APRIL 2014

KHYBER
PAKHTUNKHWA
Swat
Approximate Line of Control
ISLAMABAD
CAPITAL
TERRITORY  Jammu
and Kashmir
Peshawar
ISLAMABAD
Federally
Administered
Tribal Areas
Sialkot
Gujranwala
Sheikhupura Lahore
Lahore
Faisalabad
Kasur
PUNJAB
Quetta
Muzaffargarh
BALOCHISTAN
SINDH
Dadu
Hyderabad
Karachi
Tharparkar
Karachi
Arabian Sea

PROVINCE CAPITALS
NATIONAL CAPITAL
DISTRICT BOUNDARIES
PROVINCE BOUNDARIES
INTERNATIONAL BOUNDARIES

0   50   100  150 200 Kilometers
0   50       100      150 Miles

GSDPM
Map Design Unit
This map was produced by the Map Design Unit of The World Bank.
The boundaries, colors, denominations and any other information
shown on this map do not imply, on the part of The World Bank
Group, any judgment on the legal status of any territory, or any
endorsement or acceptance of such boundaries.

*Source:* LUMS 2011.

## Concluding Remarks

The ongoing spatial transformation in Pakistan contains both risks and opportunities. Poorly functioning urban centers with poor services and slim opportunity for gainful employment could become centers of discontent and social conflict. On the other hand, properly managed cities enjoying social services and

**Table 3.3  City Populations and Urban Agglomerations, 1990–2025**

| City | 1990 | 1995 | 2000 | 2005 | 2010 | 2015 | 2020 | 2025 |
|------|------|------|------|------|------|------|------|------|
| Faisalabad | 1,520 | 1,804 | 2,140 | 2,482 | 2,833 | 3,260 | 3,755 | 4,283 |
| Gujranwala | 848 | 1,019 | 1,224 | 1,433 | 1,643 | 1,898 | 2,195 | 2,513 |
| Hyderabad | 950 | 1,077 | 1,221 | 1,386 | 1,581 | 1,827 | 2,112 | 2,420 |
| Islamabad | 343 | 452 | 594 | 732 | 851 | 988 | 1,148 | 1,320 |
| Karachi | 7,147 | 8,467 | 10,019 | 11,553 | 13,052 | 14,855 | 16,922 | 19,095 |
| Lahore | 3,970 | 4,653 | 5,448 | 6,259 | 7,092 | 8,107 | 9,275 | 10,512 |
| Multan | 953 | 1,097 | 1,263 | 1,445 | 1,650 | 1,906 | 2,203 | 2,523 |
| Peshawar | 769 | 905 | 1,066 | 1,235 | 1,415 | 1,636 | 1,893 | 2,170 |
| Quetta | 414 | 504 | 614 | 725 | 836 | 971 | 1,128 | 1,298 |
| Rawalpindi | 1,087 | 1,286 | 1,519 | 1,762 | 2,015 | 2,324 | 2,683 | 3,067 |

*Source:* LUMS 2011.

connectivity will reap agglomeration economies and, under the right set of policies, will promote industrialization and life-changing employment opportunities.

Two sets of challenges will need to be addressed in managing the transition of urban centers into hubs of manufacturing and other economic activity. Rapid urbanization and the growing difference between rural and urban living standards will increase the incentives for rural-to-urban migration. Fresh migrants will add to the urban population that already faces problems finding adequate housing and meeting their needs for municipal services, including water, sanitation, and waste management. They may opt to live in slums in the hope of future improvement in living standards. Unattended, slums will become centers of social conflict and unrest. Well-designed programs to improve service delivery in slums will help reduce social tensions and make for a smoother transition.

The other challenge is to the urban environment that will deteriorate with increased vehicular traffic and congestion. The measures needed to abate urban environment pollution are discussed in detail in chapter 6 on infrastructure reform.

## Notes

1. 1.8 percent in 2007–08 (Government of Pakistan 2009).
2. Details on the agrarian transformation taking place within Pakistan are given by Mahmood Hasan Khan, who has done extensive research on agriculture in Pakistan. See his "Lectures on Agrarian Transformation in Pakistan," http://www.freepatentsonline .com/article/Lectures-in-Development-Economics/201617590html. Accessed May 6, 2011. Kahn observes:

    > The historical role of agriculture in the process of development is well known. It provides surplus of output and manpower to initiate industrialization. Development is initially fuelled by increased agricultural productivity and the transfer of surplus for profits and capital accumulation. This is something that is well distilled from the history of almost all societies which have economically developed. It is equally valid today.

In analyzing the current situation in Pakistan, Kahn details the capital intensification that has led to eviction or displacement by proprietors of family farmers and sharecroppers. As he observes, "increasing numbers of these unattached workers are migrating from villages to towns or cities or even to the Middle East...."

3. The manufacturing sector in 2007–08 absorbed only 13 percent of the country's labor force compared to 11.5 percent in 1999, a meager 1.5 percentage-point increase over the course of almost a decade (GoP 2009).

4. At the end of 2008, Pakistan also hosted the largest number of refugees in relation to its economic capacity. The country hosted 733 refugees per US$ 1 GDP (purchasing power parity) (UNHCR 2009).

5. Although about 40 percent of Pakistan's population is now thought to reside in urban areas, these estimated 65 million persons are concentrated in a few centers. The 1998 census showed about 200 towns and cities with more than 25,000 people, but also revealed that 8 cities with populations of over 1 million accounted for almost 60 percent of the total urban population in Pakistan, while almost a quarter of the urban population was housed in cities ranging in size from 100,000 to 1 million. This distribution is unlikely to have changed.

6. The three categories include the most-developed districts—that is, where the index is 1 standard deviation (SD) above the mean; least-developed districts—that is, where the index is 1 SD below the mean; and the medium-developed districts consisting of all other districts (LUMS 2011).

7. According to the 2011 LUMS report: The Ellison and Glaeser index is "...based on a rigorous statistical model that takes random distribution of plants across spatial units as a threshold to compare observed geographic distribution of plants. Ellison and Glaeser (1997) assume that plants make location decisions to gain from internal and external economies peculiar to a particular location. In practice, the value of the EG index indicates the strength of agglomeration externalities in an industry. Usually a $\gamma$ score of more than 0.05 indicates highly agglomerated industry; a score between 0.05 and 0.02 suggests moderate agglomeration and a score of less than 0.02 shows randomly dispersed industry. The geographic concentration of 3-digit industries performed at the district level by the Ellison-Glaeser index. As suggested by Ellison and Glaeser (1997), values higher than 0.05 are considered as high concentration, values in the range of 0.02 to 0.05 show intermediate concentration and values lower than 0.02 represent low concentration. Results of the EG index are also compared with raw geographic concentrations known as Gini index and Herfindahl index."

8. The World Bank's *World Development Report 2009: Reshaping Economic Geography* (World Bank 2008, 159) observes: "Preoccupied with urban unemployment and squalor in the fast-growing cities of the South, early research on labor migration advocated restrictions. Governments often acted on these prescriptions, instituting migration abatement policies, but to little effect: flows from the countryside to cities and from wagging two leading provinces continued unabated."

9. Arif and Hamid 2009; data based on PRHS 2001.

## References

Arif, G. M., and Hamid, S. 2009. "Urbanization, City Growth and Quality of Life in Pakistan." *European Journal of Social Sciences* 10 (2): 196–215. http://www.fcitizenforum .com/PROBLEMS-OF-A-CITY.pdf.

Breschi, S., and F. Lissoni. 2003. "Mobility and Social Networks: Localized Knowledge Spillovers Revisited." Working Paper 142, CESPRI (Centre of Research on Innovation and Internationalization), Milano. ftp://ftp.unibocconi.it/pub/RePEc/cri/papers/WP142LissoniBreschi.pdf.

CMI (Census of Manufacturing Industries). "2005–06 Plant Level Data." Federal Bureau of Statistics, Government of Pakistan.

Ellison, G., and E. Glaeser. 1997. "Geographic Concentration in U.S. Manufacturing Industries: A Dartboard Approach." *Journal of Political Economy* 105 (5): 889–927.

GoP (Government of Pakistan). 2009. Labor Force Survey 2008–09. Federal Bureau of Statistics, Islamabad.

Hamid, S. 2010. "Rural to Urban Migration in Pakistan: The Gender Perspective." Islamabad, Pakistan Institute of Development Economics. http://www.eastasiaforum.org/testing/eaber/sites/default/files/documents/PIDE_Hamid_2010.pdf.

Lahore University of Management Sciences (LUMS). 2011. A. A. Burki, K. A. Munir, M. A. Khan, M. U. Khan, A. Faheem, A. Khalid, and S. T. Hussain. *Industrial Policy, Its Spatial Aspects and Cluster Development in Pakistan.* Consultant report by the Lahore University of Management Sciences for the World Bank. Lahore, Pakistan.

OCHA. 2010. "Pakistan Humanitarian Update 18, 9 July 2010." UN Office for the Coordination of Humanitarian Affairs (UN OCHA).

Ratha, D., and S. Mohapatra. 2009. "Forecasting Migrant Remittances during the Global Financial Crisis." *Migration Letters* 7 (2): 203–13.

United Nations (UN), Department of Economic and Social Affairs, Population Division. 2011. *International Migration Report 2009. A Global Assessment.* New York: United Nations. http://www.un.org/esa/population/publications/migration/WorldMigrationReport2009.pdf.

UN HABITAT. 2011. *Global Report on Human Settlements 2011: Cities and Climate Change.* Earthscan, 234, 235.

UNHCR (Office of the United Nations High Commissioner for Refugees). 2009. *UNHCR Statistical Yearbook 2009.* Geneva, Switzerland: UNHCR. http://www.unhcr.org/4ce532ff9.html.

World Bank. 2008. *World Development Report 2009: Reshaping Economic Geography.* Washington, DC: World Bank. http://web.worldbank.org/WBSITE/EXTERNAL/EXTDEC/EXTRESEARCH/EXTWDRS/0,,contentMDK:23080183~pagePK:478093~piPK:477627~theSitePK: 477624,00.html.

## CHAPTER 4

# Skills Development

## Introduction

The two megacities and several million-plus cities emerging from the ongoing spatial transformation in Pakistan have the potential to become industrial hubs enjoying agglomeration economies. However, this will depend on how well the cities are governed and how judicious they are in investing in infrastructure to make them both livable and well connected. Importantly, this potential is more likely to be realized if the workers inhabiting the cities are appropriately skilled and can contribute to making industry internationally competitive and profitable.

The ongoing skills-development initiatives in Pakistan show two trends[1]: One set of initiatives aims to improve the skills of the poorest segment of the society as a form of social protection. The Federal Benazir Income Support Program's Waseela-e-Rozgar (focused on the poorest 20 percent of the nationwide population) is an example. The other set does not specifically target the poor, but rather aims to enhance worker capabilities in general that make the hiring firms more competitive and therefore more profitable so that they are willing to pay higher wage to workers who acquire such skills. Typically, these initiatives require, as a prerequisite, many more years of school education than the poor can afford so that the beneficiaries generally are from higher income groups than the poorest 20 percent. All the provinces have such programs, as does the federal government. These may be called industrial competitiveness and growth growth-promoting skills initiatives.

A recently introduced program, the Punjab Skills Development Fund (PSDF), on the other hand, provides skills to the vulnerable (young men and women in districts with few employment opportunities) who may lie well above the poverty line and is therefore a hybrid. While PSDF is focused on the poorest districts of South Punjab, some of the courses offered require a level of education that poor households cannot afford. Because of its interesting design features and initial success, the PSDF is being scaled up to cover all of Punjab and is likely to become the premier initiative to upgrade worker skills to make firms more competitive and thus promote industrialization and economic growth.

The next section summarizes the state of skills development in Pakistan. Following that is an introduction, in section 3, of the key players in skills development in Pakistan at both the federal and the provincial levels. Section 4 of the chapter reviews the main features of the Punjab Skills Development Fund and progress to date. Drawing insights from PSDF, section 5 recommends the reform agenda to improve other provincial and federal skills-development initiatives. Section 6 concludes with some observations on the need to strengthen education, which constitutes the foundation for building sound skills-development programs to promote industrialization and economic growth.

## The State of Worker Skills[2]

Nearly 70 percent of the firms located in Pakistan's urban clusters report that the lack of availability of skilled workers is a major impediment to productivity (Wilson and Otsuki 2004). More recently, a comprehensive survey of garment manufacturers (discussed in chapter 2) corroborated these results. As shown in the technology pyramid below, poorly skilled workers are an important factor in the intensity of the low technology that characterizes Pakistan's manufactured goods (see figure 4.1; higher levels in the pyramid represent greater technological sophistication).

A well-structured three-tiered skilled workforce would have proportions of workers in each tier as represented in the triangular shape of the pyramid in figure 4.1. Pakistan's workforce is more like the cylinder-shaped structure inside the pyramid illustrated in figure 4.2. The trainable workforce (workers with secondary-level education), given low literacy rates, is a small portion of the labor force in the lowest tier. The rest of the skilled workforce falls in the mid-tier (trained engineers and mid-level skilled workers). A tiny proportion of the workforce is in the top tier (scientists and technology entrepreneurs).

**Figure 4.1  Pakistan in the Technology Pyramid**

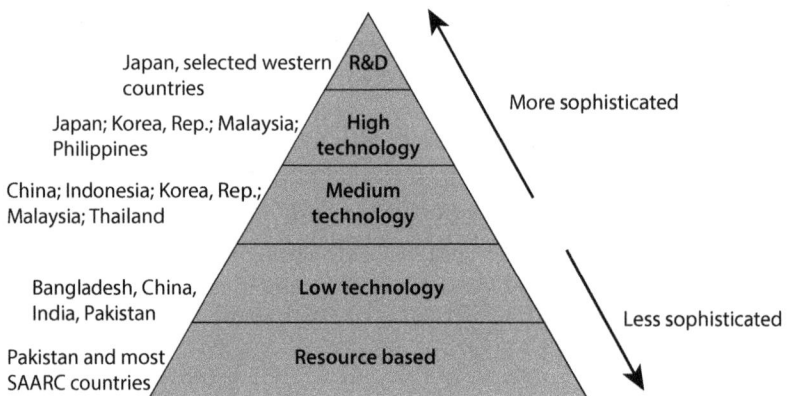

*Note:* R&D = research and development.
*Note:* SAARC = South Asian Association for Regional Cooperation.

**Figure 4.2 Pakistan in the Skills Pyramid**

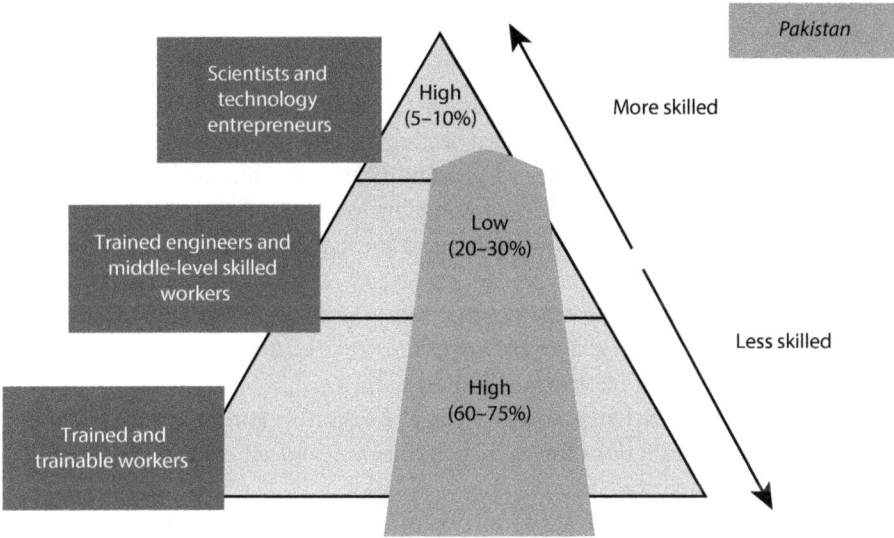

Meeting the skills challenge in Pakistan thus requires both pushing up the skills cylinder in the top tier of the pyramid and expanding it to fill the empty space in the bottom two tiers. The key to this is increasing basic literacy. In Pakistan, the completion rate for primary education of the relevant age group is 67 percent; this is abysmally low compared with India's 96 percent, Malaysia's 95 percent, and Turkey's 100 percent (World Bank 2013). A much higher transition rate from primary to secondary education will also be required. Currently, the gross secondary school enrollment in Pakistan of the relevant age group is 35 percent; this is considerably lower than India's 77 percent, Malaysia's 69 percent, and Turkey's 82 percent (World Bank 2013).

A useful recent survey of the education sector in Pakistan's Punjab province, which accounts for the bulk of Pakistan's workforce, assessed education outcomes and the interventions designed to improve them (Habib 2013). Implementing interventions that increase literacy is critical to laying the foundation for a large pool of skilled workers working in urban clusters and contributing to their agglomeration economies.

## Key Players in Skills Development

Skills development, or vocational training, in Pakistan is a shared responsibility between the federal and provincial governments. There are a number of federal and provincial departments and independent agencies working in the sector, at times performing overlapping functions. Vocational training is a term describing practical training for producing skilled workers; such training covers the ambit of vocational certificates, with entry levels ranging from primary to matriculation. Technical education, on the other hand, refers to diploma-level courses (of three years' duration) that produce technicians or highly skilled workers. An overview of the skills-sector agencies working in Islamabad and in the provinces is given below:

**National Vocational and Technical Training Commission** (NAVTTC), which was set up in 2006, is the apex standard-setting body for vocational and technical skills. The commission has the responsibility to carry out skills planning and research; define skills standards; and develop curricula, policies, and standards for areas such as accreditation, teacher training, skills testing, certifications, and so on.

**National Training Bureau**, an organization set up prior to NAVTTC, was involved in standard setting, but is now mainly educating *vocational* trainers and carrying out trade tests for institutes affiliated with it.

**National Institute of Science and Technical Education** (situated in Islamabad) performs similar functions for science and technical teachers. It is also involved in the development of curricula and textbooks.

**Skills Development Councils** are small organizations led by the private sector that were established under the National Training Ordinance of 1980 (amended in 2002). Currently, the councils carry out training and award certificates.

**Technical Education and Vocational Training Authority** (TEVTA) dominates the skills sector in Punjab. TEVTA is a large public provider that reports having instructed 38,000 vocational trainees and 33,000 technical trainees during 2012–13, and has more than 350 institutes.

**Punjab Vocational Training Council**, which, through its more than 150 institutes, delivers only vocational training. Zakat, an alms-giving program, funds the council, which was set up in 2010 and functions as a skills-financing agency to promote the delivery of private training. It currently works in four districts and is being expanded to the whole province in two phases (PSDF is discussed below in detail).

**Punjab Board of Technical Education (PBTE)** functions as an awarding body, carrying out trade tests and examinations for TEVTA and private institutes. Five hundred and twenty private institutes are registered with PBTE.

**S-TEVTA** was set up in Sindh in 2007. It manages more than 250 institutes throughout the province. These include technical, vocational, and commercial education institutes. Federal government statistics in 2005 report that there were more than 55,000 technical and vocational education training (TVET) enrollees in Sindh in that year.

**Benazir Bhutto Shaheed Youth Development Program** (BBSYDP) funds public and private sector projects. BBSYDP, which the World Bank funded in Sindh in 2008, has so far trained more than 100,000 people in that province. The International Labour Organization (ILO) reports that the employment rate of the trainees is 27 percent. In Khyber Pakhtunkhwa, TVET institutes function under the Directorate of Technical Education and Manpower Training, whereas in Balochistan, institutes have been consolidated under the fledgling umbrella organization B-TEVTA.

**Waseela-e-Rozgar**, a federal government program, is part of the **Benazir Income Support Programme** (BISP). Waseela-e-Rozgar provides technical and vocational training aimed at the poorest 20 percent of the population to enable them graduate out of poverty. In 2012–13, the program expects to graduate 150,000 trainees and has allocated Rs 4.5 billion to achieve that target. Third-party evaluations confirm that BISP's programs are well-targeted and benefits reach the intended population. However, there have been no third-party evaluations of the quality of training under Waseela-e-Rozgar or its success in improving its graduates' incomes.

The total number of TVET trainees in the country ranges between 300,000 and 500,000. No estimate exists for those trained in unregistered institutes or under informal apprenticeships. There are broadly two categories of skills development: skills development for social protection, and skills development for competitiveness and economic growth. The TVET sector has been low on the reforms agenda of successive governments and is supported by modest budgetary allocations. For example, in Punjab, the skills budget in 2011–12 was less than 1 percent of the education budget. A renewed attention to the skills sector will mean allocating additional resources linked with measurable outputs and outcomes.

## Punjab Skills Development Fund—A New Model for Funding Skills and Vocational Training

In 2010, the Government of Punjab and the Department for International Development UK set up the Punjab Skills Development Fund for providing skills training to workers. PSDF is a Section 42 company guided by a private-sector-led board of directors with a total outlay of £50 million. The board has met 13 times since it was set up in October 2010. The board's subcommittees are closely involved in giving direction to PSDF operations. The program was formally launched in 2011 with the appointment of a chief executive officer. Currently, it trains persons from four districts of southern Punjab, namely Bahawalpur, Bahawalnagar, Lodhran, and Muzaffargarh. Plans are underway to expand its operations to six additional districts of the Punjab—Lahore, Faisalabad, Gujranwala, Sheikhupura, Sargodha, and Chiniot—to test the funding model in more economically upbeat districts in growth sectors.

The objective of the fund in the four targeted districts is to train 80,000 vulnerable people over five years and restore the state's credibility in facilitating access to better-paying jobs. PSDF has launched three principal training schemes: skills for market (training for self-employment focused on rural areas), skills for employment (training for employment in small towns/rural areas/informal sector), and skills for jobs (training for employment in the formal sector). The first two categories of skills, offered to the poor and women in rural areas and small towns, are forms of social protection, while the third category is targeted at the educated unemployed—the vulnerable individuals—in urban/peri-urban areas of the four districts. The average duration of the training programs for skills for market and skills for jobs is 4 months and 6.5 months, respectively. The trainees receive a stipend of Rs 1,500 per month if the training is within the four districts and Rs 3,000 if the location is outside. As of June 2013, nearly 30,000 individuals have been trained in 90 different trades working with 60 public, private, and non-government organizations. The program is on course to meet the overall target of graduating 80,000 trainees in four years.

### PSDF's Design

PSDF's design represents a major shift in delivering public resources for skills development. PSDF identifies the courses to be taught and the trainees to be targeted, and then takes competitive bids from both public and private trainers to provide the training at specified locations. Bids that satisfy the rigorous technical and financial criteria set by PSDF are then contracted and given funds to provide the training. PSDF does not provide training on premises constructed with its resources nor by teachers hired by the fund. Nor is it a "captured" fund that funnels public money to public-sector training institutions insensitive to market demand for their training programs.

The PSDF design outlined above can work only under the following condition: PSDF spends its energy and resources in staying on top of the information flows that match, on the one hand, the demand for skills acquired by the trainees (that help to get a job in the market or improve self-employment income) with, on the other hand, the supply of training programs funded by PSDF. Thus, core functions become research on the skills needs of households and employers, gathering market information, fine tuning courses, setting technical and financial criteria for assessing bids, third-party evaluation of training programs, and tracking trainees to assess post-training employment and income status.

Given the core functions outlined above, the success of PSDF is dependent on the quality of research that supports its decision making. PSDF's sponsors have made adequate technical assistance available to PSDF to procure such research. The board ensures that a proper balance is kept between the operational needs of delivering the program according to the agreed timeline and the quality of information needed so the training that is delivered does indeed match the demand for skills. This design feature allows for ongoing monitoring and evaluation, with a feedback loop into program design, and thus facilitates timely course correction.

PSDF has defined its success in terms of the following standards:

- Select trainees who meet the criteria of vulnerability (income less than US$2 a day and marginalized women).
- Identify training courses that increase trainees' employability and productivity.
- Promote training by private trainers via competitive bidding by public and private trainers for training contracts.

- Ensure zero tolerance for "ghost" training programs and training that does not conform to contract specifications.
- Assess improvement in trainees' employability and income after completion of the training program.

## Design Features to Help Meet PSDF's Standards

How well PSDF performs on the measures listed above will be assessed in due course as the program matures and evaluations are completed. This is especially true for the last standard regarding the program's impact on income. Nonetheless, several design features are already beginning to have an impact on outcomes.

### Evidence-Based Rollout

The evidence-based program rollout utilized baseline surveys of the living conditions in the four districts currently targeted. The sample included 11,000 households surveyed regarding their preferences for skills. In addition, a survey of employers for skills demanded and a survey of networks for job placement was conducted. The surveys identified two categories of skills: skills for market (such as tailoring and home crafts) and skills for jobs (such as welding, electrician, chef, and inventory control). PSDF therefore has an effective targeting mechanism and a strong system in place to ensure employability and income generation.

### Vulnerability

The program's focus is on four districts of southern Punjab—namely Bahawalpur, Bahawalnagar, Lodhran, and Muzaffargarh, which are the province's least developed districts with respect to poverty, education, and health indicators—allows the program to meet the first standard. The selection of trainees satisfies the criteria of vulnerability in that their income is less than US$2 a day and nearly 40 percent of the beneficiaries are women.

### Course-Correcting Design Feature

Household surveys conducted in the early stages of the program revealed a high degree of enthusiasm for training by households, even for young women in these relatively conservative districts. This was followed by randomized control trials (RCTs) to assess whether the enthusiasm for training expressed in the surveys would be sustained in committing households' time to the training program. The trial involved distribution of vouchers to households with potential trainees; these vouchers would be cashed when the training was taken. The results were discouraging. The voucher uptake was an abysmal 5 percent in the general population and even lower in the targeted population (satisfying the criteria of vulnerability). Further analysis showed that the low uptake was not due to lack of demand for training, but rather due to program design factors such as inadequate information on training programs, distance from the training center, the limited number of course offerings, and low stipends. The voucher uptake was even lower for women, due to factors such as the number of household dependents both elderly and children.

PSDF's program design was adjusted in light of the RCT findings. Adjustments were made in the new round of bids for courses offered to women trainees whose uptake was very low. The adjustments involved providing more information on the program to potential trainees, specifying the location of training centers to address the distance concern, and offering courses that are more varied. The results of these adjustments are very encouraging. By adjusting distance and providing training closer to potential trainees, the voucher uptake more than doubled (figure 4.3) due to greater effort in out-of-village mobilization and provision of information. More varied course offerings were also a resounding success in increasing voucher uptake by women (figure 4.4). Furthermore, all of this occurred without increasing the stipend! These experiments have helped fine-tune the program regarding the location of training, modes of mobilization of trainees, and course offerings.

**Figure 4.3  Impact of Village-Based Training: Overall Voucher Uptake by Training (Percentage of Female Participation)**

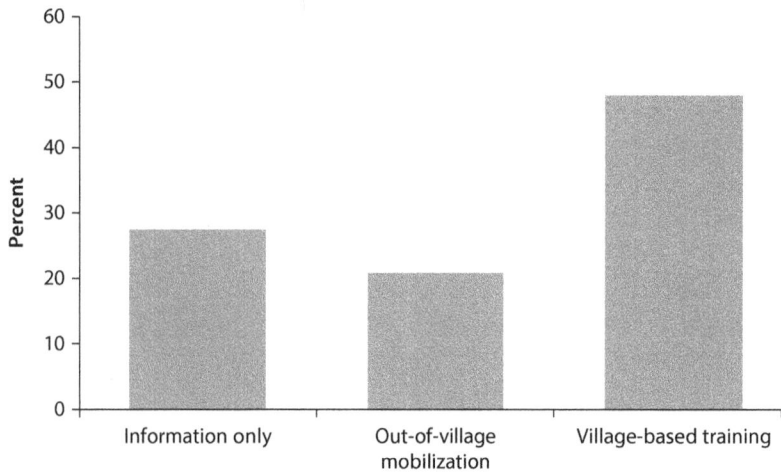

**Figure 4.4  Course Desirability Matters: Voucher Uptake in Village-Based Training by Course (Percentage of Female Participation)**

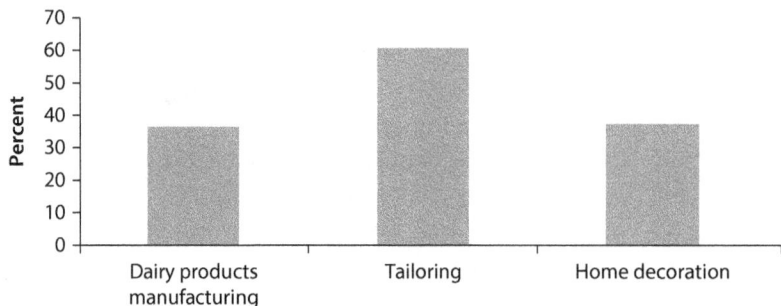

### Private-Sector Development

PSDF's strategy to develop private sector trainers seeks to create competition in the market for better results. Members of the private sector are invited to bid for all three main categories of training programs: skills for market, for jobs, and for employment. Thus far, nongovernmental organizations (NGOs) have won the most contracts (44 percent), followed by private training providers (29 percent). Public-private partnerships account for 6 percent of the contracts, whereas public training institutions have taken up 16 percent of the contracts. Thus, PSDF is creating entrepreneurship in training that, until recently, public-sector training institutions dominated. The potential for growth, as seen in low-cost private formal education in recent decades, is substantial.

### Third-Party Monitoring and Cost Effectiveness

A robust third-party monitoring system has been put in place to ensure the availability of inputs-trainers, learning materials, and trainee attendance. The fund has zero tolerance for corruption, as all bids are transparent, and carefully checks to ensure that PSDF does not fund ghost programs via ongoing third-party monitoring and independent yearly financial audits. Testing services that ensure quality of training programs are outsourced to national and international accredited certifying agencies. (see figure 4.5.)

### Going Forward

Spurred by the promising PSDF rollout, plans are underway to expand PSDF operations to all of Punjab.

By 2020, the number of trainees will increase by a multiple of 25 from the current 20,000 trainees per annum to 500,000 trainees per annum. This has important implications for the design of PSDF. First, employers located in the relatively more prosperous districts of Punjab will become important stakeholders. Catering to their training needs will imply a substantial increase in and

**Figure 4.5 PSDF Cost Effectiveness: Comparison of Four Skills-Development Programs**

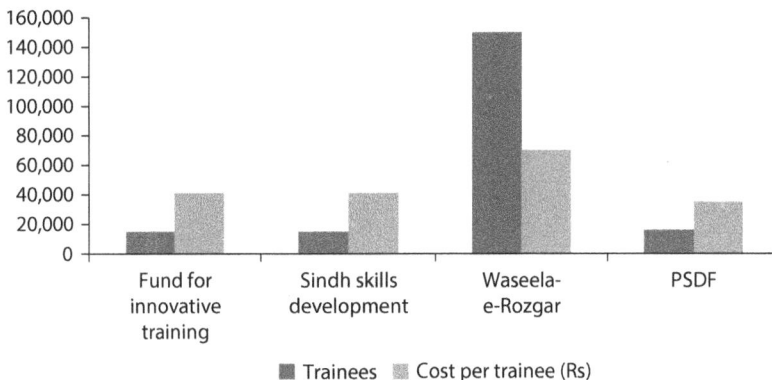

Source: Nabi 2013.
Note: PSDF = Punjab Skills Development Fund.

predominance of training courses aimed at skills for jobs. PSDF management, supported by empirical research, is consulting with key industrial clusters, starting with garments exporters, on their training needs. Courses will be designed in close consultations and then contracts will be awarded to training providers who respond cost effectively to industry demand for skills. Second, PSDF will increasingly become a program focused on economic growth as the share of training for skills for the market, and the social protection dimension of the program, declines in importance. Third, PSDF will need to be vigilant in ensuring that the social protection dimension of skills training, especially in the poorer districts, continues to receive the attention of PSDF management. Fourth, private sector trainers will be challenged to respond to the considerably larger training cohort requiring increasingly complex training courses. Finally, the capacity of PSDF itself will need to increase rapidly to manage the much larger program.

Another set of challenges is associated with the fiscal sustainability of the envisaged much larger program. Given low overall government revenue, the subsidy built into the program's current design will no longer be feasible. A public/private partnership, with the private sector and the trainees picking up a larger share of the training cost, would be one solution. The earlier stages of PSDF's rollout will have demonstrated the increase in worker productivity associated with training and the ensuing increase in employers' profits and trained workers' higher wages. These benefits to employers and trained workers will create the incentives for them to pick up a greater share of the cost of training. This, in turn, will pave the way for the government to change its role from the funding of training to providing regulatory oversight (such as setting standards, ensuring quality, and checking fraud) and facilitating knowledge exchange (on emerging skills needs) between training seekers (employers and workers) and private training providers.

## Guiding Principles for Countrywide Skills-Development Initiatives and Suggested Reforms

### Guiding Principles
The PSDF experience suggests that a successful comprehensive nationwide TVET program, in a setting of weak employment growth, has to be guided by the following principles:

- Set up a labor market information system to track industrial/business clusters in Pakistan and to track labor markets related to the importing of labor; systematically generate evidence on skills gaps and shortages.
- Strengthen linkage with employers at all levels.
- Produce quality inputs for TVET that include curricula, teaching and learning resources, and trained teachers.
- Stimulate a market for the private provision of training and, via competition, make public sector training institutions efficient.
- Target the ultra-poor via a mix of interventions in tandem with skills-training programs.

- Regulate training providers based on the principles of informed consumer choice, fair play, and accountability.
- Clarify federal and provincial government roles in skills training for efficient provision of countrywide skills training.

With the guiding principles as a backdrop, the next subsection briefly reviews the major skills initiatives in Pakistan and identifies the issues that need to be addressed.

### Improving the Countrywide TVET System
#### NAVTTC

NAVTTC currently enjoys support from a joint project funded by GIZ, the European Union, and the government of the Netherlands. The apex body's performance leaves much to be desired. It has been involved in training delivery to the neglect of its core functions. NAVTTC must focus on its core functions—namely, the development of standard curricula and, most importantly, the development of teaching and learning resources. All major skills stakeholders (industrial clusters, labor representatives, and concerned government departments) must be involved in developing and finalizing NAVTTC's work program. Implementation of skills standards and curricula should take place at the provincial level. Also required is a performance review of NAVTTC; this review should take stock of the work done so far and set goals for future activities.

#### Skills-Development Funds

Punjab's pilot project, which funds nonpublic providers though a competitive process, has been assessed to be cost effective (adds publicly funded capacity without huge capital investments). It successfully engages the private sector, and lends flexibility and relevance to the TVET system. Skills-development funds can operate in a number of areas:

- Pre-employment Technical and Vocational Training Delivery (for example, the Punjab Skills Development Fund);
- Upgrading the skills of the existing workforce (for example, the Human Resource Development Fund, Malaysia);
- Trainee scholarships, especially for technical trainees; and
- Public-private partnerships (for example, the National Skills Development Fund, India).

Skills-development funds may be set up in all provinces with joint contributions by the federal and provincial governments. Private-sector boards should lead these organizations, and competitively selected teams should manage these organizations. Provincial governments should set aside funds for these companies; these funds should be commensurate with the objective of promoting private TVET provision. The federal government should contribute from its budgetary resources. Additionally, a fixed percentage of the Workers Welfare Fund should be recommended for transfer to the Skills Development Funds by the Council of Common Interest. The Skills Development Funds should emphasize meeting the training needs of sectors and firms that focus on competitiveness and economic growth rather than poverty alleviation.

### Poverty-Focused Skills Interventions

Empirical evidence suggests that traditional TVET providers do not have a menu of courses that provide access to the less educated and to populations residing in rural areas. A survey by the Centre of Economic Research Pakistan in southern Punjab revealed that requiring a primary level of education for entry into a vocational course excludes roughly 50 percent of poor males and 80 percent of poor females.

There is strong evidence to suggest that, for the ultra-poor, training must be combined with complementary interventions such as an asset transfer. BRAC (formerly known as Bangladesh Rehabilitation Assistance Committee, then as the Bangladesh Rural Advancement Committee), an international NGO, experimented with asset transfers to accompany short-terms trainings for the ultra-poor. The interventions resulted in more than 95 percent of the ultra-poor graduating out of poverty (Consultative Group to Assist the Poor). Suggested policy actions, therefore, are

- Developing the capacity of the Benazir Income Support Fund, the Pakistan Poverty Alleviation Fund, or any other dedicated agency to roll out skills interventions that follow the BRAC model; and
- Linking training with microfinance and initiatives that provide livestock assets.

### Encourage and Fund an Employers' Association Such as the Pakistan Business Council to Play a Key Role in Skills-Sector Planning and Research

To make TVET relevant and demand-driven, a strong employer linkage needs to be developed. This may be initiated at the apex level with the active involvement and support of a nationally representative employers association, following the example of India in setting up the National Skills Development Corporation. Corporate contributions to such initiatives must be encouraged.

### Reform Public Provision

Public providers are beset with a number of inefficiencies: trainers and trainee attendance is low; equipment and buildings are underutilized; and consumables are mostly in short supply. There is no annual performance review for large public providers to track their outputs as well as outcomes. Institutions also do not have linkages with industry. The reform of the public provision of training should include the following:

- Set targets for public providers and put in place a strong monitoring system linked with incentives for institute principals. Institutes should also be assessed based on outcomes.

- Move the public sector towards competitions by encouraging individual institutes to bid for funds and collaborations with private providers.
- Push public providers towards high-value trades and technologies.

### Improve the Regulatory Environment

The quality-assurance mechanism for TVET is weak and can learn considerably from the approach taken by the Higher Education Commission. Regulating the sector would imply accreditation by the federal NAVTTC, and testing and certification by provincial or even private-sector bodies that affiliate individual institutes with them. Proposed steps are as follows:

- A clear demarcation of regulatory functions between federal and provincial government;
- An accreditation cell with NAVTTC that starts with accreditation of testing and awarding bodies and courses on the lines of Ofqual, UK (ofqual.gov.uk);
- Trade associations may be encouraged and funded to enter the skills realm by developing specialized courses and testing them. Accreditation of such bodies may also be allowed.

### Expand Internship Programs to Include Skilled Youth

Placement of skilled workers is low, and the employment rate of TVET graduates is below 30 percent (ILO). A recent United Nations Educational, Scientific, and Cultural Organization review of skills-sector evidence (UNESCO 2012) reports that countries are increasingly moving towards including on-the-job experience as part of training. Chile's Joven Program, which combines classroom-based training with work placement, is cited as an example. The following initiatives are proposed to improve placement:

- Internship programs, which offer short-term placement to vocational trainees, may be started.
- Where internship programs already exist,[3] their scope may be broadened to include TVET trainees.

### Provide Vocational Training at High Schools in Low-Income Districts

In low-income districts, to increase the take-up of vocational training programs that require several years of schooling as a prerequisite, vocational training may be instituted at the middle school and high school levels. Such programs should include vocational training scholarships to encourage retention and lower the early school dropout rate.

### Set Up Employment Exchanges

Employees and employers use their respective networks for jobs in the trades. The formal system of linkages (such as newspaper advertisements and human resource employment firms) is very limited in this sector. Employment exchanges may be set up to link the trained individuals with employers.

The employment exchange could conduct the verification parts in the process, thus "vouching" for the employee.

### Track Labor Demand in Labor-Importing Countries

To enhance the competitiveness of Pakistani workers in labor-importing countries, a labor-demand tracking system should be set up to track changes in the types of skills that are in demand. This information should inform the funding of vocational training programs and the stipulation of training courses supported by such funding.

### Reform the Apprenticeship System

The Apprenticeship Ordinance, 1962 (Ordinance No. LVI of 1962), requires all industrial establishments with more than 50 employees and more than 5 in a notified apprentice-able trade, to train at least 20 percent of those employed in apprentice-able trades. The ordinance is not being implemented according to its mandate. For example, in Punjab, the largest province, the total number of registered apprenticeships is only around 10,000. Organisation for Economic Co-operation and Development countries such as Australia and the United Kingdom have extensively reviewed and revived their apprenticeships systems to broaden their scope and have included incentives for employers and trainers. The apprenticeship system is emerging as the major delivery mode for TVET, because it directly links trainees with the world of work.

In Pakistan, a serious buy-in from employers is required to revive the system. The following steps are proposed:

- A review of apprenticeships should be commissioned to understand the system's deficiencies.
- Experience in developed countries suggests that a range of incentives is embedded in the apprenticeships schemes (for employers, trainers, and trainees). The programs also offer flexibilities, such as the choice for employers and trade associations to devise their own apprenticeship frameworks.

## Concluding Remarks

Pakistan has an established record in skills development. In recent years, there has been a renewed focus on enlarging the skills pool. This effort has resulted in new design features that emphasize private-sector development for the provision of skills and state-of-the-art, evidence-based monitoring systems. Several skills-development programs have been designed in response to poverty and unemployment, and are essentially social protection programs (see table 4.1). However, skills training is now being scaled up to respond to the needs of industrial clusters. In combination with trade reform and modernization of infrastructure (to be discussed in chapters 5 and 6, respectively), skills development can be a key instrument for realizing the

**Table 4.1  A Mapping of Skills-Development Entities/Programs**

| Province | Program | Targeted population | Trainee target/ training capacity | Total funding |
|---|---|---|---|---|
| *Skills development as social protection* | | | | |
| Punjab | Punjab Vocational Training Council | Individuals who are eligible for zakat | 34,763 (total enrolled, 2011) | Rs 1.06 billion |
| Punjab | PSDF (Phase 1) | Poorest south Punjab districts; little schooling | 80,000 | Rs 3.6 billion |
| Balochistan | NAVTTC establishment of vocational training centers in 13 tehsils of Balochistan | Poorest/marginalized groups with low-level schooling | 5,460 | Rs 103.9 million |
| Federal | BISP's Waseela-e-Rozgar | Poorest 20% of population, low-level schooling | Overall target 150,000 trainees per annum | Rs 4.5 billion budget (2012/13) |
| Federal | Fund for Innovative Training | marginalized groups; 75% trainees from poor households | — | Rs 1.32 billion (5 years) |
| *Skills development as a driver of growth* | | | | |
| Punjab | TEVTA | Individuals with minimum educational qualifications | 71,000 (includes vocational and technical) 2012/2013 | Rs 6.025 billion and Rs 1.5 billion for development |
| Punjab | PSDF (Phase II) | Vulnerable youth; have basic core skills | 55,000 | Rs 3.6 billion |
| Sindh | S-TEVTA | Individuals with minimum educational qualifications | — | Rs 1.347 billion non-development funding and Rs 1.2 billion in development funding (2012/13) (*Express Tribune* 2012) |
| Sindh | Benazir Bhutto Shaheed Youth Development Program | Educated and unemployed youth | More than 100,000 | — |
| Sindh | Sindh Skills Development Program | Technical staff/ teaching instructors | — | Rs 4.55 million |
| Balochistan | B-TEVTA | Individuals with minimum educational qualifications | 6,218 | — |
| KP | Directorate of Technical Education and Manpower Training | Individuals with minimum educational qualifications | 4,888 (current enrollment) | Rs 1.802 billion |
| Federal | National Institute of Science and Technical Education | Trainers | 125 in-service science teachers (2009/10); 453 in-service technical teachers (2009/10) | — |
| Federal | National Training Bureau | Technical trainers | — | — |

*Note:* — = not available, BISP = Benazir Income Support Programme, NAVTTC = National Vocational and Technical Training Commission, PSDF = Punjab Skills Development Fund, TEVTA = Technical Education and Vocational Training Authority.

agglomeration economies of ongoing urbanization. Appropriately designed training programs can thus be instrumental in fostering industrialization and international competitiveness.

## Notes

1. The discussion in this chapter is based on two recent papers: "The Current State of Technical and Vocational Education and Training in Pakistan and Proposed Reform for Discussion" (July 2013) by Ijaz Nabi, with support from Ali Sarfraz and Sarah Saeed (Punjab Skills Development Fund); and "Two Social Protection Programs in Pakistan" (appearing in the 2013 annual conference volume of the *Lahore Journal of Economics*, Lahore School of Economics). It also draws on the Ministry of Industry, Government of Pakistan report, "A Strategy for Industrialization" (2005; authored by Ijaz Nabi).

2. The discussion in this section is based on GoP (2005): "Towards A Prosperous Pakistan: A Strategy for Rapid Industrial, Growth," Ministry of Industries, Production and Special Initiatives, Government of Pakistan, 2005.

3. For example, Punjab Internship Programme.

## References

*Express Tribune*. 2012. "On Your Feet: Rs. 1.2 Billion Development Budget for STEVTA Approved." *Express Tribune*, July 12.

GoP (Government of Pakistan). 2005. "Towards A Prosperous Pakistan: A Strategy for Rapid Industrial Growth." Ministry of Industries, Production and Special Initiatives, Islamabad.

Habib, M. 2013. "Education in Pakistan's Punjab: Outcomes and Interventions." *Lahore Journal of Economics* 18 (September 2013): 21–48.

Nabi, I. 2013. "Two Social Protection Programs in Pakistan." *The Lahore Journal of Economics* 18: 283–304.

UNESCO (United Nations Educational, Scientific, and Cultural Organization). 2012. *Education for All Global Monitoring Report 2012*. Paris: UNESCO.

Wilson, J. S., and T. Otsuki. 2004. *Technical Regulations and Firms in Developing Countries: New Evidence from a World Bank Technical Barriers to Trade Survey*. Washington, DC: World Bank.

World Bank. 2013. World Development Indicators (database). Washington, DC: World Bank. http://data.worldbank.org/data-catalog/world-development-indicators.

## CHAPTER 5

# Challenges in Trade

## Introduction

Trade, industrial competitiveness, and urbanization are closely linked. Trade logistics are a large part of the costs of finished products and are often key to the international competitiveness of manufacturing firms. How well urban clusters are connected to each other is critical for taking advantage of openness to trade. Modern and supportive trade facilitation improves the response of urban clusters to trade opportunities. Trade policy influences costs via tariffs on inputs and industrial efficiency, and influences competitiveness via tariffs on outputs that provide protection. A supportive trade policy that does not tie up exporting firms' capital in refundable duties on imported inputs lowers costs while promoting the growth of urban clusters and the employment opportunities they create. Trade policy also affects access to markets and allows comparative advantage and industrialization opportunities to emerge. Given Pakistan's geography and history, and rapid economic changes taking place in its immediate neighborhood, trade policy that promotes regional trade contributes to the growth of regionally diverse urban clusters and the agglomeration economies they generate.

This chapter brings together themes on international trade. The following section examines the principal challenges of trade logistics. The chapter's third section focuses on trade policy. It reviews recent developments in tariff policy and discusses regional trade in more detail given its potential for sustained economic growth. Section 4 concludes with a discussion of some of the challenges that need to be surmounted for Pakistan to take advantage of the opportunities offered by regional trade.

## Logistics

A competitive network of logistics is the backbone of international trade (World Bank 2010a). Logistics encompasses a variety of essential activities—from transport, storage, and customs clearance, to payment systems—and involves both public and private agents. Unfortunately, Pakistan has yet to realize the productivity gains from developing a modernized logistics system, such as those implemented in industrialized countries. The significance of efficient logistics for trade and economic growth is widely acknowledged. Analysis based on the 2007 Logistics Performance Index (LPI) has shown that improved logistics performance is strongly correlated with trade growth, export diversification, foreign direct investment, and overall economic growth (Arvis et al. 2010). High quality and reliable logistics are particularly important for higher value products and perishable goods, but are also becoming critical to minimize inventories and reduce the risk of overstocking for low- and medium-value (World Bank 2006). Evidence from around the world indicates that the reliability of the supply chain is the most important aspect of logistics performance.

Indeed, when transport services are unreliable, exporters and importers incur extra costs, for example, by increasing inventories to hedge against failed deliveries. These induced costs can be higher than direct costs of freight, affect firm competitiveness, and can even affect countries' potential to benefit from time-intensive commodities. Quality of transport logistics is a crucial dimension of reliability, both in terms of delivery within the promised time window and the share of shipments that have no errors in cargo composition or documentation (Arvis et al. 2010).

Efficient supply chains are key to international competitiveness, especially as Pakistan strives to move to exports with higher value added. International comparisons, however, show that Pakistan ranks poorly in trade facilitation services that are central to efficient supply chains. The World Bank LPI identifies the challenges and opportunities countries face in the performance of trade logistics. According to the World Bank LPI 2012, Pakistan ranked at 71 out of 155 countries, which is worse than the ranking for India (46). Pakistan's LPI score is 2.83 (ranked 1–5, with 1 being worst), which is lower than India's score of 3.08 (table 5.1).

Pakistan's transport supply chain system is not providing the value-added services that have become the hallmark of modern logistics, such as multimodal systems that combine the strengths of different transport modes into one integrated system. In general, logistics services provided by freight forwarders are

**Table 5.1  Logistics Performance Index (LPI), 2012 (Out of 155 Countries)**

| Country | Year | LPI Rank | LPI Score | Customs | Infrastructure | International shipments | Logistics competence | Tracking and tracing | Timeliness |
|---|---|---|---|---|---|---|---|---|---|
| Singapore | 2012 | 1 | 4.13 | 4.1 | 4.15 | 3.99 | 4.07 | 4.07 | 4.39 |
| Hong Kong, SAR, China | 2012 | 2 | 4.12 | 3.97 | 4.12 | 4.18 | 4.08 | 4.09 | 4.28 |
| China | 2012 | 26 | 3.52 | 3.25 | 3.61 | 3.46 | 3.47 | 3.52 | 3.8 |
| Malaysia | 2012 | 29 | 3.49 | 3.28 | 3.43 | 3.4 | 3.45 | 3.54 | 3.86 |
| India | 2012 | 46 | 3.08 | 2.77 | 2.87 | 2.98 | 3.14 | 3.09 | 3.58 |
| Pakistan | 2012 | 71 | 2.83 | 2.85 | 2.69 | 2.86 | 2.77 | 2.61 | 3.14 |

*Source:* GCI International 2012.

simple because of the simple structure of the supply chain, which does not always utilize the most efficient mode of transport for the movement of goods. For example, rail freight generally has a competitive advantage over road freight for longer distances and for the transport of bulk commodities. Local offices or representatives of large international companies, which make up half of the logistics market, are the primary providers of integrated logistics services (World Bank 2009a). The following describes specific logistical concerns in Pakistan's port, rail, airport, and road sectors.

### Ports and Shipping

Many of the logistical inefficiencies of ports have to do with high charges, delays at the port, labor problems, and restrictive onshore cargo handling practices (LUMS 2011). Cargo handling at Pakistan's two main ports, Karachi and Port Qasim, reached 63.8 million tons in 2008–09, compared with under 20 million tons in 1989–90. However, to keep things in perspective, container port traffic in Pakistan at 1.93 million 20-foot equivalent units (TEUs) is half that of Sri Lanka. Service provided by private container terminals is preferred over those run by the government port authority. Total container handling charges of US$113 per TEU at Karachi and US$105 per TEU at Port Qasim are higher than the average of US$80 per TEU for India.

With the implementation of Pakistan Customs Computerized System (PACCS), the customs clearance time has been reduced from four to five days to less than 24 hours at the Karachi International Container Terminal. PACCS was rolled out and implemented in three other container terminals at the end of 2006. The free storage period also was reduced to four to five days from seven days. However, container dwell times (five to six days on average) are still above the international standard of three to five days, which decreases the capacity of container terminals to less than their potential. Tariffs for bulk and general cargo were relatively low (US$ 4–6 per ton) compared to other rates in the region, but tariffs on containerized cargo were relatively high.

### Trucking

The trucking fleet is predominantly outdated by several decades and runs on underpowered engines, which has implications on logistical performance (World Bank 2006, 71). High import tariffs on high-capacity multi-axle trucks protect local manufacturers producing low-capacity and low-powered trucks, and hence prevents the trucking sector from improving the trucking fleet. Over the past 20 years, revenues per kilometer have decreased, in real terms, by 1.4 percent on average per year (World Bank 2006, 67). Many trucks operate long hours and carry excessive loads while traveling at low speeds that range between 20 and 25 kilometers per hour, compared to 80–90 kilometers per hour in Europe. Journeys in Pakistan take three times longer than in Europe. Road freight takes an average of three to four days between ports and the north of the country (a distance of 1,400–1,800 km), which is twice the equivalent time in Asia and Europe (World Bank 2006, 69).

To maintain high revenues, trucks are overloaded. Such overloading and the lack of enforcement of regulations on safe operation, crew hours, truck modification, and trailer manufacture increase the risk of accidents (World Bank 2006). Trucks needing repairs due to overloading lose transport time (JICA 2006). The average time lost for non-agricultural freight trips is 4.7 hours, compared to 3 hours for passenger trips. Even though the cost of trucking freight is US$0.015–0.021 per ton-km (World Bank 2006), the quality of service is poor, especially seen from the perspective of exporters. Express service at higher rates is available, but the fleet providing the services is small compared to demand. The recent reduction in tariffs on imported vehicles will improve things, but this will take time. More recently, security concerns have mounted, especially in Balochistan and interior Sindh.

### Railways

Pakistan Railways (PR) is one of the largest organizations in Pakistan, employing 86,669 workers in 2007–08 (GoP 2010b). It has a network of 7,791 route-km, 7,346 km of which are of broad gauge, while the remaining 445 km are of meter gauge (GoP 2005). There are 625 stations with 1,043 km of total double-track sections and 285 km of electrified sections. Since 1982, no new routes have been constructed. The main line connects the five major stations of Karachi, Multan, Lahore, Rawalpindi, and Peshawar. The core railway, comprising the main north–south route and the strategic link to Quetta, comprises one-third of the total network. However, it supports 75 percent of the total trains and over 85 percent of freight traffic (World Bank 2006, 49) (figure 5.1).

Long delays and low speed are the main causes of road being preferred to railways for both passenger and freight service. The productivity of Pakistan Railway's freight services is about one-eighth of Chinese railways, one-third of Indian railways, and half of Thai railways, a network of comparable size. In addition, freight rates are not competitive compared to road transport. In contrast, Chinese rail is two to three times cheaper than road. As a result, PR has a very low and stagnant market share, carrying less than 10 percent of passenger traffic

Figure 5.1 **Freight Carried by Pakistan Railways**

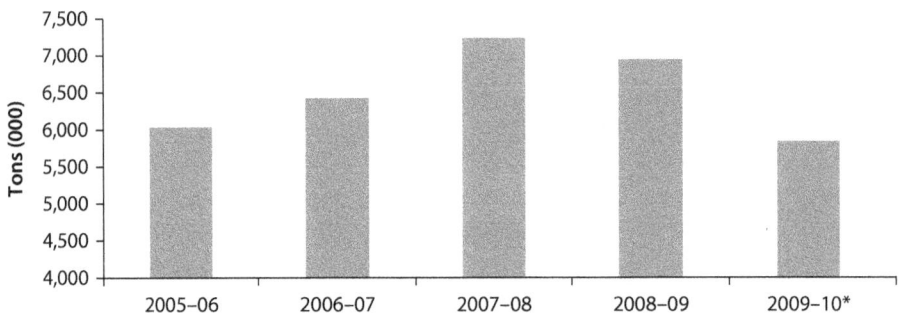

Source: GoP 2010b.
Note: * = provisional.

and 4 percent of freight.[1] In 2008/09, railway freight traffic was 5,896 million ton-km (GoP 2010a, 205). However, in 2007/08, railways carried 7,234 tons of freight, which was estimated at less than 5 percent of the total freight carried in the country.

## Aviation

Pakistan International Airline Corporation (PIA) was established in 1955 and was for a long time the only airline in the country. Pakistan has 42 functional airports out of which 10 serve international flights. Karachi is Pakistan's main airport, but Islamabad and Lahore also handle significant levels of both domestic and international cargo. Two additional international airports are coming up in Islamabad and Gwadar with the involvement of the private sector under Pakistan's policy of liberalizing the aviation industry. The Sialkot International Airport is complete; it has generated US$600 million of annual revenues from the transport of cargo and passengers. The new Islamabad International Airport is expected to handle annual traffic of 6.5 million passengers and 100,000 tons of cargo on completion.[2]

Though facing the competition from a few private airlines, PIA, the major public-sector airline, carries approximately 70 percent of domestic passengers and almost all domestic freight traffic.[3] The share of airfreight to total freight transported is quite small. A total of 319.8 million ton-km were transported in 2008 (World Bank 2009b) (figure 5.2).

Pakistan adopted an Open Skies Aviation Policy in the early 1990s. Private airlines joined the civil aviation industry in Pakistan because of the policy. Most of these airlines operated on a small scale, with limited professional management,

**Figure 5.2 Air Transport Freight**

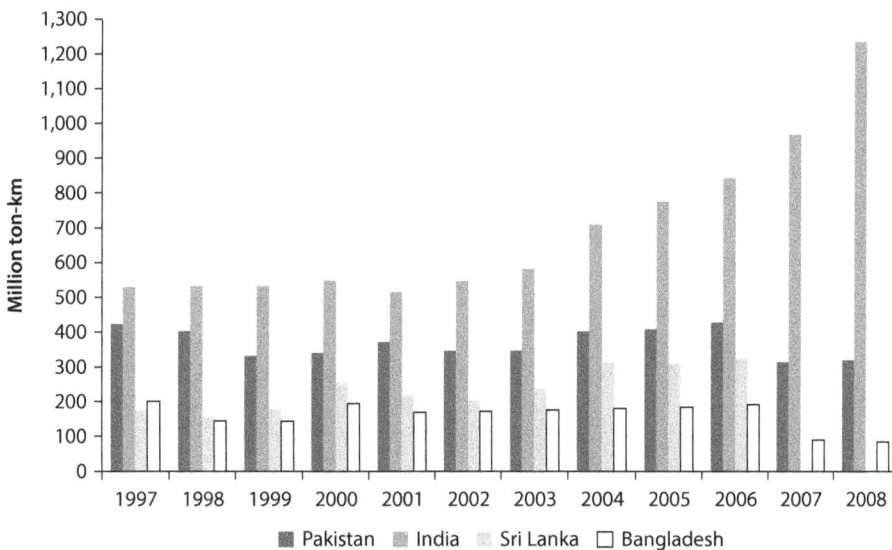

*Source:* World Bank 2009b.

and inefficient and old equipment. Stiff competition from PIA led to heavy losses for most of them, and most of the private operators could not continue services.

CAA (Civil Aviation Authority, established in 1982 to regulate aviation in Pakistan) initially made efforts to regulate the aviation industry, but met with stiff resistance from the various professional cadres of PIA. Over the years, the ongoing tussle between PIA and CAA has deepened the mistrust between the two key players in the industry. PIA has major grievances over the unilateral Open Skies Policy because it faces more competition from other airlines without getting an opportunity to penetrate foreign markets.

A 2006 Pakistan logistical cost study found that airfreight dwelling times at airports are two to three times longer than the actual transport time because of an inadequate supply of airfreight capacity on planes. There was a general delay of four to seven days. Additionally, the study found that Indian exporters have access to greater airfreight capacity than Pakistani exporters (LCG 2006, 78–81). For example, the frequency of freight air transport out of all of Pakistan's international airports—which include Karachi, Islamabad, Lahore, and Peshawar—to Frankfurt is 10 flights per week, whereas flights from Mumbai, India, to Frankfurt—including an MD-11 full freighter that flies three times per week—can accommodate 300 percent more freight export by air (LCG 2006, 81).

## Trade Policy

### Tariff Reform

Pakistan embarked on a radical trade liberalization program in 1996–97. By 2003, this program had eliminated nearly all its remaining traditional quantitative restrictions while drastically reducing and simplifying import tariffs. Real exchange-rate devaluation over the period of about 20 percent supported this liberalization. The reforms enabled exports and the economy to take advantage of the boom in world trade between 2003 and late 2007. During this period (2007/08 compared with 2001/02), exports in nominal U.S. dollars increased by 110 percent. Although this was an encouraging performance, over the same period, the exports of other developing countries grew much faster: for example, India's increased by a factor of three in nominal U.S. dollars. It can be plausibly argued that Pakistan's economic system was still not adequately efficient and flexible to take better advantage of this extraordinary opportunity because of continuing failures and rigidities in its economic policies, especially in its trade policies.

From the beginning, there were a number of important exceptions to the 1997–2003 trade policy reforms, and some backtracking on others occurred later on, especially during 2006 and after the global financial crisis of 2008. These include

- reversal of a number of the more important liberalizing reforms in agriculture, notably of wheat, and fertilizer policies;
- continuation of the long-standing ban on imports from India of products not on Pakistan's limited "positive list";

- local-content policies in the auto industry[4];
- the use of ostensibly World Trade Organization (WTO)–compatible (TBT and sanitary and phytosanitary) technical regulations, and regulations based on health and safety to restrict imports[5]; and
- the introduction of antidumping[6].

Starting in 2006/07, there were increases in the maximum level, dispersion, and complexity of Customs Duties, and in August 2008, the introduction of a number of "Regulatory Duties" on top of Customs Duties. Including the regulatory duties (but omitting outliers such as the very high tariffs in the auto sector), there are now at least nine standard "normal" tariffs, ranging from zero to 50 percent. This compares with just four standard normal rates, ranging from 5 to 25 percent, in 2002/03. The new structure has greatly increased the potential for high effective protection rates and bigger distortions across import-substitution activities, and has increased the system's general anti-export bias. Additionally, since 2006, there has been an expanded use of statutory regulatory orders (SROs). Most of these provide exemptions or partial exemptions from normal tariffs, but others provide for increased tariffs. In 2010/11, more than half (54 percent) of the total number of tariff lines were subject to at least one special condition announced in an SRO.[7] Most of these are exemptions for inputs and are confined to specified firms or groups of firms. They are not available to other importers, in particular, commercial importers. Their administration is a de facto import licensing system run by the Engineering Development Board and other ministries in conjunction with the Customs Service.

Additionally, the tariff system became more complex as a result of preferential trade agreements—especially the agreement with China effectively implemented in January 2006, and to a lesser extent from the agreements with Sri Lanka (operational from June 12, 2005) and with the other South Asian countries under South Asia Free Trade Agreement (operational from January 1, 2006). Pakistan also continued to use administratively complex and constantly changing export-subsidy programs and policies. Given positive protection for import-substitution production, there is a general case for both input tariff rebate/exemption programs and export subsidies. However, some hold the view that these programs, as actually administered in Pakistan, disproportionately benefit established exporters, discriminate against small and new exporters, and discourage export diversification.

Substantial distortion has thus crept back into the trade policy, and that distortion benefits a few chosen firms while eroding the international competitiveness of the vast majority.

### Regional Trade

In today's globalized world, growing cross-border trade between economies is increasingly important for business. To analyze the extent of trade activity in Pakistan, the World Bank's *Doing Business 2010* ranked 13 of Pakistan's main industrial cities, based on their cross-border trading, as

**Figure 5.3  Ranking of Pakistani Cities in Terms of Trading across Borders**

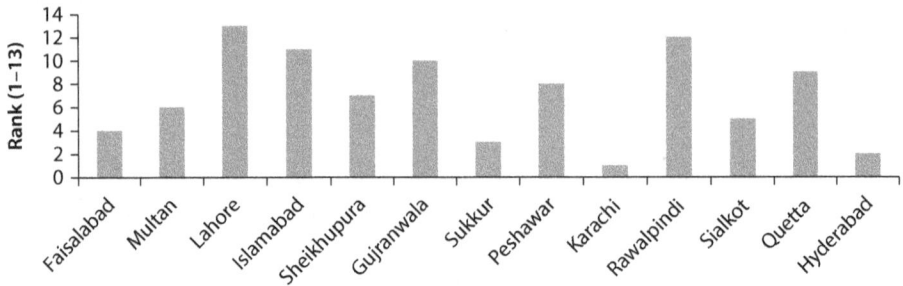

Source: World Bank Doing Business 2010b.

shown in figure 5.3 (World Bank 2010b). Karachi, which is Pakistan's largest city, houses the country's largest seaport, and is the capital of the province of Sindh, not surprisingly has the top ranking, followed by Hyderabad and Sukkur in second and third place, respectively. Both these smaller cities are located near Karachi, which may explain some of their advantage influencing their ranks, as proximity allows for greater information spillovers, access to specialized labor, and local transfers of knowledge.

Indeed, an interesting finding highlighted in *Doing Business 2010* is that a city's size may not be the controlling factor in trade. For example, a big city like Lahore fared poorly in trade compared to the relatively smaller cities of Multan and Sheikhpura city (an industrial city), which were found to be more efficient in cross-border trading (LCG 2006).

Geography allows Pakistan to take advantage of regional trade opportunities to give new growth dynamism to its large cities, thereby stimulating industrial expansion and achieving its objective of higher economic growth sustained over several decades.

### The Historical Context

Right up to the 19th century, most trade in the regions that now constitute Pakistan was regional trade over land routes. There was virtually no trade via the sea. Cities such as Lahore, Multan, and Peshawar, and those in Upper Sindh, lay on trade routes connecting lands to their west—Central Asia, China, and the Islamic Republic of Iran—and those to the east—India. As such, those cities became centers of trade, commerce, and culture, and brought prosperity to regions they commanded. Basic infrastructure and trade facilitation—such as the 16th-century Grand Trunk (GT) road, lodges for travelers along the GT road, widespread use of minted currency, and the development of Urdu, the language of the bazaar for commerce—along the east-west commerce routes promoted the trade (map 5.1).

The cultural centers spawned by the trade routes have defined themselves historically as parts of much larger regions that lie outside the borders of the modern nation-state of Pakistan. Indeed, these centers were better connected with trade and cultural centers outside the modern state of Pakistan than those

**Map 5.1 The Historical East-West Trade Routes of Pakistan**

that lie within it. As a result, the regions left a distinct and lasting stamp on South and Central Asia.

Starting in the mid-19th century, developments in colonial India began to erode the old trade routes and the infrastructure that supported them. Anglo-Russian rivalry and the long Chinese slumber cut off the land routes and markets to the west and the north, which had a long-lasting impact on the region centered on Peshawar. A rich tapestry of economic transactions between South Asia and the Central Asian territories, bringing substantial prosperity to the Punjabi and the Pashtun and northern areas of modern Pakistan, was unraveled. The British Indian government, focused on developing trade via the sea route, had no interest in cultivating trade with Persia along the old land routes, which negatively affected upper Sindh. These developments changed the regions of modern Pakistan from being at the center of east-west trade routes, to the status of a peripheral region of the south subcontinent tucked away in the northwest.

Independence in 1947 and the ensuing disputes with India cut off trade routes to the east. Pakistan, bordering four historically significant regions for trade transactions and cultural exchange (Afghanistan, China, India, and the Islamic Republic of Iran), was no longer connected in any meaningful way with the geographical region in which it lay.

There was, however, a positive aspect to this isolation. The economic managers of newly created Pakistan, building on the initiatives under colonial rule, invested heavily in modernizing the infrastructure (roads, railways, and other modes of connectivity) that developed the intra-Pakistan north-south trade corridor. For the first time in history, Pakistan's historical regional centers achieved a high degree of connectivity, defining an Indus Basin market across the length of modern day Pakistan (map 5.2).

The infrastructure investments in the Indus Basin market facilitated the big growth vents that yielded gross domestic product growth rates of 6 percent or more for several decades. The major growth vents that helped increase productivity for sustained periods of time were the spread of canal irrigation, import-substituting industrialization of the 1950s and the 1960s, successful adoption of high yield variety crops (the so-called green revolution), and internal and overseas migration. Without the infrastructure investments that created the industrial/commercial clusters of Karachi, Lahore, Faisalabad, Gujranwala, Multan, and Peshawar up and down the Indus market (map 5.2), such improvement in productivity and the 6 percent growth rate sustained over several decades would not have been possible.

### Towards Becoming a Regional Economic Hub

There is a widespread view that the major growth vents, and the logistics infrastructure investments and trade policy that supported them, have run their course. Modernizing the frayed trade logistics discussed in section 3.1 will help, as will the upgrading of other key components of infrastructure. However, a new "big idea" regarding growth is also needed on the scale of the previous major growth vents to increase productivity and investments significantly. Regional trade in a much-changed current setting has the potential to be a big idea growth vent.

As recently as the 1980s, it did not matter that the old east-west trade routes discussed earlier lay abandoned. China was performing far below its capabilities as a potential economic giant. Western China, in particular, was mired in low growth, and that was the more relevant China for Pakistan. In Central Asia, the mineral wealth was exploited in the interest of Communist Russia. In addition, India, with its low "Hindu" growth rate, was shackled to a heavy-handed and stifling regulatory framework and a decaying colonial bureaucratic heritage. In the last thirty years, all this has changed.

**Map 5.2 Pakistan's Indus Basin Market along the North-South Trade Corridor**

China is undergoing a major restructuring to deepen growth beyond the Pacific coast to western China and thus bring it to Pakistan's land border in the north. India, on an impressive growth trajectory of 7–8 percent growth per annum and now recognized as a major emerging economic power, lies along the long eastern land border. Across the northwestern border, beyond troubled Afghanistan and Pakistan's own volatile tribal belt, are the Central Asian republics, rich in natural resources and keen to exchange their mineral wealth for goods and services to satisfy growing consumption of their citizens. Beyond the western border lies the Islamic Republic of Iran, rich in oil and natural gas that it would be free to sell to needy South Asia in exchange for skilled workers and consumption goods once its strategic interests are allied with the welfare of its citizens.

Trade across Pakistan's land border thus presents great possibilities. With appropriate infrastructure investments in place, several trade flows are likely. One, of course, is trade in goods flowing from the east (India) and north (China), to Central Asia and the west (the Islamic Republic of Iran, the Persian Gulf, and beyond). A counter-flow of trade in energy that brings much-needed fossil fuels to fuel-deficient South Asia is also highly likely. With an educated and skilled workforce concentrated in clusters along the trade and energy routes, the cost advantage of locating industry in Pakistani urban clusters to serve a much larger South and Central Asian region will become obvious. Initially, a facilitator of regional trade in goods and energy flows, Pakistan will attract (given the high savings of India and China, and assuming improvement in Pakistan's investment climate) technical knowledge (via joint ventures) to stimulate Pakistan's industrialization.

Reopening and modernization of the traditional east-west trade routes and their interaction with a much-improved north-south trade corridor will give a new vigor to the Indus Basin market, increasing manifold economic transactions within the market and the prosperity that comes with it (map 5.3).

### Trade with India

Becoming a regional hub entails normalizing economic relations with India. The transactions dynamics of a T-junction (regional trade without India) pale in comparison to those of a hub (regional trade with India included). Rigorous analytical work demonstrates the benefits of liberalizing trade with India (Nabi 2011; Nabi and Nasim 2001; Naqvi and Nabi 2008). The seminal report by the Ministry of Commerce (GoP 1996) provided a careful assessment of gainers and losers at the sectoral level from liberalizing trade with India and strongly recommended the liberalization of Pakistan-India trade. The influential recent study by Pakistan Business Council (Pakistan Business Council 2013) takes the argument further by elaborating the broader economic gains of liberalizing trade with India (box 5.1). This analytical work, combined with recent geopolitical developments, has resulted in Pakistan taking steps towards granting most favored nation status (MFN) to India. This has resulted in moving from a positive-list-based highly restricted trade to a negative-list-based trade (about 1,200 items are on the negative list). This has given a new momentum to the steady normalization of trade (despite the dips due to non-economic factors) between India and Pakistan (figure 5.4).

### What Will It Take to Become a Regional Economic Hub?

The east-west economic routes (that go beyond trade in goods and include energy flows and movement of workers and flows of investment), and the growth vent associated with them, will not be realized until there is peace in Afghanistan, Pakistan's tribal belt straddling the Afghan border is stabilized, and Balochistan re-engages with the federation constructively.

Normalizing trade with India is critical for Pakistan's Indus Basin market to get the full benefit of an economic hub taking advantage of economic transactions

**Map 5.3 Enhanced Vibrancy of the North-South (Indus Basin) Trade Flows from Reopening of the Historical East-West Trade Routes**

with the billion-plus people vibrant economies of China and India in the north and the east, and the resource-rich economies to the northwest and the west. This requires building on the momentum of opening up in the recent past.

### Moving Forward on Trade with India

The announcement of a long and unwieldy negative list of 1,200 items accompanied the granting of MFN status to India. It was stated that the list would be phased out in a year. This timetable must be adhered to. The establishment of a bilateral commission must accompany MFN status to India. The commission would address the issues closely tied to India and Pakistan having a normal

## Box 5.1  Pakistan-India Trade Case Studies

The three case studies below (taken from Pakistan Business Council 2013 report and based on research by Ijaz Nabi) demonstrate the industrialization stimulus likely to result from normal India-Pakistan trade.

*An Indian Importer (Mr. Pradeep Sehgal, partner in SINOCHEM)* SINOCHEM, established in 2001 and headquartered in Amritsar, distributes chemicals throughout Northern India. Annual turnover is US$35 million, of which imports from Pakistan (US$20 million of chemicals) are a large share.

Mr. Sehgal's first visit to Pakistan was in 2001 at the invitation of Lahore Chamber of Commerce. The first business deal was in 2008 importing soda ash from Olympia (Munnoo group). Trade was allowed only via railway. SINOCHEM initially imported 1,000 tons of soda ash per month limited by railway wagon capacity. Railway freight was a major bottleneck. In 2011, trade was allowed via road transport. This reduced freight time considerably. SINOCHEM's imports from Pakistan increased to 2,500 tons per month and then to 4,000 tons per month in 2012. Now the imports include soda ash, hydrogen peroxide, and caustic soda. It took a year but the firm eventually received clearance from the Ministry in Delhi for back-to-back loading of liquids, which is essential for chemicals. This will facilitate growth of imports of chemicals considerably. SINOCHEM is planning to set up a packaging plant close to the border to facilitate onward distribution in India. SINOCHEM imports in the future could be as high as US$100 million a year. Showing ingenuity and demonstrating potential spillovers from bilateral trade, SINOCHEM bought an abandoned railway station in Gujrat, Pakistan, close to the manufacturing unit, to haul chemicals, and developed close relations with DESCON chemicals (a part of DESCON group) to set up a repackaging factory near Amritsar.

Mr. Sehgal considers having a local, well-connected, and knowledgeable partner critical for the success of his venture. On establishment's attitude, he said that on the Indian side, senior officials are supportive but working-level people can cause difficulties. He found the Pakistani establishment very supportive, but working-level people have the same mindset as in India. A few other Amritsar- based entrepreneurs are looking at possibilities. One imports gypsum and processes it to plaster of paris just across the border.

*A Pakistani Exporter (Mr. Imran Ashraf, CEO Hilbro Instruments)*
Hilbro, established in 1989 and headquartered in Sialkot, manufactures and exports surgical and medical instruments to Europe, the United States, Japan, Asia, and Africa. Annual turnover is US$10 million (employing 1,000 workers) of which exports to India are US$240,000. Mr. Ashraf first visited India as a member of Pakistan Minister of Commerce delegation to a South Asian Association for Regional Cooperation exhibition in Delhi. He was allotted a small stall at the exhibition, and this introduced Mr. Ashraf to Indian buyers. The first business deal was in 2006 with a Delhi-based distributer, Dental Instruments traders and distributors and involved export of dental, oral, and orthodontist instruments. It was a single US$2,000 consignment sent via Pakistan International Airlines (PIA) airfreight on a Lahore-Delhi flight. There were no customs or freight problems in either Lahore or Delhi. In 2012, Hilbro exports increased to US$20,000 a month via airfreight, and the firm now exports to four Delhi-based companies

*box continues next page*

**Box 5.1 Pakistan-India Trade Case Studies** *(continued)*

supplying them with both dental and general surgical instruments. The Delhi-based dental instruments company is large and has many suppliers, but one of the surgical instruments distributers is small and Hilbro is its largest source. The instruments are being sold in government hospitals and private clinics/hospitals with "Made in Sialkot, Pakistan" written on them. They are competitive because of quality as they conform to much tougher European, U.S., and Japanese standards. Given the rapid growth in the Indian health services including medical tourism, the potential for growth is substantial and could be as high as US$2 million for his firm alone. He does not believe there is much export of surgical instruments to India by other Sialkot-based firms. Hilbro plans to partner with an Indian surgical instruments importing company to set up a small manufacturing plant (about 50 workers initially) in India to export unfinished instruments that would be finished in the Indian plant. Visas are a big issue, as are Pakistan-India political tensions that introduce uncertainty and cloud business prospects.

### A Pakistani Importer (Mr. Khalid Mahmood, CEO GETZ Pharma Pvt. Ltd.)

GETZ Pharma, established in 1995 and headquartered in Karachi, manufactures a range of branded generic medicines to treat cardiovascular and metabolic diseases, hepatitis C, ulcers, and other infectious diseases. The medicines include various types of interferon, insulin, and antibiotics, among others. The annual turnover is US$110 million of which US$35 million is exports destined for many Southeast Asian, Central Asian, and African countries and Afghanistan. GETZ Pharma is the largest exporter of medicines from Pakistan for the past seven consecutive years. It employs 4,500 workers worldwide (3,200 in Pakistan), and 83 percent of the workforce is highly skilled consisting of graduates, masters, PhDs, medical doctors, MBAs, and accountants.

Mr. Khalid Mahmood first visited India in 1996 to explore importing a molecule, Omeperazole, to manufacture RISEK capsules prescribed for treating GERD, reflux, dyspepsia, and ulcers of the stomach, conditions sharply on the increase in Pakistan. The molecule was initially imported from Europe until it was discovered that the European company imported it from India and relabeled it under its own brand name, and in the process charged about 8 times higher prices. As a result of purchasing the raw material for this drug directly from the Indian manufacturer (after extensive testing for quality), GETZ Pharma was able to reduce the market price of the capsule from Rs 39 per capsule to Rs 12 per capsule and sales jumped tenfold. In 1997, imports from India for the company were US$25,000 and by 2012 had shot up to US$20 million. Imported raw materials require climate-controlled conditions and are sent by airfreight or by sea. Road/rail freight would be a lot cheaper, but climate control is not assured and thus overland import is not feasible. Import by air and sea is trouble free.

The potential of benefitting from India's expertise in pharmaceuticals is considerable. Of the US$1 trillion global market for medicines, half consists of generic medicines. Developing countries research and develop nearly US$50 billion of generics, with India accounting for US$20 billion. Both China and India are good sources for the three core aspects of pharmaceutical manufacturing—namely, raw materials, machinery, and Contract Research and Marketing Services. The last is critical in this knowledge-intensive manufacturing activity.

*box continues next page*

**Box 5.1  Pakistan-India Trade Case Studies** *(continued)*

GETZ Pharma benefitted from Indian technical expertise to improve its manufacturing processes, quality assurance, and cost effectiveness via two- to three-week visits by Indian consultants to its Karachi factory to train Pakistani pharmacists, chemists, and engineers. Cultural affinities and cost competitiveness made such consultancies highly attractive, and they explain GETZ Pharma's success in Pakistan and in international markets. The consultancy visits declined sharply after the Mumbai incident and have not resumed. GETZ Pharma's case shows how trade with India benefits Pakistan's global trade balance even though the bilateral (Pakistan-India) trade balance worsens. Raw material, machinery, and technology transfer from India is one-tenth the cost compared to European sources. Indian imports increase the international competitiveness of Pakistani pharmaceuticals and thus contribute to export earnings and improve the trade balance further.

***Some Insights from the Case Studies***

- A major bottleneck in promoting Pakistan-India trade is freight infrastructure, especially Pakistan Railway, without which the full range of the benefits of geography can be realized.
- Senior members of the policy establishment are generally supportive while working-level officials are trapped in an obstructionist mindset mainly for kickbacks.
- Ease of travel is critical for small businesses to seek out profitable opportunities, acquire local knowledge, and develop partnerships based on trust.
- Indian technical expertise can help Pakistan improve its overall trade balance even as the bilateral balance deteriorates.
- Internationally competitive Pakistani exporters see India as a huge market.
- Political tensions must not be allowed to disrupt business travel and supply lines.

---

economic relationship that results in sustained benefits. The commission would focus on the following:

- *Goods and services-related non-tariff barriers.* The objective would be to use the WTO framework for addressing Indian (and Pakistani) non-tariff barriers and then bring these into the strategic regional trade policy framework outlined above. Develop institutional capacity (National Tariff Commission) to address non-tariff barriers and antidumping complaints with a view to promoting trade rather than hindering it.
- *Land routes.* The maximum benefits from a more liberal trade regime with India will come from land routes that minimize response time to market forces; open up as many land routes as possible, building on the old road and railway networks all along the border from the Kashmir region to the Arabian Sea.
- *Travel.* Travel (visa services and air/road/railway transport) must be facilitated to promote competitive trade in goods and services that benefits small- and medium-sized firms, to tap into the large pool of Indian skilled workers, gain access to Indian farm and other technology, and encourage cross-border tourism.

**Figure 5.4 The Evolution of Pakistan-India Trade**
*Millions of US$*

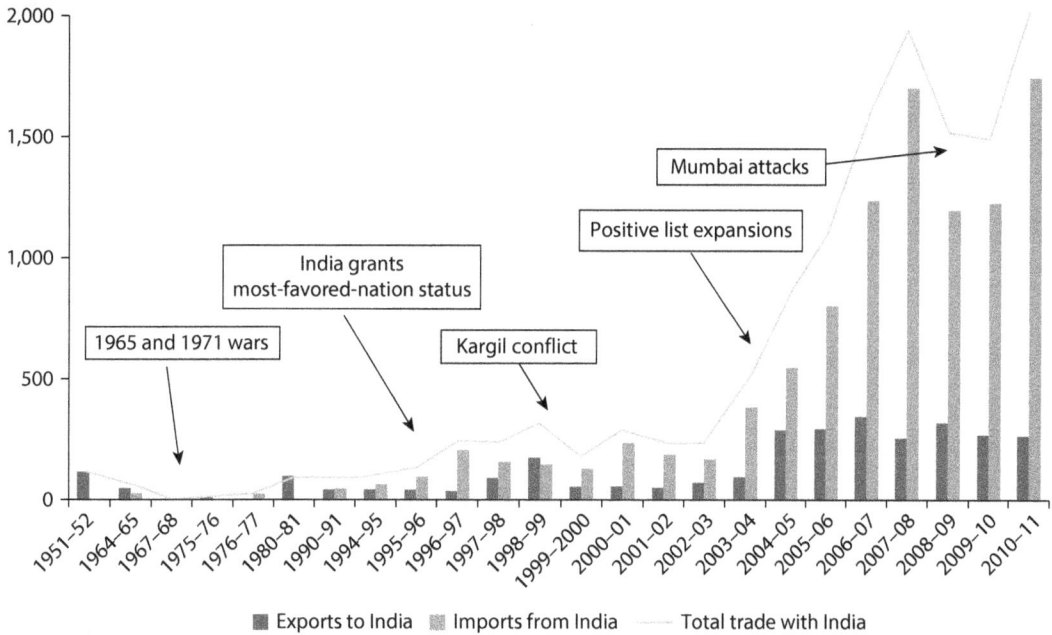

Source: Gopalan, Malik, and Reinert 2012.

To create a sustained momentum for liberalizing trade and investment flows, it would be useful to set up a regional trade forum (comprising the private sector, academia, and the media), that monitors the working of the bilateral commission mentioned above. The forum should identify barriers to trade embedded in the trade policy, the payment system, and communications (including travel); the forum should also help identify losers from liberalizing trade with India and suggest ways to compensate them and should help in formulating a broader regional trade and investment promotion strategy.

India has an important role in promoting bilateral trade with Pakistan and South Asian regional trade.[8] Paths to economic development and prosperity do not have go through sweatshops that cater to affluent western consumers. A large and vibrant Asian regional market would constitute a significant and, given demographic shifts, growing part of global demand for products. India's long-term strategic interest is to help create that Asian market. That, in turn, requires strengthening Pakistan to be an effective regional hub that connects the Asia-wide market.

Successful management of the new liberalized India-Pakistan trade regime to scale it up to a full-fledged economic relationship will be key. In the short term, it may well mean exercising voluntary restraint on exports that hurt small- and medium-sized Pakistani manufacturers. It would also require focusing on export of machinery and technology to Pakistani firms that currently import these at high cost from more expensive developed country sources. Setting up production units for the Asia-wide market requires the development of joint ventures and other investment strategies. The visa regime will have to be liberalized and travel facilitated so that small entrepreneurs develop cross-border business linkages, and so that there is wider sharing of gains from liberalization.

### Improvement in Trade Infrastructure and Trade Facilitation at the Land Borders

Cross-border connectivity will be critical for Pakistan to enjoy the economic benefits of becoming a hub for economic transaction in the region. Pakistani ports can provide the closest access to sea for these sub-regions. In fact, creating a vertical connect between the coastline wharfs and the markets of the region can optimize Karachi's (and other ports on the Arabian Sea coast) gateway potential. A trade connection with India represents access to a market twice that size. The current state of cross-border transport nodes is inadequate to meet the requirements of a regional economic hub. The Pakistan Business Council's 2013 regional trade report points out the following trade facilitation and infrastructure challenges that need to be overcome if Pakistan to become a regional economic hub (the list confirms the logistics challenges discussed in section 3.1) (box 5.2):

*Sea (Shipping Services):* Pakistan does not have any container shipping company. With a coastline of around 1,100 km it has three ports—Karachi Port, Port Qasim, and the more recent Gwadar Port. Karachi Port has two container terminals, Port Qasim has one container terminal, and Gwadar Port is still in its infancy.

*Air (Airfreight Services):* The national airline operates a freight service; however, there are no dedicated freighters. There are seven international airports; however, the absence of organized logistics centers at the airports is felt strongly.

---

### Box 5.2  A Case of Poor Trade Facilitation on the Indian Border

Until recently, overland trade could take place only by railway, which involved significant delays and payments of "speed money," thus eroding the advantage of geography. Moving a railway wagon from Lahore to Amritsar, a distance of 50 kilometers, could take 60–90 days. It would take 15–20 days to have a wagon allocated in Lahore (with speed money up to Rs 5,000 per wagon). The wagon was then loaded, inspected by customs, and sealed in Lahore. However, attaching the wagon to the rake and moving it to Mughalpura station also causes delay and involves speed money of up to Rs 5,000 per week, per exporter, to stay in the good books of officials who allot the engine to move the rake to the border. The rake is then moved to the border and on to Amritsar, where it should arrive by 5 PM on a workday (for security clearance), or it would be sent back to the border for delivery the next day. The poor condition of Pakistan Railways' engines often causes delays. Customs clearance in Amritsar is on the same day (for chemicals, speed money is fixed at Rs 900 per ton).

---

*Land (Road Transport Services):* The trucking business is in the informal sector and there are hardly any companies of size in the sector. Total number of trucks is around 250,000 trucks.

*Railways:* There are eight inland dry ports. The network connects all the dry ports across the country; however, the railways carry only 3 percent of the national freight.

*Waterways (Rivers and Canals):* This node would be seasonal—that is, operating when the water levels in the rivers and canals are high. Furthermore, the existence of dams and barrages limits the use of waterways to short stretches; it would require extensive work to create bypasses.

*Pipelines (Oil and Gas Transport):* Although Pakistan has cross-country pipelines to carry its oil from the south to the north, and to carry gas from the mid-west to the rest of the country, it does not have cross-border capabilities. Regional countries offer potential for this; but here the decisions are not based on economics alone.

*Transmission Lines (Electricity):* Here again Pakistan has an established national distribution system but no cross-border transmission capabilities.

## Notes

1. World Bank, "Pakistan Transport Sector: Overview," World Bank, Washington, DC (accessed January 23, 2011), http://go.worldbank.org/7CYYM39VG0.

2. The construction of the new Islamabad International Airport is expected to be completed by 2013.

3. World Bank, "Pakistan Transport Sector: Overview," World Bank, Washington, DC, (accessed January 23, 2011), http://go.worldbank.org/7CYYM39VG0.

4. These were replaced in July 2006 by very high and steeply escalated tariffs that effectively kept almost the same system in place, and enabled the detailed interventions of the Engineering Development Board to continue.

5. These include bans and restrictions on imports of secondhand products (for example, consumer durables such as passenger cars, motor cycles, air conditioners, and various types of industrial machinery and equipment) where the protection of local industries is clearly the dominant motive.

6. This started in a small way in 2002, but subsequently expanded rapidly during and after 2008/09.

7. Fifty-seven percent of agricultural tariff lines and 53 percent of non-agricultural tariff lines.

8. This discussion is based on Nabi (2012).

## Bibliography

Arvis, J.-F., M. A. Mustra, L. Ojala, B. Shepherd, and D. Saslavsky. 2010. *Connecting to Compete 2010. Trade Logistics in the Global Economy: The Logistics Performance Index and Its Indicators.* Washington, DC: World Bank. http://siteresources.worldbank.org /INTTLF/Resources/LPI2010_for_web.pdf.

GCI (Global Competitive Index) International. 2012. World Economic Forum.

GoP (Government of Pakistan). 1996. "Transition to the GATT Regime." Ministry of Commerce, Islamabad.

———. 2005. Ministry of Railways, Islamabad. http://www.railways.gov.pk/.

———. 2010a. *Pakistan Economic Survey 2009–10*. Islamabad: Ministry of Finance.

———. 2010b. *Pakistan Railways Yearbook 2009–10*. Islamabad: Pakistan Railways.

Gopalan, S., A. Malik, and K. Reinert. 2012. *Pakistan-India Trade: Economic Opportunities and Policy Challenges*. Draft report, International Growth Centre-Pakistan. London and Oxford, UK: London School of Economics and University of Oxford.

JICA (Japan International Cooperation Agency), National Transport Research Centre (NTRC), and Ministry of Communications, Government of Pakistan. 2006. *Pakistan Transport Plan Study in the Islamic Republic of Pakistan. Final Report*. Tokyo: JICA. http://www.ntrc.gov.pk/PTPS-reportSDJR06013FinalReport01.pdf.

LCG (Logistics Consulting Group). 2006. *Pakistan: Logistics Cost Study*. Final Report. Denmark: Logistics Consulting Group. http://www.nttfc.org/reports/Logistics_costs _study_Pakistan_report_June_06.pdf.

Lahore University of Management Sciences (LUMS). 2011. A. A. Burki, K. A. Munir, M. A. Khan, M. U. Khan, A. Faheem, A. Khalid, and S. T. Hussain. *Industrial Policy, Its Spatial Aspects and Cluster Development in Pakistan*. Consultant report by the Lahore University of Management Sciences for the World Bank. Lahore, Pakistan.

Nabi, I. 2011. "Economic Growth and Structural Change in South Asia: Miracle and Mirage." Development Policy Research Center Monograph, Lahore University of Management Sciences, Lahore.

———. 2012. "Lifting the Indo-Pak Trade Game." *The Hindu*, March 28. http://www .thehindu.com/opinion/lead/lifting-up-the-indopak-trade-game/article3251761.ece.

Nabi, I., and A. Nasim. 2001. "Trading with the Enemy: A Case for Liberalizing Pakistan-India Trade." In *Regionalism and Globalization: Theory and Practice*, edited by S. Lahiri, 170–97. London: Routledge.

Naqvi, Z., and I. Nabi. 2008. "Pakistan-India Trade: The Way Forward." In *Hard Sell: Attaining Pakistan's Competitiveness in Global Trade*, edited by M. Kugelman and R. Hathaway, 149–171. Washington, DC: Woodrow Wilson Center.

Pakistan Business Council. 2013. "Pakistan Economic Forum–II. April 2013." Pakistan Business Council, Karachi. http://www.pbc.org.pk/assets/pdf/regional_report .pdfp.

Private Power Infrastructure Board. Ministry of Water and Power, Government of Pakistan, Islamabad. http://www.ppib.gov.pk.

World Bank. 2006. "Transport Competitiveness in Pakistan—Analytical Underpinning for National Trade Corridor Improvement Program." Energy and Infrastructure Operations Unit, World Bank, Washington, DC.

———. 2009a. *Second Trade and Transport Facilitation Project. Project Appraisal Document*. Report 48094-PK, Sustainable Development Unit, Pakistan Country Management Unit. Washington, DC: World Bank.

———. 2009b. World Development Indicators (database), World Bank, Washington, DC. http://data.worldbank.org/data-catalog/world-development-indicators.

———. 2010a. "Global Trade Logistics: South Asia Needs More Progress to Spur Faster Economic Growth." http://www.worldbank.org/en/news/feature/2010/03/02/global -trade-logistics-south-asia-needs-more-progress-spur-faster-economic-growth.

———. 2010b. *Doing Business 2010*. Washington, DC: World Bank. http://www .doingbusiness.org/.

———. 2012. *Logistics Performance Index. Global Rankings 2012*. Washington, DC: International Finance Corporation and World Bank Group.

## CHAPTER 6

# Infrastructure Modernization

## Introduction

Given the manifold increase in the size of the economy and the number of trade and logistics transactions in the last six decades, the infrastructure that helped to create the Indus Basin market is now frayed and needs modernization. Well-functioning cities that enjoy agglomeration economies and become manufacturing hubs for employment generation and international competitiveness require modern services such as reliable and low-cost energy, well-maintained roads, and wastewater treatment that lower the cost of production. Upgraded and adequate infrastructure services that improve sanitation, access to clean drinking water, and public transport improve livability of cities and reduce congestion and other social costs of urbanization. Trade, especially the revival of regional trade, requires state-of-the-art infrastructure spanning inter-city and cross-border roads, railways, air transport, and telephones for regional connectivity. Efficient ports and shipping is an integral part of the national trade corridor. Cross-border standardization of freight transport regulations, improvements in the trucking fleet, and road safety standards are key to promoting regional trade. These themes, and the economic strategic objectives underpinning them, come together to provide the stimulus for upgrading Pakistan's infrastructure throughout the national economic corridor and provide a much needed vibrancy to the Indus Basin market.

This chapter focuses on what it will take for Pakistan to modernize its infrastructure. The next section reviews the current state of Pakistan's infrastructure. Sections 3 and 4 discuss the infrastructure and trade facilitation reform programs, respectively. Section 5 discusses mitigation measures to address emerging externalities (social, environmental, and institutional capacity challenges) associated with rapid urbanization and infrastructure expansion.

## The State of Pakistan's Infrastructure

Investment climate surveys and competitiveness indexes consistently point to inadequate infrastructure and poor trade logistics as key bottlenecks to both the formation of well-functioning clusters of economic activity and international competitiveness of Pakistani firms. Indeed, the empirical literature has identified both trade and infrastructure as being correlated with economic growth performance. The ease with which exporters can access both domestic and international markets depends considerably on a variety of country-specific factors, including macroeconomic conditions, protective policies, corruption, reliable supply of hard infrastructure, and trade logistics performance, among others. Reaching the optimal environment for the exchange of goods mandates minimum barriers to business operations and activities.

Evidence indicates that transport bottlenecks occur in all modes of transport infrastructure and services. Some major challenges in transport include poor quality of roads, underinvestment in railways, poor intraregional connectivity between national road networks, lack of cross-border transport infrastructure to link cities, and inadequate road and rail connectivity of ports with the rest of the economy. Moreover, a lack of access to reliable energy also has severe implications for industrial production and growth potential.

The infrastructure inadequacies are even more worrisome given the discussion in chapter 5 on the potential for gain from Pakistan becoming a hub of regional economic activity. To take advantage of its location and benefit from the growing prosperity in countries that border Pakistan, state-of-the-art infrastructure and regional connectivity will be essential.

### Energy

Access to consistent and affordable electricity is imperative for the success of industry. According to the Government of Pakistan (GoP): "Pakistan is facing an unprecedented energy crisis due to surging demand and supply gap," and this is occurring under low service coverage (GoP 2013a). Only 67 percent of the population has access to electricity, below South Asia's 71 percent, and well below East Asia's 92 percent (Andres, Biller, and Dappe 2013). Even when connected, power is highly unreliable, which is significantly stifling industrial growth. Lack of energy has implications on firm productivity, domestic and foreign direct investment, and export performance. According to the Global Competitiveness Report 2011–2012, the biggest obstacles reported for doing business in Pakistan include government instability/coups; corruption; policy instability; inadequate supply of infrastructure; and inefficient government bureaucracy; followed by poor access to funding.

Roughly 75 percent of Pakistani firms identified lack of electricity as a major constraint that affects their performance.[1] Managers of energy failed to anticipate the sharp increase in consumer demand, which increased from little over 12,500 megawatts (MWs) in 2003 to almost 25,000 megawatts in 2011 (Aziz 2013). With declining public expenditure on energy, electricity demand has outstripped supply by a significant margin for the past few years (figure 6.1), resulting in an estimated gap of 5,500 MW for 2010. In effect, supply has been flat at around 15,000 MW for the past 7 years (GoP 2013b).

Acute energy shortages have resulted in an unreliable power supply and frequent load shedding, which have in turn placed a huge burden on the

**Figure 6.1  Electricity Demand and Supply, 2003–10**
*Megawatts (MW)*

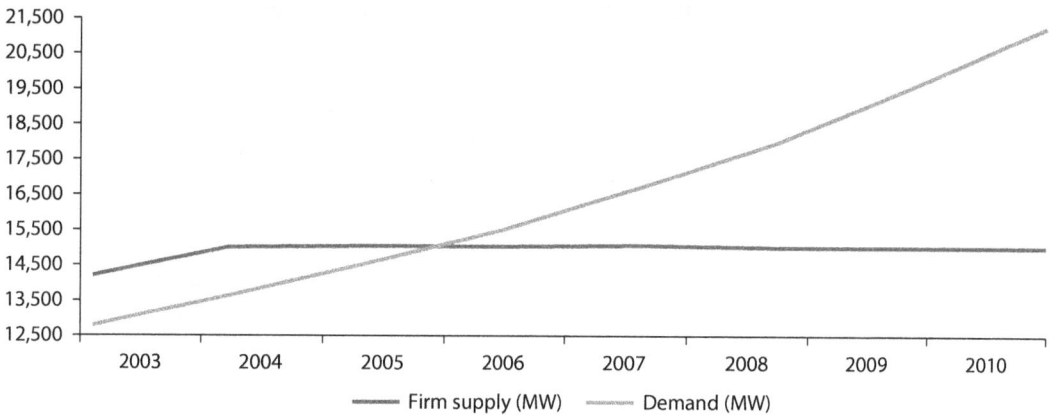

— Firm supply (MW)    ------ Demand (MW)

*Source:* Private Power Infrastructure Board, http://www.ppib.gov.pk.

manufacturing sector. Particularly badly affected are electricity-intensive sectors such as textiles, basic metals, leather products, rubber and plastic goods, as well as pulp and paper products and capital-intensive industries. The total cost of outages to the industrial sector is substantial—an estimated Rs 157 billion (Ghaus-Pasha 2008). This is equivalent to 9 percent of the total industrial value added, and constitutes a 7 percent decline in production and an employment loss of 300,000 jobs. In addition, the slowdown in manufacturing activity has affected other related economic activities such as wholesale and retail trade, transport, communications, banking, and insurance. Considering this short-run multiplier effect, the total cost of industrial load shedding was an estimated Rs 210 billion, which is about 2 percent of gross domestic product (GDP).

Independent power producers (IPPs) could have filled the supply gap.[2] However, delays in tariff adjustment and the failure to prevent theft and technical line losses did not improve the incentive regime for the needed IPP investment to add to capacity and upgrade technology. Circular debt—that is, failure of PEPCO to make timely payments to power producers, who were then unable to pay the oil and gas companies—has become endemic. These deferred payments led to a reduction in production and an accumulation of Rs 872.41 billion in the so-called circular debt[3] (Aziz 2013; GoP 2013a).

Energy pricing policy has systematically discriminated against manufacturing firms that pay the highest tariffs, while commercial, agricultural, and household consumers are subsidized. Fertilizer producers, an exception among manufacturers (the aim is to subsidize farmers) and household consumers received subsidies of Rs 14 billion and Rs 9 billion, respectively, in 2003 and continue to enjoy high subsidies. Energy subsidies have been a focus of the International Monetary Fund's recently completed article IV consultations. They are estimated at around 1.8 percent of Pakistan's GDP (IMF 2013).

Due to the lack of both private and public investment in the power sector, the condition of the transmission and distribution system is poor. In 2006, it cost Pakistan an estimated Rs 4.3 billion for each percentage point of line loss. According to the World Development Indicators, the situation has slightly improved during the last decade, with transmission and distribution losses declining from 26.1 percent in 2001 to 20.9 percent in 2008. However, Pakistan's losses are still the second largest in South Asia—India's are highest at 23.3 percent. Another indicator of the system's inefficiency is the delay in getting an electricity connection. The procedure can take 206 days, compared to 145 days for South Asia, 67 days in India, and 51 days in Malaysia (World Bank 2012). Moreover, the waiting time has deteriorated drastically from 2002, when it was 32 days. On a national level, the situation has actually worsened in three out of four provinces, with delays in Khyber Pakhtunkhwa (KP) now almost three times those of 2002. At the firm level, medium-sized firms suffer most with delays of up to 140 days.

Given the acute energy crisis, the GoP must develop a comprehensive energy framework that addresses potential sources for energy over the long term and resolves key issues, particularly pertaining to circular debt. The country's primary energy supplies heavily depend upon the imported crude oil and petroleum products, which have generated an import bill that exceeds US$14.5 billion. To address this issue, the government is pursuing policies of attracting private investment in the energy sector with greater reliance on domestic resources. It has recently introduced several new policies targeting the energy sector to attract investment and ensure energy security at affordable price (GoP 2013a). The country also needs to address the issue of energy subsidies, and the Government of Pakistan has a plan to bring down the current subsidy rate to 0.3–0.4 percent of GDP in three years. This gradual decrease would be implemented in four phases and it is broadly in line with successful energy reform strategies (IMF 2013).

The energy crisis is hitting the industry at multiple levels. Energy tariff increases are forcing businesses with low margins and those who are unable to generate their own power (particularly small and medium enterprises [SMEs]) to close down. Unannounced load shedding and voltage fluctuations damage machinery worth millions of dollars, and the unavailability of electricity harms productivity of the workforce. Given the energy crisis, the GoP needs to explore new sources of energy supply to cater to industry, particularly developing cleaner sources of energy as an alternative to its limited gas sources. The GoP also needs to resolve current transmission and distribution losses, invest in thermal and hydel (hydroelectric) plants, utilize coal as an alternative source of energy (as is done in India), and import energy sources from neighboring countries, including gas from the Islamic Republic of Iran.

Areas with a heavy presence of industry—both large-scale and SMEs—should be given the status of industrial corridors, and these corridors should only experience load shedding when absolutely necessary. The government should make it a priority to supply reliable power to the industrial clusters, especially in industrial cities like Karachi and Faisalabad. The approach to energy-related problems is in GoP's proposed new industrial policy, and includes the following elements advocated by the Ministry of Industries and Production (GoP 2011a). There is a need for sector-wide energy audits, beginning with heavy-load industries. Based on audit recommendations, the industry should receive incentives to shift toward more energy-efficient production methods and technology. There is need for peak-load pricing schedules in the industrial corridors. A comprehensive program that focuses on reducing technical losses and improves the reliability of the distribution system is required. In the medium to long run, there should be a shift in energy mix. The development of localized, cheaper machinery for hydroelectric, thermal, and coal-based power plants may help this shift. Captive power generation should be allowed in special economic zones, science parks, and industrial estates. At the same time, action is necessary to facilitate the local development of wind turbines and solar energy technology in industrial estates. For this purpose, pilot research projects should be initiated bringing together universities, industry, foreign and local experts, and relevant government departments.

Cross-border energy corridors can help promote both regional economic cooperation and access to energy resources. Developing a cross-border energy corridor with the Islamic Republic of Iran for the construction of the Iran-Pakistan gas pipeline will help address the energy crisis in the medium and long run. In addition, the development and implementation of the proposed Iran-Pakistan Gas Pipeline and the Turkmenistan-Afghanistan-Pakistan (TAP) Natural Gas Pipeline project have important implications for helping Pakistan meet its energy demands. The Iran-Pakistan project, signed in 2009, is expected to deliver gas from the Islamic Republic of Iran's South Pars gas field through Pakistan's Balochistan and Sindh provinces.[4] The TAP project consists of a gas pipeline of roughly 1,800 kilometers that can transport up to roughly 33 billion cubic meters of natural gas per year from southeast Turkmenistan to Afghanistan, Pakistan, and India (ADB 2012). The projects will link energy-deficit economies such as Pakistan to the relatively richer hydrocarbon Central Asian economies. Furthermore, the projects will also provide Pakistan with cheaper and cleaner energy sources to help meet current and future energy demands, and help overcome shortages in electricity (ADB 2012). However, problems pertaining to political, security, technical, and funding challenges have stalled the TAP project's implementation, and solutions for dealing with these issues have yet to be resolved. To date, construction work on the Iran-Pakistan gas pipeline is currently in progress.

## Transport Infrastructure

Facilitating trade and spatial connectivity is effective only with the support of adequate transport infrastructure, which helps to *facilitate* the production and distribution of products and services. As previously discussed, transport is an essential component to the success of trade logistics and growth. Indeed, roads are one of the top infrastructure concerns for businesses worldwide. In the absence of institutional barriers, transportation infrastructure is a critical

Revitalizing Industrial Growth in Pakistan • http://dx.doi.org/10.1596/978-1-4648-0028-3

element to improving industrial competitiveness as it expands the markets of individual industrial producers.

Transport sector inefficiencies cost Pakistan's economy an estimated 4–6 percent of GDP every year.[5] According to the 2011–2012 Global Competitiveness Report, the quality of Pakistan's overall infrastructure is ranked 115 out of 142 countries. Although the transport sector is functional, its inefficiencies with long waiting and traveling times, high costs, and low reliability are hampering the country's economic growth. These factors also reduce the competitiveness of the country's exports, increase the cost of doing business in Pakistan, and constrain Pakistan's ability to integrate into global supply chains, which mandate just-in-time delivery.

### Roads and Highways

The total road network in Pakistan is approximately 259,618 km, of which 12,000 km consists of national highways and 2,207 km of motorways under the responsibility of the federal government. As of March 2010, there were an estimated 216,043 trucks in Pakistan plying on 180,000 km of high quality roads. Pakistan ranks 79 out of 142 countries on quality of roads—a ranking lower than China and Sri Lanka (figure 6.2). Road density in Pakistan is among the lowest in the region. Road density stands at just 33 percent, compared to 113 percent in India, and 150 percent in Sri Lanka (World Development Report 2009; World Bank 2008).

Pakistan's reliance on obsolete and inefficient fleets has implications for road quality. A major challenge is the trucking fleet that consists mainly of 2-axle (70 percent) and 3-axle (20 percent) vehicles and on some main sections of the major highway (N5) accounts for 70–80 percent of the total flow. Trucking companies are primarily small (less than five vehicles) and unregistered (informal, non-taxpaying), and depend on freight brokers and subcontracting to large companies to secure business. To maintain high revenues, trucks are overloaded, which damages road quality and increases the demand for higher road investment. Poor quality and overloaded fleet, in turn, implies high cost of road

**Figure 6.2  Quality of Roads**

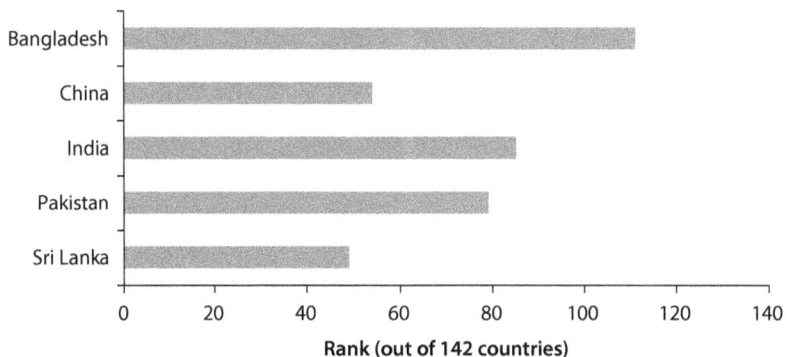

*Source:* World Economic Forum 2011.

maintenance. Recent fiscal problems have reduced funding for road maintenance, and at the current allocation of Rs 25 billion per year, it will take 8 years to clear the backlog of road maintenance.

### Railways

The poor condition of the railways infrastructure is one reason for its poor performance—while the public sector has made significant investments in road infrastructure, the same has not been true for rail. Pakistan Railways (PR) is unable to service its debt, and to cover its full operating costs plus pension payments, and thus is in no position to invest in renewal and maintenance of its rolling stock. Signaling and telecommunications equipment are in need of repair. Freight wagons are old, and in poor condition with a small capacity designed for general cargo, while much of freight transport is now moving towards containerization. Other PR shortcomings include running numerous unnecessary lines, cross-subsidizing passengers from freight and the non-core network from the core network, and offering supply-driven services.

Railway business began to slow down in 2008, as the economy slowed down and internal security issues intensified. Issues with infrastructure also stalled growth; for example, they affected freight traffic by the non-availability of locomotives and non-procurement of spare parts. In 2009/10, freight traffic decreased by 13.1 percent.

### Air Transport

Pakistan ranks 85 out of 142 countries on air transport infrastructure quality (figure 6.3). Aviation infrastructure is not at par with international competitors. Cargo handling facilities need major upgradation, and parking and landing facilities are inadequate and limited. Moreover, there is no airline in Pakistan dedicated solely to the transport of cargo for both exports and imports. Private airlines are not able to respond to the high demand in freight or passenger transport due to government's close collaboration and protection of Pakistan International Airlines (PIA), which carries almost all domestic freight traffic.[6]

**Figure 6.3 Quality of Air Transport Infrastructure**

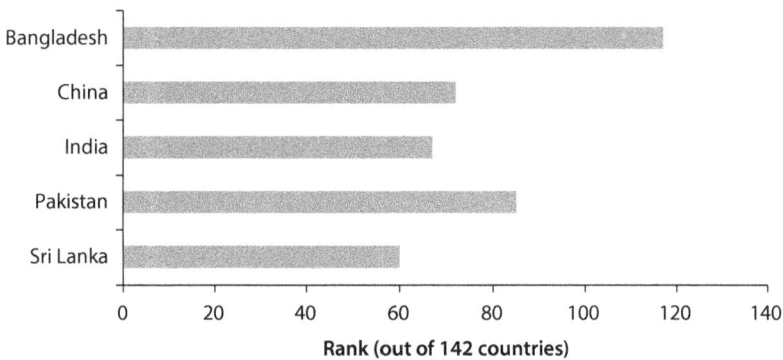

*Source:* World Economic Forum 2011.

The major beneficiaries are the international airlines that fill the demand gap for transportation of cargo. The patronage given to PIA by the government is a major disincentive for other private airlines to enter the industry and de-motivation for PIA to improve its efficiency and the quality of services that it provides.[7] PIA also operates as a monopoly on certain routes, for example, for Haj traffic. For these reasons, Pakistan ranks 126 out of 140 countries on airport density (World Economic Forum 2011).

## Infrastructure Reform Program

### Absence of a Reform Program for Energy

A lack of power has drastically affected the industrial sector, with some figures pointing to drastic reductions in industrial production and increases in unemployment levels. Indeed, a recent report by the Asian Development Bank (ADB) notes that "Losses arising from power and gas shortages held down GDP growth by 3–4 percentage points in FY2011 and FY2012." The increase in power tariffs has also hurt industry by increasing costs. Lack of fuel, particularly in the case of PR and Pakistan International Airways, has hurt the services sector.

The Government of Pakistan is currently working on a formal and comprehensive plan or long-term vision to resolve the ongoing chronic energy crisis that is hindering the growth of its economy. The energy crisis is a multifaceted problem plagued with political, technical, security, and financing challenges that have made seeking both short- and long-term solutions difficult. The GoP has engaged in a variety of high-level discussions centering on finding solutions for the energy crisis. Topics included power generation from alternative sources (for example, coal, renewable, and hydroelectric from domestic sources) and international sources of energy (for example, gas imports from neighboring countries, including the Islamic Republic of Iran) for meeting short-term and long-term energy demands; the circular debt problem; upgrading and rehabilitating transmission and distributing systems; and electricity theft. However, to date, no formal national energy plan has been formulated that addresses solutions for the energy crisis. An inefficient logistics system, an inadequate supply of infrastructure, and the ongoing energy crisis have decreased the competitiveness of industry, resulting in substantial losses of productivity, profit, employment, and hence exports growth. Given that the growth and development of a country is positively linked to industrialization and investment, Pakistan's systematic poor performance in industrial growth is a major cause of concern. Therefore, it is vital to develop and implement policies that promote trade and provide the appropriate infrastructure to reduce the cost of doing business. Given that industrial sectors are primarily located in urban centers, a key objective is to efficiently link these clusters with domestic and international markets to enhance trade growth. The following recommendations are not part of the GoP's reform program and can be adopted in the GoP's industrial strategy for reducing and mitigating industrial losses due to trade and infrastructure inefficiencies.

## Transport Sector Reform

Upgrading and rehabilitating the national road network and railway links that connect cities—particularly industrial clusters—to each other must take priority. It is critical to maintain existing transport infrastructure and services in good working order while simultaneously investing in improved physical infrastructure to reduce transport costs for industrial clusters. Efforts should focus on improving regional connectivity between industrial clusters, including the movement of containers and the cross-border movement of goods in order to reduce transport bottlenecks (box 6.1). The upgrading of infrastructure (for example, at Gwadar Port) is also crucial for promoting regional trade flows and will allow Pakistan to act as a transfer channel for goods moving between the Middle East and China.

---

### Box 6.1  Signing Convention on International Transport of Goods to Promote Regional Connectivity

The information in this box is based on a note prepared for the Pakistan Business Council's Regional Trade Report 2013. The Pakistan National Committee of the International Chamber of Commerce (PNC-ICC), also known as ICC Pakistan, has been promoting Pakistan's accession to the International Transport of Goods (TIR) Convention since 2000. ("TIR" is the acronym for the French "Transports Internationaux Routiers.") In February 2002, the PNC-ICC hosted a major international foreign direct investment conference in Karachi, with over 600 delegates attending from over 20 countries, in addition to government officials, federal ministers, legal experts, and the trade. Because of this conference, the Karachi Business Declaration included in its final recommendations to the government, "the ratification and implementation of the TIR Convention for transit trucking and the Istanbul Convention on ATA Carnets for temporary admission."

The Federal Cabinet resolved on June 15, 2002, to accede to both conventions. It was recommended to first accede to the Istanbul Convention on ATA Carnet (that allows the holder to temporarily—up to one year—import goods without payment of normally applicable duties and taxes) as the pilot program restricted to exhibitioner materials and professional equipment. Signing the TIR Convention for transit trucking would allow this. The expectation was that the implementation of the Istanbul Convention would help the various regulatory authorities and the customs to familiarize themselves with the concept of temporary admission in utilizing a WCO international guarantee system. The more extensive and widely used TIR Convention overseen by the International Road Transport Union (IRU) would then follow.

Pakistan acceded to the Istanbul Convention and deposited the instrument of accession for the TIR Convention 1975 on October 21, 2004. The accession to the Istanbul Convention was successful; however, the accession to the TIR Convention was rejected owing to a reservation made by the Pakistan Foreign Office under Article 8 Paragraph 4 of the TIR Convention.

*table continues next page*

**Box 6.1  Signing Convention on International Transport of Goods (TIR) to Promote Regional Connectivity** *(continued)*

The TIR Commission has since been working to facilitate the re-accession process. The matter was first referred to the Ministry of Law on February 18, 2006, and then to the attorney general of Pakistan. However, there has been progress and the matter is pending at various government departments/ministries.

In February 2007, Pakistan International Freight Forwarders Association organized a logistics conference with participation from the highest levels of the Government of Pakistan, in addition to representations from China and Kazakhstan, as well as the president of FIATA (Freight Forwarders Association: Fédération Internationale des Associations de Transitaires et Assimilés), and the IRU leadership. At the conference, there was detailed discussion of the ratification of the TIR.

The ATA Carnet system has been implemented in Pakistan for over 4 years. Efforts at overcoming the hurdles to signing the TIR Convention are ongoing, not only through the National Trade and Transportation Facility, but also in direct interactions between members of the TIR Convention and government officials. The IRU, in its international deliberations—especially in the context of the ECO (Economic Cooperation Organization whose members are Afghanistan, Azerbaijan, the Islamic Republic of Iran, Kazakhstan, the Kyrgyz Republic, Pakistan, Tajikistan, Turkey, Turkmenistan, and Uzbekistan)— has recommended the TIR Convention as the most important international transit system for the ECO region. Meanwhile, the 10 ECO states endorsed the TIR Convention to be their main international transport convention.

Pakistan becoming a full-fledged signatory of the TIR Convention is critical to achieve the degree of connectivity needed to benefit from regional trade.

---

The key reforms include[8]

- Modernize and streamline trade and transport logistics, practices, and customs.
- Improve port efficiency, reduce the costs for port users, and enhance accountability of port management.
- Create a commercial and accountable environment in PR, and increase private sector participation in the operation of rail services.
- Modernize the trucking industry and reduce the cost of transport and other externalities.
- Sustain delivery of an efficient, safe, and reliable national highways system.
- Promote and ensure safe, secure, economical, and efficient civil aviation operations.
- Increase export of perishable commodities (such as fruits, vegetables, and livestock) through establishment of an efficient and viable cool chain supply system.
- Develop an energy corridor linking China and Afghanistan with the Central Asian Republics.
- Develop inland water transport through link canals and the Indus River as alternative and economical modes of transportation.

To implement the program, the GoP has set up a National Trade Corridor Task Force (NTCTF) headed by the Deputy Chairman of the Planning Commission. Task force members are the federal secretaries of the Ministries of Communications, Railways, Ports and Shipping, Defense, Petroleum, and Industries; as well as representatives of the Federal Board of Revenue the National Highway Authority (NHA), and the Civil Aviation Authority. In addition, the three development partners—the World Bank, the ADB, and the Japan Bank for International Cooperation—supporting the program are represented on the NTCTF. Ten committees operate under the task force to oversee implementation of specific activities.[9] The government has also set up the NTC Management Unit in the Planning Commission to act as the supervisory agency for the initiatives under the program.

Pakistan's transport supply chain system might provide the value-added services that have become the hallmark of modern logistics: *multimodal systems* that combine the strengths of different transport modes into one integrated system. Pakistan's freight transport system needs to shift towards integration and complementarities of rail and trucking to improve efficiency and decrease environmental impacts. Rail freight generally has a competitive advantage and lower costs over road freight transport via trucks for longer distances. The adoption of a multimodal freight transport system, utilizing rail for long hauls and road freight for shorter distances, is a strategy for enhancing the sustainability of freight transport. Given that rail is more environmentally sustainable than road, the case for integrating rail more significantly into freight logistic itineraries for goods is critical.

### Trucking Sector

Overloading is endemic in the industry and truckers claim that it is critical for profitability given that the fleet consists mostly of 2-axle vehicles. This causes both accidents and road damage. NHA has prepared a truck weight control action plan, which envisages setting up of weigh stations at goods loading points and at entry points of highways, as well as using data from a proposed central data repository (CDR) with details of motor vehicle registration to be able to identify owners of offending vehicles.

The 2007 Trucking Policy recognized that the 2- and 3-axle vehicles, which dominate the sector in Pakistan and are often assembled in backstreet operations with no regard for minimum quality standards, are harmful for the environment, consume more fuel, and damage road infrastructure. As such, the policy sought to effect a modernization of the fleet, encouraging use of multi-axle vehicles that meet minimal European emission standards. Subsequent to the finalization of the Trucking Policy, this reform has become imperative as the Pakistan Environment Protection Agency (Pak-EPA) notified new National Environmental Quality Standards (NEQS) for motor vehicles in 2008, which specify that all local diesel vehicle manufacturers must meet Euro II emission standards by end June 2012. In addition to the notification of fuel emission standards, the government has also prepared national standards for manufacture of trailers and semi-trailers that have been sent to the Pakistan Standards and Quality Control Authority (PSQCA) for finalization.

The key policy incentive for modernizing the fleet was the rationalization of tariffs on vehicle assembly kits in the budget of 2006/07. This rationalization brought tariffs down from levels of up to 60 percent (on completely built units and completely knocked down [CKD] for rigid trucks) to 10 percent, with duty on CKD kits for some categories of prime movers removed altogether. In order to make the policy regime predictable, a five-year timetable for additional reduction of duties was also given. In addition, in the Trade Policy of 2007–08, the government allowed import of used heavy-duty vehicles as long as they met certain specifications. Even with these incentives, however, the average price of a truck meeting Euro II specifications is about Rs 7 to 8 million, well above the Rs 1 to 1.5 million charged for a truck assembled by a manufacturer in the informal sector using secondhand materials.

The government also wants to move towards instituting industrial estates for truck assembly in an effort to check truck body making in the informal sector, where bodies are built onto Hino or Bedford chassis with little regard for the need to adhere to safety regulations or minimal quality standards. Trucking was recognized as an industry in January 2008, in a bid to better regulate the sector, and open up opportunities for sector stakeholders to access credit.

Provincial governments house the vehicle-registration and certification systems, but the 2007 Trucking Policy highlights the need to create a CDR to facilitate data transfers and exchange across provinces, a vital function in an environment when vehicles cross provincial boundaries regularly. The proposed CDR would house data on the origin of the vehicle, its registration and identification particulars, as well as details of taxes paid, fitness certifications, axle load control, and a host of other variables. The proposed design would ensure that the roles and functions of the federal and provincial governments are delineated clearly, and that the federal government acts as a database manager, but does not take on operational responsibilities for vehicle regulation.

The creation of a database on vehicles in general and trucks in particular would also facilitate motor vehicle examination and fitness certification systems, which are for all practical purposes nonexistent at the moment, in spite of the legal requirements of the Motor Vehicles Ordinance of 1965.[10] Motor vehicle examiners are not trained or equipped to test vehicle fitness according to the requirements of international or even newly instituted domestic standards. The Trucking Policy proposes the establishment of vehicle fitness testing stations, possibly with public-private partnership (PPP), as part of a revamped system of vehicle testing and certification.

In addition to vehicle fitness, a revamped regulatory system would also institute systems for driver's training and licensing, to ensure the testing of drivers regarding their knowledge of traffic rules and physical fitness, as per the requirements of a job with long hours spent in navigation, often in difficult conditions. Instituting such a system will require setting up training schools for drivers of heavy vehicles, instituting tests for licensing, and maintaining a database of infractions linked to license numbers. The system would also help in checking against substance abuse among drivers—a common problem that has potentially extremely dangerous implications.

### Pakistan Railways

To allow rail to operate on a commercial basis, PR might be split into two different organizations: one responsible for freight and the other for passenger services, without any sort of subsidization.[11] This would allow PR to be relieved of costs of operating the large non-commercial network of lines and services. PR should, over time, separate core and non-core activities with a view of having the company focus on its core function of providing rail transport rather than on management of its non-operational land assets, such as factories and workshops.

The government is keen to reduce rail-related costs to the economy, at a time when it is paying between US$65 million to US$130 million in subsidies to keep PR afloat (World Bank 2006, 3). The key strategy in this regard is to encourage private sector participation by implementing a track access policy that allows private operators to run both passenger and freight services on selected routes. Investment in new rail lines for freight transport should be made based on PPPs sharing risks and using the highest economic, financial, social, and environmental standards. Planned activities that fall broadly under this heading include instituting systems to mechanize track maintenance, a human resource management system that would enhance capacity of existing staff, a design for rehabilitation of main bridges, and plans to enhance the productivity of workshops. Overall, such measures can help revitalize the rail freight sector, and enhance its reliability and performance, as well as its business reputation. The capacity building of employees is crucial not only to ensure efficient service in a revamped PR, but also to improve the long-term employment prospects of railway workers to prepare them for a future where private service operators may play a more prominent role. By allowing private entry into the railways sector, the GoP can correct some of the inefficiencies that have led to the view that rail transport is a transport modality that cannot compete, on a cost or convenience basis, with highway transport.

### Air Transport

Proposed policy interventions in the air transport sector are at a planning stage and will depend on the findings of sector and infrastructure assessments and assessments of regulatory safety oversight. Overall, trade and transport reforms will lend support to further sector restructuring and modernization, including implementation of Global Navigation Satellite System approaches and further sector restructuring, including encouraging private sector involvement in airport and services management as per the Civil Aviation Policy of 2008; and restructuring of PIA. PIA's restructuring has been anticipated for some time, but the issue may have assumed greater urgency since June 2010, when the Prime Minister emphasized the need to restructure eight organizations seen as white elephants that the public exchequer could no longer support. Job losses in the aviation industry, particularly for flight crew and maintenance staff, will have a strong negative impact, given the lack of viable alternatives in the sector. Again, as in the case of railway workers, these losses are unlikely to be effected without payment of compensation, which should somewhat mitigate the effects.

### Private Sector Participation in the Transport Sector

Increasing freight transport productivity requires private sector participation. Due to federal budget constraints, bringing in private participation (particularly in rail and aviation) is required. Private-sector participation in the rail industry could serve to correct some of the deficiencies resulting from the current management, including subsidization that leads to artificially high freight transport rates and poor track maintenance. Even though the major share of trucking in Pakistan is private, the National Logistics Cell (NLC) owns by far the largest trucking company in Pakistan. The NLC, established in 1978 to transport public imports of wheat and fertilizer, operates some 1,400 trucks and employs more than 7,000 workers. To provide a level playing field, the government might consider developing a regulatory framework for ensuring market competition in the rail and air transport sectors, including provisions for entry and exit of private operators. This regulatory framework could facilitate intermodal connectivity and private sector participation. The regulatory structure should include responsibilities on cross-cutting issues such as environment and social management, project and concession contract development, and monitoring and evaluation. An apex regulatory organization could take over responsibilities such as regulatory policies and promotion of private sector participation.

## Reform of Trade-Facilitation Ports Shipping

### Trade Facilitation
### Simplification of Trade Documents

These initiatives include measures to ensure that all trade-related documents in Pakistan conform to the United Nations Layout Key, an international standard for simplified documents, as well as checking commercial and official familiarity with Electronic Data Interchange for Administration, Commerce and Transport. Other planned activities include assessing the efficiency of documentary credit systems and identifying the extent to which trade and transport delays cause payment delays.

### Facilitation of Trade Operations

Activities planned include improvements in official regulations covering movement of goods across borders (that is, facilitation and tracking of cargo in transit trade operations); support for clearance procedures at dry ports; capacity building of freight forwarders; and development of cold chain logistics, among other things. The two pilot projects to be initiated—the development of an electronic trading platform and transit/cargo tracking systems—can be included in this broad set of measures.

The freight-forwarding and logistics sector has traditionally had little access to sources of financing, since Pakistan's banks are more geared towards working with production houses that can offer collateral in recognized forms. In the longer run, governmental officers, entrepreneurs, and other stakeholders in the trade and freight transport sector need to start a dialogue with financial institutions to explore the possibility of extending business development credit to logistics professionals in keeping with their expanding role in an economy increasingly dependent on strong domestic and international transport links.

Some key concerns regarding ATA relate to security and require the strong implementation of security protocols. However, the loss of business for Pakistani truckers is also a key concern, particularly in an atmosphere of heightened insecurity. An important mitigation strategy here will be to ensure that Afghan drivers operate under the same regulatory regime that applies to Pakistani businesses, therefore providing them with less of an opportunity to engage in a price war with local concerns.

### Reform of Ports and Shipping

In 2008–09, the last year for which published data are available, the Karachi Port had 291 officers and 4,893 workers (KPT 2009), whereas Port Qasim had 1,666 employees in 2007 down from 2,213 in 2000 (PQA 2007). As mentioned earlier, these represent significantly lower levels from previous years as rationalization of staffing has been a feature of administrative changes at both ports in recent years. Further reduction in staff numbers has not been mentioned in the business plans of either port, or in interviews conducted by NLTA consultants with port authorities, but further private sector involvement in port operations may necessitate further cuts—a fact that has been alluded to in the Project Appraisal Document (PAD).[12]

Limiting the scope of, and ultimately wrapping up, the Karachi Dock Labor Board (KDLB) has been on the agenda of the Ministry of Ports and Shipping for some time (World Bank 2006). Initially the government had planned to fund severance packages for KDLB registered workers, as well as labor redeployment services. The plan could not, however, go very far as workers registered with KDLB are not public sector employees. As of July 2010, the KDLB is very much functional, although its future remains uncertain.

Port Qasim has always operated as a landlord port, and the Karachi Port is moving closer to that status through the implementation of a Landlord Strategy developed by the Ministry of Ports and Shipping. The Karachi Port Trust (KPT) is in the process of developing a deep-draft container terminal at Keamari, whose operation will be on build-operate-transfer (BOT) basis. The reconstruction of berths 10 to 17 is proceeding, and at least two of these berths are likely to handle bulk cargo when the reconstruction is complete. Other plans include setting up an independent dredging company as a wholly owned subsidiary (which may later be privatized) of KPT, with a chief executive officer hired from the market, and outsourcing of tugs and pilot services, as approved by KPT's board in 2006.

### *Rationalization of Port Tariffs and Improved Marketing*

The Ministry of Ports and Shipping regulates port charges, but with the proposed corporatization of port authorities, this function will transfer to the respective boards managing the two ports. Both the Karachi Port and Port Qasim are committed to further reductions in port charges. In August 2009, a 10 percent reduction in wet charges was announced for Karachi Port, while recommendations were made to KPT's Board of Trustees to freeze the annual increase of handling, marshaling, and storage charges of containers.[13] The Karachi Port has set up a costing cell to examine further reductions in charges, which will be sent to the ministry for approval.

Depending on the charges reduced, the impact of tariff rationalization on end users and service providers at ports would be positive. If the tariff reduction increases port usage in the long term, the positive effects will multiply and could extend to employment creation not only at the ports themselves, but also among ancillary service providers and in the wider economy. Rationalization of port charges and an improvement in port services may also result from the proposed corporatization of ports and the transfer of greater autonomy to port authorities—a process that should result in ports competing for business. Once again, a spirit of competition among the ports should be good for business and for end users.

### **Mitigating Negative Externalities**

Henderson (2003) examines the implications of excessive urbanization, particularly the impact of "urban primacy" (the share of a country's urban population that is in its largest city) on congestion, housing, and the environment. He argues that cities that have excessive urban primacy are those that have expanded to a point in which additional agglomeration creates more congestion costs than benefits. However, Henderson also finds several examples with cities that have "suboptimal primacy" in the 1990s, primarily European countries such as Switzerland, Belgium, and the Netherlands. His research finds that deviations from optimal urban primacy in either direction (suboptimal or excessive urban primacy) considerably reduce economic growth. In the case of excessive urbanization in a city, very large commuting and housing costs strain the entire urban system by diverting scarce resources from other cities to reduce the congestion and environmental costs in congested cities. Henderson (2002) documents an additional cost: excessive primacy not only implies very large commuting and housing costs in the largest city, but also strains the entire urban system by diverting resources from other cities to the largest city in order to reduce congestion and environmental costs (Henderson 2002).

The *World Development Report 2003* (World Bank 2002) further addresses the implications and solutions of urbanization levels that are not optimal:

> Disproportionate urban concentration often results from an imbalance in national institutions for signaling and balancing interests, especially across regions and levels of government. Democratization, fiscal decentralization, and investments in intercity roads, waterways, and communication can significantly reduce such concentration, permitting wider access to urban assets across the country.

To better develop and implement urban development strategies that respond to Pakistan's spatial transformations and that take into consideration the development of transport infrastructure to better develop cities, capacity building is required at least in two tiers of government (provincial and district). Pakistani cities have inadequate infrastructure to meet current needs, let alone an ability to respond to growing demand. In addition, cities are characterized by inefficient spatial structures (low-density ribbon development), restrictive land use regulations, rent control, and limited supplies of land for commercial, industrial, and residential development. As a result, land is relatively expensive and people and businesses tend to locate in farther locations and/or informal areas. Within large cities, there is fragmentation—both spatially and institutionally—of responsibilities for service delivery, and fiscal capacity is limited. Addressing these challenges will be crucial to respond to the current urban population's needs, as well as to prepare for continued urbanization. Energy infrastructure will also need study and enhancements because, in some areas, infrastructure forms a bottleneck to growth that is similar to the role played by suboptimal transport infrastructure.

### Social Challenges

While the benefits expected from the reforms are undeniable, some groups may nevertheless find themselves adversely affected by some of the direct and indirect consequences of the reforms discussed above. Increases in transport productivity might affect rural non-farm and urban poor households, and might correlate with negative social impacts such as social conflict, urban sprawl, reduced business opportunities in small trucking businesses, transmission of HIV/AIDS, and involuntary resettlement. In addition to identifying the possible social and environmental impacts of specific policy actions, a discussion on the impact of the trade and infrastructure reforms is incomplete without a broader assessment of what trade and transport facilitation can mean for communities living along the existing trade corridor as well as its proposed extensions. Focus groups were conducted in a small number of selected locations across the country, with an emphasis on finding communities where the transport sector was a major employer, and where the impacts of upgradation or extension of the trade corridor would be immediately apparent.[14] As explained below, there is a need to streamline provincial and federal laws and regulations to ensure social and environmental sustainability, and a smooth rolling out of the investment plans for roads and railways.

Pakistan's demographic growth heightens social conflicts, which manifest themselves as sectarian or ethnic strife. Reforms in the freight-transportation sector, for example, can be expected to affect disproportionately one specific ethnic group. Such a situation presents a potential for social unrest. In the trucking sector, a mitigation strategy for specific ethnic groups of small and obsolete trucks likely to be negatively affected by the enforcement of the trucking policy needs to address two concerns. The first is how to provide a business climate that keeps such businesses profitable or finds alternative means of employment.

The second is how to promote social inclusion. Access to vocational training and/ or micro-loans to those workers should be considered as measures to facilitate the adjustment and limit the risk of social tensions. In addition, better access to information about employment opportunities can facilitate the match between workers and new or growing private firms operating in the sector.

Small operators in the trucking sector have a low probability of losing business to new and larger enterprises due to trade and transport reforms. Ensuring that they have access to credit and insurance, and are allowed to operate on a level playing field that allows their services throughout the country (including major routes) would help reduce the risks facing small operators. Businesses linked to the current trucking sector—particularly those of rural non-farm and urban poor households as well as women and youth—might benefit from the implementation of the trucking policy and the modernization of the railways and ports sectors. Modernization will create new opportunities for smaller trucking firms, provided they have access to credit and are not forced to quit operating on major inter-city routes.

In the case of reforms in the port, shipping, and trucking sectors, there is a risk that youth (especially from non-farm households and urban poor households) could be directly affected either through direct retrenchment or indirect loss of jobs, as well as through the loss of job prospects they had envisioned and invested in through the *Ustad Shagird* arrangement (Master-Apprenticeship). The importance of starting off right is important for young people since it is the initial transition to the labor force that is an important determinant for their future economic (and social) well-being and, if taken collectively, a determinant of the overall level of economic development in Pakistan. Without the proper foothold to start out in the labor market, young people will have less choices that will improve their own job prospects and those of their future dependents, thus perpetuating the cycle of insufficient education, low-productivity employment, and poverty, from one generation to the next. Finding a new job will be harder for youth who entered the labor market young and have limited education and skills, making the attainment of a stable and secure job all the more difficult. Furthermore, youth who are not in education, employment, or training (NEET), roughly 36 percent of the total youth population in 2005–06, could also be affected by other members of their family and community losing sources of income, which increases their chances of being discouraged and locked in poverty,[15] which may result in increased social conflict.

The modernization of the trucking sector and adaptation of a multimodal transport system will help curb the spread of HIV originating from the trucking sector. In addition, public health initiatives to control the spread of HIV by changing behavioral risks of truck drivers are recommended. Important components would include the provision of services in geographically defined areas at greatest risk for HIV transmission (such as major trucking stopover locations). The services include information campaigns and behavior change communication aimed at improving truck drivers' knowledge, attitudes, and behaviors regarding HIV; voluntary counseling and HIV testing; and proper management of sexually transmitted diseases. Such a component has been found cost effective in Pakistan.

Ensuring social safeguards will be crucial to mitigate the negative impacts of reforms in the trade and transport sector. The creation and implementation of a uniform national resettlement policy enforced across Pakistan might ensure the safeguarding of rights of persons directly affected by any transport program. In addition to the mitigation measures included in the design of the reforms, there is a need for effective grievance redress mechanisms to ensure that no further harm occurs. The basis for decisions should be considered, consultative, and inclusive planning. Regional and international policies and law precedents are available. In addition to measures for prompt compensation and support for livelihood development along with appropriate and effective grievance redress mechanisms at the local level, transparent mechanisms for determining compensation, supported by effective and extensive public information campaigns, are critical.

Reforming the Land Registration Act to ensure security of land titles and mandate the complete computerization of all land records in the provinces with mechanisms for transparency and third-party validation built in is crucial. The establishment of secure land and property rights and preventing malpractice in the real estate markets is not only vital for protection of existing land holders, but will provide incentives for new businesses and asset owners to invest in new lands. Such investment is an element of the increasing amount, and geographical spread, of market-activity stimulation expected from trade and transport reforms.

Upgrading slums and improving service delivery in urban settings should be a priority to manage and take advantage of Pakistan's spatial transformation. As mentioned before, the envisioned reforms are likely to increase existing incentives for rural-to-urban migration. Under current circumstances, migrants will add to the urban population that already faces problems finding adequate housing and meeting their needs for municipal services, including water supply, sanitation, and waste management. Clearly designed programs to improve slums and service delivery, with adequate resources and political support, would not only improve the quality of life of most urban residents, but would also reduce the social risks identified in this report, including those related to social tensions and conflict.

Road conditions and human behavior are the most relevant variables affecting road safety in Pakistan. Available information indicates that risk factors include poor road quality and lack of appropriate signage. The trucking sector is likely to be involved in a high number of accidents because of practices such as overloading, modification and poor conditions of trucks, inadequate driving skills, and driver exhaustion caused by long hours behind the wheel. Until recently, obtaining a driver's license in Pakistan was relatively easy, as it did not require formal training and the process involved a few formalities with provincial authorities. The 2007 Trucking Policy should be implemented, as it contemplates measures to provide training to drivers and establish a new system enabling the cumulative counting of penalty points, resulting in suspension or cancellation of driver's licenses. Additional measures that the GoP might consider include allocating a dedicated budget for road safety and building the capacity of police officers to enforce existing laws.

### Environmental Challenges

Freight transportation reforms might consider a number of environmental policy options to enhance the positive effects and mitigate the negative consequences of trade and freight transport reforms. Accelerating the implementation of the 2007 Trucking Policy would lead to the substitution of the obsolete, poorly maintained, and highly polluting trucks for larger and modern trucks. These newer trucks, besides being technologically more efficient, cost effective, and less polluting, would reduce the number of trips required to move a given amount of cargo.

The maximum allowed content of sulfur for all fuels used in Pakistan originally was scheduled to drop from 10,000 to 500 ppm by 2008, but the stricter standard was postponed until 2010, and then again until July 1, 2012. The main reason for the postponements was that companies needed more time to retrofit refineries. However, Pakistan can take advantage of ultralow sulfur fuels as they become increasingly available in international markets. Pakistan currently imports about 3.5 Mt of diesel a year from Kuwait, whose content in sulfur is 2,000 ppm. Importing diesel from Oman, Qatar, Bahrain, or the United Arab Emirates could reduce sulfur contents of diesel used in urban centers to 500 ppm.

Systematic air quality monitoring in urban centers (especially of particulate matter $[PM]_{2.5}$ and $PM_{1.0}$) helps track progress of the enforcement of vehicle emission standards. Air quality monitoring is essential to identify the changes in air quality over time, and to determine if there is proper enforcement of vehicle standards. Ambient air pollution in medium and large urban centers in Pakistan is very serious, and very little has been done to address the problem. The high levels of dangerous pollutants, such as fine particulate matter and sulfur dioxide, cause significant health risks to urban populations. The GoP needs to revise its strategy regarding ambient air quality management by regularly monitoring the most important pollutants, including $PM_{2.5}$, which according to available evidence plays the largest role in damaging human health.

Pakistan needs comprehensive legislation to control environmental noise pollution. The NEQS for motor vehicle exhaust and noise only apply to noise generated from motor vehicles. There are no national standards for regulating noise limits for residential, industrial, and commercial areas. Road traffic noise is another major source of noise pollution in urban areas. Aircraft noise is a significant source of pollution primarily in the major airports that are located inside or very close to densely populated urban areas. Given that excessive noise is a health risk, there is a need to design, implement, and enforce a comprehensive regulation on noise pollution control that includes standards for controlling noise generated from sources such as airplanes and locomotives, as well as noise standards for residential, industrial, and commercial areas.

Pakistan needs a national framework to manage the transport of hazardous materials. The goal is to create and implement a regulatory framework that covers all aspects of hazardous material transport. Key measures that the GoP could adopt include

- designing standards for the construction of vehicles used to transport hazardous materials;
- updating information on new chemicals/substances that are transported on Pakistan's roads and railways;
- enhancing institutional capacity and clarifying legal responsibilities for relevant agencies;
- mapping of transportation routes and vulnerable points; and
- providing resources to help the police and local fire departments to properly enforce regulations pertaining to the transport of hazardous materials.

The GoP should consider international best practices in developing its national framework for hazardous materials management. Key examples include the technical guidelines for sound environmental management of various types of waste developed by the Basel Convention (to which Pakistan acceded in 1994),[16] the International Maritime Dangerous Goods Code,[17] and the Model Regulations on the Transport of Dangerous Goods prepared by the United Nations.[18]

To avoid or mitigate biodiversity loss and natural habitat fragmentation due to construction of new freight transportation infrastructure, Pakistan's Environmental Impact Assessment (EIA) system could be reformed. While Pakistan's legal framework for EIA and the Guidelines for Preparation and Review of Environmental Reports have been in place for a number of years, there is a need for a number of actions to ensure its effective and efficient use as a planning tool. An important first step would be requiring all public and private projects that require an EIA to comply with the existing guidelines.

A modernized trucking sector and the use of railways for long hauling would help reduce greenhouse gas (GHG) emissions. Changing the modal split for inland freight transportation to 30 percent rail and 70 percent road (currently it is 4 percent rail and 96 percent road) would reduce annual GHG emissions to 36.8 TgCO$_2$eq. This would be a 23.3 percent reduction or a reduction of about 11.2 million tons of GHG discharged into the atmosphere. Emphasis on the rail freight sector would result in an annual reduction in the consumption of diesel fuels by the inland freight transportation sector in Pakistan, of about 1.06 million metric tons by the year 2025/26. These savings in diesel consumption would imply a yearly reduction of about 6,116 metric tons of sulfur burned in internal combustion engines in the country.

The lack of environmental and social planning capacity at transport agencies should be rectified with a program of institutional strengthening and capacity building. Environmental and social units should be established in all organizations that still lack them. These units should be integrated into the planning and decision-making process of their organization, so they possess the ability to influence construction and operation in such a way as to take into account environmental and social considerations (particularly early on in the planning process when such considerations can be dealt with more efficiently).

### Institutional-Capacity Challenges

Organizations in Pakistan's infrastructure sector have limited capacity to address the environmental and social issues that arise during the construction and operation of transport infrastructure. Strengthening their institutional capacity to incorporate environmental and social consideration at the earliest planning stages and address issues as they arise would generate significant benefits to Pakistan's population. In addition, given that reforms in the spatial transformation and industrial sector will have countrywide effects, they will put a burden on Pakistan's environmental management framework. Strengthening the institutional capacity of environmental agencies (particularly after the devolution of environmental responsibilities to the provincial governments because of the Eighteenth Constitutional Amendment) should be an utmost priority, particularly as evidence indicates that the freight-transport sector's environmental externalities are already significant.

## Notes

1. World Bank, "Pakistan Enterprise Surveys, Pakistan 2007," World Bank, http://www.enterprisesurveys.org/Data/ExploreEconomies/2007/pakistan#infrastructure, accessed July 13, 2012.

2. It is important to note that it is not a feasible alternative to install generators to supply electricity when there is an outage. The cost per unit of electricity is significantly higher when using generators, which is why only around 6 percent of domestic energy production is provided by generators.

3. It should be noted that estimates on the circular debt vary according to the time when they are calculated. Total liabilities of the sector are higher.

4. The roughly 2,775-kilometer gas pipeline will be supplied from the South Pars field in the Islamic Republic of Iran. The main line will start from Asalouyeh, the Islamic Republic of Iran, and is expected to stretch over 1,100 kilometers through the Islamic Republic of Iran to reach Pakistan. In Pakistan, it will pass through Balochistan and Sindh. In Khuzdar, a branch would connect to Karachi, with the main pipeline continuing towards Multan. See http://ipripak.org/factfiles/ff124.pdf, for more details.

5. GoP 2011b, 13. http://www.finance.gov.pk/survey_1011.html. Accessed November 15, 2011. In many developed countries, transport contributes between 6 and 12 percent of national GDP (Rodrigue, Comtois, and Slack 2009). In India, the transport sector contributed between 5.7 and 6.4 percent of GDP between 1999 and 2005 (ADB 2007).

6. http://web.worldbank.org/WBSITE/EXTERNAL/COUNTRIES/SOUTHASIAEXT/EXTSARREGTOPTRANSPORT/0,,contentMDK:20699058~menuPK:869060~pagePK:34004173~piPK:34003707~theSitePK:579598,00.html.

7. PIA has the highest employee-to-aircraft ratio in the world, at 434 per aircraft. Indian airlines have 276 employees per aircraft. The highest employee-to-aircraft ratio in

the United States is at United Airlines, with fewer than 120 per aircraft (http://www
.historyofpia.com/forums/viewtopic.php?f=1&t=13287).

8. As listed on the website of the NTC Management Unit: http://115.186.133.3/pcportal
/NTCIP/index.html.

9. These committees cover railways, highways, trucking, aviation and air-transport, ports
and shipping, trade facilitation, cool chain, energy, public-private partnership, and
project interventions.

10. Under the associated Motor Vehicles Rules, 1969 (specifically Rule 35), motor vehicle
examiners are required to assess the fitness of commercial vehicles annually.

11. The analyses of passenger transport in general and train passenger services in particular
are beyond the scope of studies discussed in this book.

12. More specifically, the PAD says that KPT "expects to reduce its staff numbers by
30 percent." See World Bank (2009, 29).

13. Wet charges include berth fee, pilotage, tug charges, and storage charges. On the other
hand, dry or land charges include costs of wharfage, use of dock labor, and dues paid
to terminal operators.

14. An important omission here was Balochistan. Field teams were to visit selected locations
across the province, close to the proposed new road and rail links to be built under the
investment component of the National Trade Corridor Improvement Program. However,
the law-and-order situation in the province did not allow the fieldwork to proceed.

15. Although on a declining trend since 1999–2000, the NEET rate in Pakistan is very
high in comparison with other regions, with respect to both the low end of the income
per capita range, such as sub-Saharan Africa (27 percent), and at higher levels of
income per capita, such as Central and South America (21 percent). If the list of prob-
ing questions aiming to net-in marginal economic activities in the labor force survey
were taken into account, then the female NEET rate in Pakistan would be reduced,
because more women would be counted as employed. It is important to keep in mind
that this measure contains both unemployed non-student youth and youth who are
inactive for reasons other than educational enrollment, including discouragement
(that is, inactive non-students).

16. See *Basel Convention Technical Guidelines* at http://www.basel.int/TheConvention
/Publications/TechnicalGuidelines/tabid/2362/Default.aspx. Accessed December 9,
2011.

17. See *International Maritime Dangerous Goods Code* at http://www.imo.org
/blast/mainframe.asp?topic_id=158#1. Accessed December 9, 2011.

18. See *UN Recommendations on the Transport of Dangerous Goods— Model Regulations*
at http://www.unece.org/trans/danger/publi/unrec/rev14/14files_e.html. Accessed
December 9, 2011.

## References

ADB (Asian Development Bank). 2007. *Transport Sector in India—Focusing on Results.*
Reference Number: SAP: IND 2007–09. Manila: ADB.

———. 2012. *Turkmenistan–Afghanistan–Pakistan–India Natural Gas Pipeline Project, Phase 3.*
Technical Assistance Report, Project Number: 44463-013. Asian Development Bank,
Manila. http://www.adb.org/sites/default/files/projdocs/2012/44463-013-reg-tar.pdf.

Andres, L., D. Biller, and M. H. Dappe. 2013. *Reducing Poverty by Closing South Asia's
Infrastructure Gap.* Washington, DC: World Bank.

Aziz, R. 2013. "Building an Efficient Energy Sector." Pakistan Policy Note 1. World Bank, Washington, DC.

Benmessaoud, R., U. Basim, A. Cholst, and J. R. López-Calix. 2013. *Pakistan: The Transformative Path*. Washington, DC: World Bank.

Favaro, E., and F. Koehler. 2009. *A Fresh Look at the Crisis and Policy Priorities*. Washington, DC: World Bank.

Ghaus-Pasha, A. 2008. *Economic Cost of 'Power Outages.'* Lahore: Institute of Public Policy. http://ippbnu.org/RR/Cost%20of%20Power%20Outages.pdf.

GoP (Government of Pakistan). 2005. Ministry of Railways. http://www.railways.gov.pk/.

———. 2011a. *National Industrial Policy 2011: Implementation Framework*. Islamabad: Ministry of Industries and Production.

———. 2011b. *Pakistan Economic Survey 2010–2011*. Ministry of Finance, Islamabad. http://finance.gov.pk/survey_1011.html.

———. 2013a. "Chapter 10: Energy Security and Affordability, Annual Plan 2013–14." Planning Commission, Ministry of Planning and Development, Islamabad. http://www.pakistan.gov.pk/gop/index.php?q=aHR0cDovLzE5Mi4xNjguNzAuMTM2L2dvcC8uL3BkZnMvSW5kXN0cmlhbF9Qb2xpY3lfSW1wbGVtGVtZW50YXRpb25fNiAwX01heTE4XzIwMTEucGRm. AwX01heTE4XzIwMTEucGRm.

———. 2013b. *Power System Statistics 2012–2013*. National Transmission & Despatch Company, Islamabad. http://www.ppib.gov.pk/Power%20System%20Statistics.pdf.

Henderson, J. V. 2002. "Urban Primacy, External Costs, and Quality of Life." *Resource and Energy Economics* 24 (1–2): 95–106.

———. 2003. "The Urbanization Process and Economic Growth: The So-What Question." *Journal of Economic Growth* 8 (1): 47–71.

IMF (International Monetary Fund). 2013. "Pakistan: 2013 Article IV Consultation and Request for an Extended Arrangement Under the Extended Fund Facility." IMF Country Report 13/287, IMF, Washington, DC.

KPT (Karachi Port Trust). 2009. http://www.kpt.gov.pk/.

PQA (Port Qasim Authority). 2007. *Port Qasim Business Plan 2006–07 to 2011–12*. Islamabad: Ministry of Ports and Shipping.

———. 2011. http://www.pqa.gov.pk/.

Rodrigue, J.-P., C. Comtois, and B. Slack. 2009. *The Geography of Transport Systems*. 2nd ed. New York: Routledge.

Singru, N. 2007. *Profile of the Indian Transport Sector*. Manila: Asian Development Bank. http://www.iptu.co.uk/content/trade_cluster_info/india/indian-transport-profile.pdf.

World Bank. 2002. *World Development Report 2003. Sustainable Development in a Dynamic World: Transforming Institutions, Growth, and Quality of Life*. Washington, DC and Oxford, UK: World Bank and Oxford University Press. http://www.dynamicsustainabledevelopment.org/showsection.php?file=chapter7c3.htm.

———. 2006. "Transport Competitiveness in Pakistan: Analytical Underpinning for the National Trade Corridor Improvement Program." Report 36523-PK, World Bank, Washington, DC.

———. 2008. *World Development Report 2009: Reshaping Economic Geography*. Washington, DC: World Bank. https://openknowledge.worldbank.org/handle/10986/5991.

———. 2009. "Second Trade and Transport Facilitation Project." Project Appraisal Document. Report No: 48094 – PK, World Bank, Washington, DC. http://web.worldbank.org

/WBSITE/EXTERNAL/EXTDEC/EXTRESEARCH/EXTWDRS/0,,contentMDK: 23080183~pagePK:478093~piPK:477627~theSitePK:477624,00.html.

———. 2012. *Doing Business 2012: Doing Business in a More Transport World.* Washington, DC: International Finance Corporation and World Bank.

———. World Development Indicators (database). World Bank, Washington, DC. http:// data.worldbank.org/data-catalog/world-development-indicators.

World Economic Forum. 2011. *Global Competitiveness Report 2011–2012.* Geneva, Switzerland: World Economic Forum.

## CHAPTER 7

# Greening Pakistan's Industry

## Introduction

Improved industrial environmental performance is essential if Pakistani firms are to be competitive in export markets like the European Union (EU) in which business customers demand high environmental compliance from their suppliers and often require certification to international standards, such as ISO 14001. Pakistan is behind its competitors in export markets with respect to environmental management. A significant number of Pakistani firms are not even aware that Pakistan has environmental regulations that they are supposed to meet. It will be impossible for Pakistani firms to remain competitive and for Pakistan to meet its goals for expanding exports unless the firms and the Government of Pakistan (GoP) become much more proactive about enhancing industrial environmental performance. Furthermore, clean production, crucial for internationally competitiveness, also helps improve overall production efficiency, thus lowering costs and raising profitability even for those firms producing exclusively for the internal market.

The next section below summarizes the state of the environment in Pakistan and industry's impact on it. The section following that makes the business case for environmental compliance grounded in international competitiveness and overall production efficiency. Section 4 evaluates the response to the business case in terms of industrial pollution abatement initiatives. Section 5 discusses the importance of strengthening the environment infrastructure to improve compliance. Section 6 concludes with recommendations.

## The Current State of Industrial Pollution in Pakistan

A 2008 World Bank study estimated the total cost of environmental risk factors in Pakistan at about 9 percent of gross domestic product (GDP). A more recent 2011 World Bank study estimated that in the province of Sindh, environmental degradation, including both natural resource degradation and the effects of pollution on human health, had a cost equivalent to 15 percent of the province's GDP. These figures reflect direct and indirect costs linked to different aspects of environmental degradation, such as water pollution, forest degradation, agricultural soil salinity and erosion, and lead exposure, among others. Industrial activities figure prominently in this estimate. Consequently, a key element of the industrialization challenge facing Pakistan is to capture all of the advantages of economic expansion while minimizing the cost due to externalities.

Industrial activities, particularly those using fossil fuels, are a significant source of air pollution. Outdoor air pollution is most severe in urban areas, where the concentrations of industrial activity, vehicles, and other sources of air pollution are the highest in Pakistan, and contribute with pollutant concentrations significantly exceeding World Health Organization (WHO) guidelines (World Bank 2008, 168). In Pakistan, more than 35 percent of the population lives in urban areas, most of them in cities of more than 1 million inhabitants. The industrial sector in Pakistan generates significant environmental pollution that is reducing the quality of life; such pollution includes a significant percentage of fine and ultrafine percent of particulate matter $(PM)_{2.5}$. Given that air pollution, particularly from $PM_{2.5}$, has been linked with negative health effects, there is a need to implement interventions aimed at improving urban air quality (Colbeck, Nasir, and Ali 2010; Ghauri 2010; Ilyas 2007).

Manufacturing activities such as tanneries, textiles, pharmaceutical, paper, cement, fertilizer, and sugar generate a lot of air pollution. Many units burn furnace oil that is high in sulfur content and generates significant amounts of air pollutants, including fine and ultrafine particle emissions. For leather production, concentrations of PM emissions are high due to dust emissions from shaving and buffing machines. PM containing fly ash and unburned bagasse particles found in the boilers' flue gases are the major issues in most of the sugar mills. Inefficient boilers and generators generate PM and sulfur and nitrogen oxides. Pulp and paper mills are major sources of air pollutants. The main sources of the air pollutants in paper-processing factories included boilers and continuous digester blow tanks (Khan 2011). A wide range of small to medium-scale industries (including brick kilns, steel re-rolling, steel recycling, and plastic molding) cause a disproportionate share of pollution through their use of dirty "waste" fuels, such as old tires, paper, wood, and textile waste. Although data are limited, sporadic monitoring of air pollutants in industrial areas in Pakistan suggests that international standards for fine and ultrafine PM and sulfur and nitrogen oxides are frequently exceeded.

Industrial activity also generates surface and groundwater contamination. The industrial activity present in Sialkot serves as an example. Rapid industrialization, along with urbanization and agricultural activities in its surroundings areas, has degraded Sialkot's surface water and groundwater (Qadir, Malik, and Hussain 2008). Major industries in Sialkot include textiles, surgical instruments, tanneries, beverages, diesel engines, drugs and pharmaceuticals, and iron and steel rolling mills. More than 264 tanneries, 244 leather and garment manufacturing units, 900 leather sports good manufacturing units, 14 flourmills, and 57 rice-husking units operate in Sialkot. Most of these industries are scattered in and around the city. All the industrial units consume large amount of water which, together with dissolved toxic substances (including heavy metals), is discharged after processing into nearby ponds, agricultural lands, rivers, streams, open ditches, and open land. Discharge of effluents from tanneries was found to be roughly 1.1 million liters per day (Khan 2011). Toxic effluents have implications for water supply safety, since they seep into the soil and thereby contaminate aquifers and pollute potable water supplies.

Contamination of groundwater due to heavy metals is one of the most serious concerns receiving attention at regional, local, and global levels because of their impacts on public health and ecosystems. Industrial pollution in Sialkot affects the quality of groundwater (Ullah, Malik, and Qadir 2009). Research results revealed that, by 2005 and 2006, the groundwater in 57 percent of the total sites sampled had high levels of lead (Pb) and other heavy metals, which exceeded the WHO and Pakistan Standards and Quality Control Authority (PSQCA) permissible limits. The concentration of lead was found to be between 0.11–0.81 mg/L in all zones, which exceeded the WHO and PSQCA guidelines of 0.01 mg/L. Lead is a serious cumulative body poison that can cause chronic health effects such as blood disorders, including hypertension, brain and nerve damage, kidney damage, and digestive problems (SDWF 2003). The study emphasized the need to reduce heavy metals contamination caused by industrial activities in order to reduce human morbidity and mortality through adequate regulations and pollution control laws, mainstreaming of environmental considerations into industrial production processes, and proper management of waste (Ullah, Malik, and Qadir 2009).

Industrial activities have been associated with increases in lead poisoning, which is one of the most significant environmental health threats affecting children in Pakistan. Even low levels of lead exposure are associated with impairment of childhood cognitive function and abnormal infant behavior (Mendelsohn et al. 1999). The U.S. Centers for Disease Control and Prevention states that a blood lead level (BLL) of 10 µg/dL or greater is a cause for concern for health. However, several studies have recently documented neuropsychological effects of intelligence quotient (IQ) losses in children less than five years of age with BLL *below* 10 µg/dL.[1] A study by Khan, Ansari, and Khan (2011) found that in areas located near industries in Punjab, 30 percent of children had BLL >10 µg/dL. The same study found that the mean BLL (µg/dL) for children between the ages one to six located 30 km from industries in Punjab was 10.9. A study of children living around automobile and battery repair workshops in Lahore found an average BLL of 10.9 µg/dL in children one to four years of age, with 52 percent of children with BLL >10 µg/dL (Ahmad et al. 2009). A study in Punjab found an average BLL of 9.0 µg/dL among children one to six years of age living near smelters/battery recycling plant industries in Wah/Gujranwala, and 6.5 µg/dL among children living 30 km from the industrial areas (Khan, Ansari, and Khan 2011). In light of the above studies, the average BLL in children less than five years of age today is roughly estimated to be 7–8 µg/dL in cities. For BLLs > 10 µg/dL, Lanphear et al. (2005) report an incremental IQ decrement of 1.9 (0.19 per 1 µg/dL) over the range of 10–20 µg/dL. They report a decrement of 1.1 (0.11 per 1 µg/dL) over the range of 20–30 µg/dL for concurrent BLLs. Total yearly losses of IQ points in children under five years in

Sindh are estimated in the range of 1.7–4.9 million, with a midpoint estimate of 3.1 million. Various studies find that a decline of one IQ point is associated with a 1.3–2.0 percent decline in lifetime income.[2]

Lack of consideration for worker safety and health in industries is a factor that not only contributes to poor human health, but also limits firms' worker productivity and output levels. The textile-processing sector is one of the most important sectors of the textile industry of Pakistan in regards to production, exports, and labor employment (Anjum, Mann, and Anjum 2009). An analysis of health effects of working in the weaving industry in Pakistan that sampled 100 units in Faisalabad found that, in general, workers did not wear safety equipment such as facemasks, earplugs, or gloves. None of the facilities provided facemasks to employees, which are crucial in providing protection to workers from cotton dust (6 percent of the workers sampled were suffering from tuberculosis) (Ambec and Lanoie 2007, 28; Anjum, Mann, and Anjum 2009). A less-polluted workplace is expected to decrease labor costs due to a reduction in the costs of illness, employee absenteeism, turnovers, and recruitment (Anjum, Mann, and Anjum 2009). A healthier environment will thus increase worker productivity (de Backer 1999).

While agglomeration economies can generate significant economic benefits, they can also result in congestion and air pollution, among other public "bads." Industries tend to agglomerate in a few geographic locations where there is availability of specialized labor, inter-industry spillovers, higher road density, local transfer of knowledge, and access to international supplier and buyer networks. These factors enhance firm competitiveness and largely explain the clustering of large-scale manufacturing and high employment levels around the metropolitan areas of Lahore and Karachi. Unless appropriate remedies are implemented to reduce air and water pollution through pollution prevention and control efforts, pollution because of industrial activity will continue to disproportionately affect the health and productivity of poor people in Pakistan. Despite strong evidence indicating an urgent need to improve Pakistan's urban air quality, the issue has received little attention, and it is yet to be included as a priority in the country's policy agenda. Given the already severe damages caused by air pollution and the possibility that environmental conditions might worsen because of growing industrialization and urbanization, the GoP might consider adopting priority interventions in the short term, and building the institutional and technical capacity to adopt additional measures over the medium and long term.

## The Business Case for Clean Production
### Export Competitiveness
Environmental concerns expressed by international buyers and other stakeholders (governments of importing countries, nongovernmental organizations [NGOs], and so on) have increasingly caused firms to give greater emphasis to environmental performance (see, for example, Christmann 2004; Klassen and McLaughlin 1996; Paulraj 2009). Adoption of cleaner production methods yielded financial gains independent of advantages in facilitating regulatory compliance (Bansal and Roth 2000, and papers cited therein). Moreover, many firms

are finding it profitable to use environmental management as a central element of their business strategy (see, for example, Hart and Milstein 2003; Rugman and Verbeke 1998). Doing so can open up new markets, cut production costs, and reduce environmental risks and liabilities.

### Environment-Related Constraints Imposed by Governments of Importing Countries

In March 2009, the U.S. Food and Drug Administration (U.S. FDA 2009) refused entry to several items of surgical equipment and a number of other export items from Pakistan, because production did not conform to applicable requirements. This is illustrative of how an exporting firm's non-compliance with World Trade Organization (WTO)-sanctioned rules on standards in international trade can affect export performance. Pakistan is a member of the WTO and is therefore subject to WTO agreements governing international trade. Two WTO agreements are particularly important in this context:

- The Agreement on Technical Barriers to Trade (TBT) recognizes the importance of international standards and conformity assessment systems in improving efficiency of production and facilitating international trade; at the same time, the agreement emphasizes that such measures should not be taken with the effect of creating unnecessary obstacles to international trade (Foss 2002).
- The WTO Agreement on Sanitary and Phytosanitary Measures (SPS) allows WTO members to restrict international trade based on regulations to ensure food safety and to prevent the spread of diseases among animals and plants. At the same time, that agreement also aims to ensure that unneeded health and safety regulations are not used as disguised trade restrictions that protect domestic producers.

A notable illustration of the government imposition of environment-related constraints on imports is the EU's 2007 Regulation, Evaluation, Authorization, and Restriction of Chemicals (REACH) legislation, which restricts chemicals in goods made in or imported into EU member countries. REACH requirements are being phased in over 11 years (starting in 2007), and they are expected to have major impacts on many firms exporting to the EU (Wilson and Schwarzman 2009). This sweeping new law applies to both new *and* existing chemicals produced in or imported into the EU (in quantities over 1 ton per producer per year). This law will clearly affect chemical manufacturers, because they must supply information on the identity and properties of their products. However, REACH also affects exporters outside the chemicals industry, because those in supply chains must communicate information about chemical uses and risks (Foth and Hayes 2008). Under the circumstances, REACH will affect Pakistani exports to the EU from textiles, leather, and many other sectors.[3]

In October 2010, China promulgated a new law, "China-REACH," which is similar to REACH in the EU. Therefore, reporting requirements relating to chemical information will apply not only to products exported to the EU, but also to products exported to China. However, China-REACH excludes the approximately 45,000 substances currently listed on the "Inventory of Existing Chemical Substances Produced or Imported in China." In addition to applying to new substances on their own, China-REACH also applies to new substances used as ingredients or intermediates for pharmaceuticals, pesticides, veterinary drugs, cosmetics, food additives, and feed additives.[4]

### Green Supply-Chain Management by Business Customers

Increasingly, international firms supplied by Pakistani manufacturers are demanding that the environment be considered in all aspects of a product's lifecycle, and this will affect business-to-business transactions. Because of increased emphasis by multinationals on greening their supply chains, the pressures to improve environmental performance currently faced by Pakistani firms engaged in exports will eventually affect firms that do not export themselves but supply exporters.

Many companies, including well-known multinationals, have developed codes of conduct that include environmental provisions they expect their suppliers to follow. For example, the Gap, Inc., code of conduct includes provisions requiring that all factories selling to Gap "shall comply with all applicable environmental laws and regulations."[5] As another example, the code of conduct for Nike, Inc., requires that its contractors protect "human health and the environment by meeting applicable regulatory requirements including air emissions, solid/hazardous waste and water discharge."[6] Sometimes companies work together in developing requirements for their suppliers. For example, in 2011, the Adidas Group, C&A, H&M, Li Ning, Nike, and Puma released a discussion draft of the "Joint Roadmap: Towards Zero Discharge of Hazardous Chemicals." This statement, which prescribes meeting a zero discharge goal in supply chains, was intended to demonstrate the companies' "commitment to collaborate and lead the apparel and footwear industry toward zero discharge of hazardous chemicals [including endocrine disruptors and carcinogens] for all products across all pathways by 2020."[7] Another example involving multiple firms is the "Code of Conduct for the Procurement of Goods to Ensure Protection of Welfare Standards," which the Foreign Trade Association of the German Retail Trade enacted. This document emphasizes labor issues, but it is also concerned with environment-related matters. One characteristic of the initiative is its emphasis on assisting suppliers so they can comply with the code of conduct (Jorgensen et al. 2003).

In an effort to protect their reputations, some large firms, instead of simply relying on ISO 14001 certifications, send their own auditors to evaluate the performance of their suppliers. An example is IKEA, which purchases from several textile companies in Pakistan and does not permit use of hazardous chemicals such as cadmium or certain azo dyes in textile products. The Walt Disney Company, another major buyer of Pakistan's textile products, provides another example of a business customer with its own environmental protection requirements (Small & Medium Enterprises Development Authority, undated).

While they are not technically considered as non-tariff barriers, ISO's voluntary industry standards, imposed by firms on suppliers can serve as de facto non-tariff barriers: failure to comply with standards may exclude Pakistani exporters from trading with international business customers that require compliance with ISO standards by suppliers. Of all the ISO standards, the two of greatest relevance to Pakistani exporters are ISO 9001 (from the ISO 9000 series of *quality* management system standards) and ISO 14001 (from the ISO 14000 series of *environmental* management system standards).[8] ISO 9001 and ISO 14001 contain specific requirements for a management system, against which an organization's system can be "certified"; certification requires third-party verification by an accredited body that an organization's quality (or environmental) management system meets the standard.

Of the two ISO standards, ISO 9001 is older and many more organizations have adopted it. Both ISO 9001 and ISO 14001 are *generic* in that they can be applied to any organization, regardless of size or sector. The focus here is on ISO 14001, because it concerns environmental management.[9] In the Pakistani context, certification to ISO 14001 requires that an organization be cognizant of its National Environment Quality Standards (NEQS) compliance status and have a plan to meet the standards if it is currently noncompliant.

As was the case for ISO 9001 (Anderson, Daly, and Johnson 1999; Corbett 2008), importing firms can use ISO 14001 to exert pressure directly on suppliers and indirectly on firms further "upstream" in supply chains.[10] This pressure by downstream business customers can take two forms: (a) excluding non-certified firms from bidding for supply contracts (as has been the case with ISO 9001), and (b) including questions about certification status in vendor selection questionnaires. International business customers who are intent on greening their supply chains may cause diffusion of ISO 14001 *within* Pakistan in the following way: Pakistani firms exporting to such business customers may exert pressure on their own suppliers in Pakistan to become ISO 14001 certified. In other words, supply chain linkages may eventually cause Pakistani firms not engaged in exports to feel pressure to become ISO 14001 certified.

### Overall Gains in Efficiency and Cost Reduction

One reason why many multinationals are pursuing green supply chain management is the growing body of evidence (Cohen, Fenn, and Naimon 1995; Porter and van der Linde 1995; Rao and Holt 2005) that green production improves efficiency and synergy among business partners and their lead corporations, and helps to enhance environmental performance, minimize waste, and achieve cost savings and marketing exposure. In addition, a growing body of empirical literature concludes that improved environmental performance enhances financial performance (for example, Hart 1995; Porter and van der Linde 1995). Cohen, Fenn, and Naimon (1995), for example, demonstrate a strong correlation between environmental performance and firm profitability. Russo and Fouts (1997), in their study of 243 firms, found that there are positive links between environmental performance and return on assets, and that returns related to environmental performance are higher for high-growth industries. Nehrt (1996) analyzed the relationship between the intensity of investment in pollution prevention and timing on firm profit growth in a sample of 50 pulp and paper firms. His findings confirm a positive relationship between early movers in pollution prevention and profit growth.

A study by Rao and Holt (2005) conducted in Southeast Asia empirically confirmed that there is a significant correlation between greening the supply chain, and the competitiveness and economic performance of the firms involved. This research provides a theoretical basis and an empirical analysis to investigate the link between green supply chain management and economic performance. For this study, a conceptual model was developed from literature sources, and data from a sample of ISO 14001 certified firms in Southeast Asia were collected using a structured questionnaire. The findings reveal that greening production significantly leads to greening operations, which enhances competitiveness and economic performance of firms, because of savings in raw material, energy, and water usage.

Pakistani firms in general, not just exporters, can cut production costs by using "cleaner production" (CP), a term often characterized using the language in United Nations Environment Programme's definition: "...the continuous application of an integrated, preventive strategy to processes, products and services to increase efficiency and reduce risks to humans and the environment" (Basu and van Zyl 2006). In less formal terms, using cleaner production involves making changes in production processes, products, and services that enhance the efficiency of resource use and thereby generate less waste and reduce environmental risk and liability. CP measures range from low-cost options (such as simple housekeeping measures like fixing water leaks and preventing chemical spills), to more expensive measures (such as replacing inefficient boilers and installing facilities in tanneries to recover and reuse chemicals like chromium).

## Responding to the Business Case for Improved Environment Management

### ISO 9001 and ISO 14001 Certification in Pakistan

In countries throughout the world, the number of certifications for ISO 14001 is lower than those for ISO 9001, but in Pakistan, the numbers are *much* lower. In 2010, there were about 251,000 firms certified to ISO 14001 worldwide compared to about 1,110,000 certified to ISO 9001. For that year, the ratio of ISO 14001 certifications to ISO 9001 certifications worldwide was about 0.23. In Pakistan, the corresponding ratio was about 0.12, slightly more than half the ratio based on global statistics in 2010. These relatively low levels of ISO 14001 certifications in Pakistan persist despite efforts of the Pakistan Environmental Protection Agency (Pak-EPA), provincial environmental protection agencies (EPAs), and others to promote ISO 14001.

As shown in figure 7.1, the number of ISO 14001 certified firms in Pakistan is low, and the rate of increase over time has not been impressive. To put the latest data in figure 7.1 in perspective (258 certifications in 2010), consider the corresponding 2010 ISO 14001 certification statistics for some of Pakistan's

**Figure 7.1  Number of Industrial Firms Certified to ISO 14001 in Pakistan, 1999–2010**

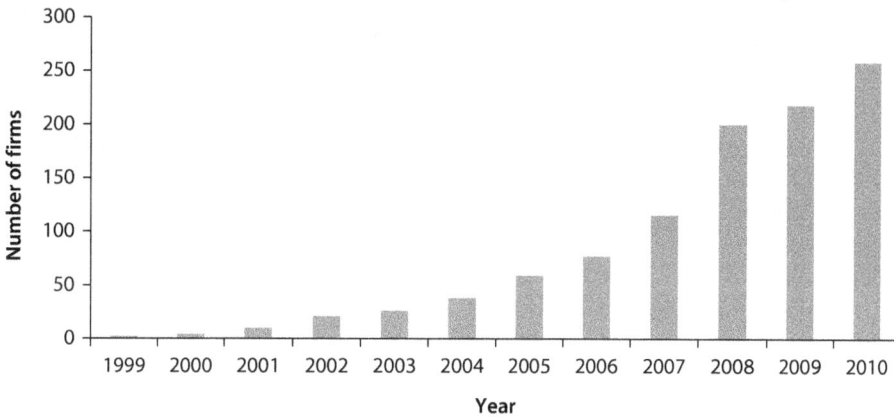

*Source:* ISO Survey of Certifications 2010.

competitors in exports: China, 69,784; the Republic of Korea, 9,681; and India, 3,878. What is equally interesting is the relatively slow growth in number of certifications in Pakistan. These three competitors experienced much more rapid growth in numbers of certifications, with growth in China being the most striking. Indeed, in 2010, China had more ISO 14001 certified firms than any other country, and nearly twice as many as Japan, which had the second-largest number.

Ali's (2011) survey of tanneries and textile processing firms provides further insights into the extent of ISO 14001 certifications. He found that most surveyed small and medium enterprises (SMEs) had not implemented environmental management systems (EMS), some had never heard of ISO 14001, and very few had become ISO 14001 certified. The situation was different in large firms. Many were engaged in exports, and saw the link between ISO 14001 certification and competiveness. Although the majority of these firms were not ISO 14001 certified, many were working toward certification. Not surprisingly, the large firms working toward certification typically were in the textiles sector and had notable export operations, and some indicated they were working toward certification because of pressure exerted by their foreign business customers.

In the future, Pakistani firms will have trouble remaining competitive and face challenges in meeting export expansion goals, unless the firms and the GoP become significantly more proactive in enhancing industrial environmental performance. Competitive pressures will only increase in the future: governments in target export countries are likely to place increasingly stringent requirements on imports to protect public health, and multinationals will demand higher levels of environmental performance of suppliers in order to protect their reputations and respond to consumer preferences. Notwithstanding the threats posed by these pressures, the pace of improvement in industrial environmental performance in Pakistan has remained low. Factors contributing to the slow rate of improvement include weak enforcement of environmental regulations by EPAs as well as firms' lack of information on environmental requirements, slow uptake of cleaner production as a management strategy, financial constraints, and the paucity of effluent treatment plants capable of meeting NEQS requirements for wastewater discharges.

### National Environment Quality Standards

Certification to ISO 14001 requires progress toward meeting the NEQS that represents a major obstacle for many firms, particularly SMEs. Based on his survey, Ali (2011) found that many firms were out of compliance with NEQS. Interestingly, surveyed firms did not comment on problems meeting the NEQS for air pollutants, but this is not because air pollution issues do not exist for leather tanneries and textile processing firms. The lack of comment on air pollution standards reflects the absence of EPA monitoring of air pollution releases. NEQS for gaseous emissions were initially issued in 1994 and then revised in 2009. They were notified for implementation in November 2009, but they had not yet been effectively implemented in the 2009/10 period during which Ali conducted the survey.[11] Under the circumstances, the recommendations below interim NEQS relate to wastewater discharges.

Firms surveyed by Ali (2011) explained their failure to meet the NEQS by indicating they could not afford the "secondary" wastewater treatment plants needed to meet the discharge standards.[12] Moreover, many firms lacked the land needed for such plants. A number of respondents complained that the NEQS for wastewater were unreasonably stringent given the economic and public safety challenges faced by Pakistan. Moreover, several survey respondents characterized the building of wastewater treatment facilities as a "dead investment"—one that would yield no financial returns.

In addition to the aforementioned difficulties in meeting the NEQS, motivations to meet the standards are low because requirements are not well enforced. That is unlikely to change quickly because of the many issues that need to be resolved in devolving environmental responsibilities to the provinces. Enhancing environmental enforcement will also require increased personnel and monitoring capacity at the provincial EPAs, and an enhanced commitment by the GoP to environmental protection.

### Creating Interim National Environment Quality Standards for Wastewater Discharges

It is difficult to predict when and how issues linked to devolution and strengthening of provincial EPAs will be resolved. However, the following steps can enhance the feasibility of firms complying with applicable environmental standards: revision of the NEQS on an interim basis, construction and operation of combined effluent treatment plants (CETPs) and revival of the long-dormant system of pollution discharge fees.

Consider, first, the revision of the NEQS, which can be accomplished by forming the equivalent of the Shamslakha Committee, created in the late 1990s to reform the NEQS (Khan 2003). The committee consisted of experts and stakeholders, and did its work by consulting extensively with representatives of enterprises, industry associations, NGOs, and the public sector. An analogous standard-setting committee could be formed and charged with determining *interim* NEQS for wastewater that are realistic for firms to meet in the short term, while the more time-consuming process of designing, financing, and building CETPs takes place. The new committee could also determine the number of years when interim standards are to apply, and the permanent NEQS that would apply after this interim period. By proceeding in this way, firms will be able to comply with the interim NEQS and therefore enhance their chances of receiving ISO 14001 certification. By having the committee also determine permanent standards, designers of CETPs will have the information needed to design facilities that meet the permanent standards.

Although provincial EPAs will not be well positioned to enforce the interim NEQS in the short term, firms that are motivated to enhance their export competitiveness will be motivated to meet the interim standards so they can certify to ISO 14001 and satisfy green supply chain management requirements imposed by their international business customers. In developing interim NEQS, top priority could be given to setting pollution limits at levels that protect human health, avoid notable nuisance conditions, and prevent damage to important ecosystems. The permanent NEQS can be more rigorous and protect both human and environmental health in the broadest sense.

A recommendation to relax the wastewater discharge requirements would encounter many protests in a country such as the United States, where outcries against "backsliding" would be expected.[13] However, in Pakistan, such criticism would not be warranted for two reasons. First, it is pointless to insist on rigorous standards when they are routinely ignored and violations go unpunished. Second, Pakistan cannot be expected to move rapidly from current circumstances, in which most wastewater is untreated, directly to secondary treatment. It took industrialized countries many decades to reach the high levels of wastewater treatment that prevail today. For example, in the United States, most wastewater was discharged untreated in the late 1800s, and even in the 1950s, most treatment systems were quite basic, not the secondary treatment plants needed to meet the NEQS.[14] In addition, even after the passage of the Clean Water Act in 1972, it took at least another decade before there was the equivalent of secondary treatment at most wastewater sources.

### Constructing Common Effluent Treatment Plants and Imposing Environment-Related Taxes

A key step in enabling large numbers of firms to comply with the NEQS is construction of CETPs to serve firms in industrial clusters.[15] A public body, an industrial association, commercial venture, or public-private partnership can own and operate CETPs. Pakistan's record in constructing CETPs is weak, and thus the construction process is likely to take time.[16] Luken (2009) noted that the 10 to 20 existing major industrial clusters are without effective wastewater treatment. Even at the CETP for tanneries at the Korangi industrial area—one of the few cases where a CETP is operating—poor operations have plagued the plant, because of difficulties in getting firms to pay their share of treatment plant operating costs.[17] While SMEs will need to rely on CETPs to attain standards, large firms outside of industrial clusters should be in a position to construct their own wastewater treatment works. However, even for large firms, much work remains. According to Luken (2009), only 50 to 100 effluent treatment plants exist in Pakistan, and there are over 8,000 firms with significant pollution loads.

Synergies exist between cleaner production (discussed below) methods and effluent treatment: CP methods can be used to minimize the generation of wastes at the firm level, thereby making it less costly to treat wastes. This is especially notable for pollutants like heavy metals that disrupt the functioning of widely used wastewater treatment processes.[18]

Another step for speeding NEQS compliance involves reviving and revising Pakistan's long-dormant pollution charge system.[19] The system can be restructured so that firms pay charges based on both the concentrations and mass flow rates of wastewater discharges. The mandate to the committee formed to revise the NEQS for wastewater can include the work of this restructuring.

A pollution charge scheme could generate revenues to help fund EPAs, thereby incentivizing improvements in discharge monitoring by EPAs. Revenues could also support construction of CETPs, but based on experience in many other countries, charge-based revenues will not be enough to construct the needed CETPs (Bongaerts and Kraemer 1989). Therefore, other funding sources need to be accessed (for example, provincial governments and industry associations as well as international aid institutions). If the charges are set high enough, as they are in the Netherlands, they can provide a significant incentive for firms to cut pollution.

Because leather tanneries are small and numerous, it will be especially difficult for EPAs to monitor and control their wastewater releases using traditional regulations. A possible response to this challenge that is worth considering involves imposition of a tax on chromium sulfate, a basic input to the leather tanning process. A tax on a chromium sulfate would result in higher prices to tanneries, thereby providing them with incentives to reuse and recycle chromium.

Organisation for Economic Co-operation and Development countries have imposed hundreds of environment-related taxes on inputs such as pesticides, but a search of the literature suggests that a product tax on chromium sulfate as a pollution control measure has not been used elsewhere. Pakistan would be in the position of having to learn by doing, if it imposed such a tax. Before moving forward with such a tax, the GoP would need to analyze the risks associated with being a pioneer in taxing chromium sulfate as a waste management policy. The GoP would also need to explore three other issues in depth: the potential negative impact of a chromium tax on the competitive position of Pakistan's leather exports, other sectors (for example, electroplating) in which output prices could rise, and ways to offset these adverse effects on output prices by subsidizing chromium recycling and reuse.

Once CETPs are constructed, and cost and operations details are sorted out, firms served by those facilities will be in better position to meet more rigorous NEQS for wastewater. Moreover, by the time the period of applicability of the interim NEQS has elapsed, the capacity of provincial EPAs should be such that they can effectively conduct enforcement. This would further motivate firms' compliance.

### Clean Production Centers

One of Pakistan's more ambitious environmental protection initiatives, which began during the 1990s, was the creation of three clean production centers (CPCs): The Cleaner Production Center at Sialkot serves leather tanneries. The Cleaner Production Institute, with offices in Punjab and Sindh provinces, primarily serves leather tanneries and textile-processing mills. The National Cleaner Production Center—Foundation, which is an affiliate of the Attock Oil Refinery, Ltd., primarily serves the oil and gas sector. During the past 15 years, the work of these centers has focused on assisting firms by conducting environmental and energy audits, providing technical assistance to industries in adopting clean production (CP) measures, and raising awareness of CP.

The survey of firms served by Pakistan's CPCs conducted by Ali (2011) mainly involved leather tanneries and textile-processing mills served by two of Pakistan's CPCs: the Cleaner Production Center and the Cleaner Production Institute. For both centers, Ali's results make it clear that the centers were the main source of information on CP for the surveyed firms. Without guidance from the centers, many of the firms would have missed the many financially advantageous CP measures they implemented. Ali (2011) showed that surveyed firms adopted many CP methods at either no cost or low cost and achieved notable reductions in materials and energy use. Indeed, Ali found that very low-cost approaches often cut production costs by 10 to 15 percent at surveyed firms.

One of the impediments to CP adoption by Pakistani firms, especially SMEs, is that they are unfamiliar with environment and energy audits, and other cleaner production techniques. Prior to the interventions by the CPCs, firms had often failed to consider the suggested CP measures as ways of enhancing productivity. However, once firms were presented with CP options, they quickly identified those yielding net cost savings. Ali (2011) found that firms he surveyed typically adopted 50 percent or more of the cleaner production options presented by CPCs, based on environmental and energy audits.

The results reported by Ali are consistent with many examples from the literature indicating that firms can save money and improve competitiveness using CP methods; see Bansal and Roth (2000); Hamed and El Mahgary (2004); Paulraj (2009); and Warren and Ortolano (1999). More specifically, a study by Cagno, Trucco, and Tardini (2005) of 134 industrial projects aimed at preventing pollution found that the average internal rate of return on the projects was 77 percent, and the range was from 1 percent to 433 percent. For most, but not all, projects, the cost savings alone justified the activity, and implementation of the measures enhanced competitiveness. The researchers also found that, increasingly, the main motivation for adopting cleaner production methods was cost reduction, followed by waste minimization. Cutting regulatory compliance costs was typically a secondary factor. Adopting CP methods can yield lower regulatory compliance costs, because adopting CP methods means generating lower quantities of waste that eventually require treatment. As shown by Cagno, Trucco, and Tardini (2005), many firms recognize that cleaner production measures can cut costs, independent of the reduced costs of meeting environmental regulations.

The experience of firms using Pakistan's CPCs, suggests that, notwithstanding valuable advice those centers provided, the centers can do much more to advance CP. The incomplete nature of services provided by the centers is evident in the number of firms served by the centers that had little understanding of basic CP concepts (Ali 2011). Many firms in Ali's study viewed CP as nothing more than conducting audits and implementing measures suggested by the audits. This reflects a very narrow perspective. Firms with a more advanced understanding think in terms of integrating cleaner production and EMS into their core business strategies for enhancing competitiveness (Rugman and Verbeke 1998).

While the CPCs' accomplishments are notable, Pakistan's challenge in this regard is to change the *long-term behavior* of firms, and not just the few hundred firms served by existing CPCs. The challenge is to reach the much larger number of company owners and managers in the several thousand industrial firms that have significant individual waste discharges as well as the several hundred thousand SMEs in the manufacturing sector, which cumulatively release substantial quantities of waste.

In the short term, the existing CPCs are well positioned to move beyond their current focus on conducting energy and environmental audits, and presenting CP measures. In addition, the centers can

- help firms develop EMS and integrate them, along with CP, into their business strategies;
- assist firms in understanding that ISO 14001 certification requires having a plan for meeting NEQS, and that such certification can enhance competitiveness and increase market share; and
- instruct firms on the relationships between CP, EMS, end-of-pipe waste treatment, and ISO 14001 certification.

As Ali's (2011) survey results demonstrate, many SMEs are unaware of the advantages of establishing EMS and becoming certified to ISO 14001; indeed, many have not even heard of ISO 14001. Firms need to be made aware that developing a reputation for good environmental performance can enhance their sales. This is not just the case for firms engaged in exports. As international business customers increase their emphasis on green supply chain management, customer demands for improved environmental performance will affect Pakistani firms that do not themselves export but supply firms that do.

The CPCs together with industry associations and provincial EPAs can join together to diffuse CP concepts and methods to firms that existing centers do not serve directly. This can be done, for example, by supporting the formation of "waste minimization clubs," which consist of companies brought together to receive CP training and share information on CP-related practices in industrial clusters. Such clubs have been used effectively in several countries, such as South Africa and the United Kingdom.[20]

CPCs could also be made stronger by creating advisory boards that include key stakeholders, such as industrial associations, provincial EPAs, and international aid institutions that have provided long-term support to the CPCs. These boards can assist the centers in identifying new revenue streams and developing business plans to ensure their financial sustainability. The boards can also identify how best to expand the centers' missions to include helping firms to create EMSs and become certified to ISO 14001. In the short term, Pakistan would also benefit from having CPCs that focus on additional export sectors, such as sporting goods and surgical instruments. In the long term, the GoP's creation of a national cleaner production center could also yield benefits. A national center could promote information sharing among subnational CPCs, create a national CP plan, and engage in international information exchanges with other national CPCs in Asia.

## Strengthening the Infrastructure for Environment Quality Management

Creating interim NEQS, building CETPs, and strengthening CPCs will make it easier for Pakistani firms to meet environment-related requirements of international business customers and countries receiving Pakistani exports. However, other complementary measures are necessary. One involves information dissemination and the other concerns institutions linked to the process of becoming certified to international standards and meeting environment-related non-tariff barriers to trade. As mentioned, the key environment-related WTO rules are those under the agreements concerning TBT (Technical Barriers to Trade) and SPS (Sanitary and Phytosanitary Standards).

Information dissemination problems exist because of the huge number of technical regulations and standards used in international trade. These are issued by dozens of organizations, including international NGOs such as ISO; formal standard-setting organizations such as ASTM International (formerly the American Society for Testing and Materials),which issues standards for materials such as steel and concrete; and ad hoc industry groups, such as the Internet Engineering Task Force, which issues protocols for the Internet (OECD 1999). In addition, governmental regulations, such as REACH, and environment-related requirements issued by individual business customers and industry consortia can also affect trade. Keeping track of the many environment-related technical requirements that can affect firms' ability to export is a daunting problem for Pakistani enterprises, particularly SMEs.

Pakistani exporters face considerable problems due to the country's limitations regarding institutional and technical capacity to certify compliance with standards, a process that necessitates, among other things, testing by accredited laboratories. Certification and testing require what is termed "quality infrastructure," which refers to internationally recognized accreditation and certification bodies and laboratories for metrology,[21] standardization, testing, quality management, and conformity assessment that exporters use to comply with international rules applicable to their products. In 1996, GoP recognized quality infrastructure as "an essential building block for industrial development" by creating the PSQCA as the national standardization body (Soomro 2007).

Among PSQCA's objectives, the following are particularly relevant to meeting ISO and other technical standards important to Pakistani exporters: inspecting and testing products and services for their quality specifications and characteristics, and testing and assessing industrial raw materials to establish their conformity with national and international standards specifications in various fields (Soomro 2007). In addition, PSQCA functions as Pakistan's "National Enquiry Point" under the WTO's Sanitary and Phytosanitary and TBT Agreements. As such, PSQCA is obliged to inform WTO of Pakistan's technical regulations and standards and conformity assessment procedures, and respond to external inquiries concerning these subjects.

Notwithstanding the existence of PSQCA and other elements of quality infrastructure, Pakistani exporters have faced challenges in satisfying SPS requirements sanctioned by the WTO's Sanitary and Phytosanitary Agreement. According to the EU-funded Trade Related Technical Assistance II Program, "[i]n Pakistan's SPS institutions, there is a widespread lack of understanding and awareness of modern SPS management systems, which hampers development of the control system."[22] As examples, the program cited the absence of internal controls effective enough to allow Pakistani fisheries to reach export markets and the high level of rejections of plant products based on international requirements, such as rejections based on aflatoxins in chilies.

Problems in meeting international standards for the textiles sector provide another example of quality-related challenges faced by Pakistani exporters. According to a representative of Textile Testing International, less than 5 percent of the 816 textile standards developed by PSQCA were harmonized with the ASTM standards.[23] He argued that textile-related sector committees and division councils of PSQCA should adopt or harmonize "PS textile standards" with those of the American Association of Textile Chemists and Colorists, because 70 percent of the foreign market demands conformity with the association's standards.

As Pakistan's National Enquiry Point under WTO's TBT and SPS Agreements, PSQCA is well positioned to assist in disseminating information on standards by serving as a communications bridge between international standard setters and Pakistani exporters. To be an effective bridge, PSQCA would need to create more linkages for supplying information to, and receiving information from, export-oriented firms. To carry out this bridging function, PSQCA would need to design and implement a system to collect and disseminate information concerning applicable overseas environmental standards and other requirements for Pakistan's main export products. The bridging function would also require PSQCA to learn and transmit the views of Pakistani exporters as inputs to the standard-setting process during the comment periods mandated by the WTO's Agreement on TBT.

The NEQS set forth pollution standards for Pakistan's industries. The provincial EPAs enforce these standards, which set limits on a wide variety of pollutants. However, these agencies are largely incapable—due to a lack of funding and staff—of meeting their regulatory responsibilities and are unable to enforce mandatory compliance with the NEQS. Hence, firms comply either on a voluntary basis or not at all. Among firms, NEQS compliance is low; many firms do not understand the NEQS requirements or are completely unaware of them.

### Environmental Management Agencies
#### Environmental Management Institutions in Flux
Prior to enactment of the Eighteenth Amendment to Pakistan's Constitution in 2010, the federal government had enacted the Pakistan Environmental Protection Act (PEPA), 1997, which established a comprehensive framework for environmental management. The 1997 law, which is applicable to numerous forms of pollution, empowered the GoP to develop and enforce regulations to protect the environment. Among other things, PEPA, 1997, included provisions for creating provincial sustainable development funds, establishing environmental tribunals, and developing an environmental impact assessment (EIA) system.

After passage of the Eighteenth Amendment, institutions at the provincial level began to replace this environmental management framework.[24] Although the path for the devolution process is not entirely clear, it appears that provincial legislation (Cochrane 2011) will establish a number of laws and institutions (for example, PEPA and the environmental tribunals set up under PEPA). Per the amended constitution, while devolution occurs, all environmental laws, regulations, and other legal instruments having the force of law can "continue to remain in force until altered, repealed or amended by the competent authority."[25]

Until recently, the overarching responsibility for environmental priority setting and policy formulation in Pakistan rested with Pakistan's Ministry of Environment (MoE). However, pursuant to the Eighteenth Amendment, the MoE was eliminated in 2011 and many of its staff members and functions were transferred to a newly created Ministry of Disaster Management. On the other hand, Pakistan EPA moved to the Capital Administration Division, which limited its geographical coverage from across Pakistan to the capital territory alone. In April 2012, the Ministry of MDM was renamed the Ministry of Climate Change, and the Pakistan EPA transferred back to it. Another aspect of devolution that was unclear concerned the status of the Pakistan Environmental Protection Council (PEPC), to which PEPA, 1997, transferred responsibilities for overall leadership on environmental matters. PEPC has now been placed with the Ministry of Climate Change. The council, which had included top-level officials from MoE, had major responsibilities for supervising implementation of national environmental policies. Notwithstanding these important duties, the council was largely inactive. PEPC not only failed to meet at least twice yearly as required under PEPA, 1997, but also failed to meet *at all* between 2004 and 2010.

Provinces have assumed their full responsibilities for environmental protection under the Eighteenth Amendment, while the umbrella responsibility for regulatory enforcement rests with the Pak-EPA as before. Prior to the Eighteenth Amendment, Pak-EPA had been responsible for overseeing the implementation of PEPA, 1997, an activity mainly carried out by the EPAs in each of the provinces. In addition to overseeing PEPA, 1997, implementation, Pak-EPA had functions that included environmental monitoring and the preparation of an annual national environmental report.

The Eighteenth Amendment requires that provincial governments take on responsibilities for the environment previously held by the federal government, a process that is proceeding haltingly. In the time since the adoption of the Eighteenth Amendment, provincial governments have assumed new environmental management responsibilities in an ad hoc manner, and the extent of inter-provincial coordination is unclear.[26]

Decentralizing environmental management responsibilities to the provinces offers a number of benefits, including the capacity to respond more effectively to local priorities, but it also poses significant risks. For example, inconsistent interpretation and enforcement of environmental standards across provinces could lead to highly uneven levels of environmental degradation in different parts of the country. The devolution process has also introduced uncertainties, inasmuch as it is unclear how provincial entities will carry out the responsibilities of Pak-EPA—with its established institutional structures and diverse professional competencies. Questions also arise about how the administrative disruptions during the transition period will affect environmental quality.

Even before passage of the Eighteenth Amendment, each provincial EPA was responsible for undertaking environmental management tasks in its province (for example, implementing rules and regulations of PEPA, 1997). Their responsibilities included regulatory and monitoring functions, such as enforcing environmental regulations, handling complaints relating to the environment, and operating laboratories for monitoring environmental parameters. The provincial EPAs did not have the capacity to attend systematically to all their responsibilities before the Eighteenth Amendment, and it is unclear how they will carry out their added responsibilities under the amendment.[27]

### Shortfalls in Implementing Environmental Regulations

The provincial EPAs, which are charged with implementing the existing federal regulatory framework, have ambitious mandates, but they generally face obstacles because of insufficient staff, small budgets, low political prestige, little administrative autonomy, and high staff turnover rates. Rarely has there been adequate staffing of agencies with experts to monitor and enforce ambient air, water, and soil quality standards, and review EIAs of major projects and monitor projects' environmental impacts. In general, the enforcement of environmental regulations is lax, and stricter penalties that are sometimes available in laws are almost never imposed for a variety of reasons, such as lack of technical capacity to provide sound evidence of infractions.

In addition to problems associated with limited human resources, inadequate funding, and so forth, provincial EPAs face another challenge: under Pakistan's current conditions, many firms cannot meet the NEQS, which govern releases of pollutants. In addition, because follow-up enforcement efforts are weak, compliance rates are low.

Several studies have documented shortfalls in the implementation of environmental policy. According to an assessment by Azizullah et al. (2011), there has not been effective implementation of the NEQS requirements. That study argued that implementation is weak because of "insufficient budgetary allocations and lack of effective coordination and communication among the responsible authorities, like federal, provincial and local entities."

Luken (2009) also documented the poor enforcement of NEQS. He found that that in the years since enactment of PEPA, 1997, the provincial EPAs had not issued discharge licenses because they were still waiting for guidance from Pak-EPA, and the only monitoring of waste releases was in response to public complaints. Luken (2009: 3480) also noted that "provincial authorities have undertaken very few enforcement actions and the Pak-EPA has yet to issue guidance on how to go about enforcement actions and [apply] civil and criminal sanctions."

The weak enforcement and compliance with NEQS reported above is consistent with data gathered in a 2009–10 survey of firms conducted by Ali (2011). The survey involved structured interviews with CEOs and senior managers at firms in four cities: Sialkot, Faisalabad, Lahore, and Karachi. Results demonstrate a striking lack of compliance with NEQS. According to Ali (2011), about 79 percent of the more than 40 leather tanneries surveyed in Sialkot were either unaware of the NEQS or not in compliance; similarly, four out of the five tanneries surveyed in Lahore were out of compliance. In contrast, four out of the five surveyed tanneries in Karachi complied with NEQS, but they were able to do so by discharging their wastewaters to the CETP in the Korangi Industrial area, one of the few CETPs in Pakistan. Ali's results for the 30 textile processing firms he surveyed were similar: 76 percent of the surveyed firms were out of compliance. A striking outcome of this survey is the large number of firms that were completely unaware that the NEQS even existed. Indeed, many firms, especially the SMEs, had never had contact with staff members from an EPA (Ali 2011).

Nadeem and Hameed (2008) give other evidence for the failure of Pakistani EPAs to implement environmental requirements.[28] In explaining the poor performance of the EIA system, the study pointed to inadequate capacity of EIA approval authorities, poor coordination among line departments and environmental agencies, deficiencies in identifying projects requiring EIAs, poor quality of EIA documents, and weak post-project monitoring.

According to Khan (2003), Pakistan was making steady progress to improve its approach to environmental management during the 1990s, but that changed around 1999, when a major falloff in implementing the NEQS occurred. Political transition in Pakistan and regional/global events from 1999 onwards resulted in weakening interest of the government in matters pertaining to the environment.

Pakistan's gaps in terms of compliance with NEQS and other environmental requirements are well known,[29] and there have been many recommendations on how to close the gaps. A typical example is a 2000 United Nations Industrial Development Organization report that recommended enhancing EPA staffing and monitoring capabilities, enhancing accountability in implementing environmental laws, and providing increased budgets for regulatory agencies (Aftab et al. 2000). It is difficult to argue with such policy recommendations. However, given all the work needed to successfully devolve environmental responsibilities to the provinces, such recommendations will not likely be effective in the short term.

Enhancing the capacity of environmental authorities is important, but it will be a long-term effort. As elaborated in the discussions in chapter 4, a more effective short-term strategy is one that complements efforts to strengthen EPAs with interventions that capitalize on the ability of firms to improve their competitiveness by enhancing their environmental performance.

### Public Disclosure and Information Dissemination

In the final analysis, an informed citizenry, an active press, and emerging environmental NGOs can move Pakistan in the direction of providing the kinds of support that EPAs will need to enforce compliance with environmental regulations. The Pak-EPA and provincial EPAs can foster the creation of an informed citizenry by distributing information regarding firms violating environmental regulations, as well as data on the health impacts of environmental degradation. There are models of how information about firms violating environmental regulations can galvanize citizens to put pressure on polluters to clean up; a widely emulated example is the program referred to as PROPER (Program for Pollution Control, Evaluation, and Rating), which was developed in Indonesia.[30] The provision of information to the public on health impacts of pollution also empowers citizens to place pressure on industries. In the short term, the Pak-EPA and provincial governments should lend support to environmental NGOs (for example, WWF-Pakistan) and news outlets interested in environmental issues by providing them with information on firms releasing pollutants affecting human health and, more generally, on the costs to Pakistan of continued environmental degradation. At the provincial level, EPAs can consider whether and how the PROPER program, which several developing countries have adopted, can be employed in Pakistan.[31] One profitable avenue might be to map out pollution hot spots, their spatial extent, the most polluting industries within these spatial zones, and the firms/factories within the identified industries that account for the majority of the pollutant effluents/emissions. Such targeting might help identify the extent to which it would be a cost-effective strategy to focus enforcement efforts on only the most-polluting firms.

Infrastructure linked to quality management at firms consists of standardization, metrology, testing, inspection, certification, and accreditation. It is often expensive, time consuming, and complicated for firms to gain access to this infrastructure. Providing these services is a crucial element to maintaining Pakistan's export competitiveness. Pakistani firms can go abroad to access the needed quality management infrastructure, but this poses special challenges for SMEs; they seldom use overseas service providers if there is no domestic capability. Sending equipment overseas for calibration is excessively burdensome. Moreover, using overseas quality management auditors for ISO 9001 certifications and overseas EMS auditors for ISO 14001 certifications are impediments for firms interested in obtaining those certifications. In addition, it is challenging for firms to use overseas auditors in trying to meet restrictions imposed under WTO Agreements on Technical Barriers to Trade. For these reasons, Pakistan should view the development of quality-related infrastructure needed by firms as a high priority element in the country's export strategy.[32] Pakistan has made a good start on infrastructure development by creating the PSQCA, Pakistan National Accreditation Council, and the National Physical and Standards Laboratory; however, these organizations do not yet have the capacity needed to effectively serve Pakistani firms engaged in exports. In the short term, there should be significant strengthening of the capacity of PSQCA, which is Pakistan's National Enquiry Point under WTO's TBT and SPS agreements.

PSQCA should serve as a communications bridge between standard setters and exporters; this will involve enhancing the vertical linkages needed to supply information to, and receive information from, export-oriented firms. The bridging function has two main elements: PSQCA should (a) make Pakistani exporters aware of trade and environmental issues so that they can make necessary adjustment in a timely way, and (b) provide information representing the perspectives of Pakistani exporters to organizations engaged in setting standards. To carry out this bridging function, PSQCA should design and implement a system to collect, track, and release information concerning foreign environmental standards and requirements for products; in the case of government-set standards, PSQCA should educate exporters about standards that are currently under development. The bridging function also requires PSQCA to solicit, collate, and relay the views of Pakistani exporters as inputs to the standard-setting process during the comment periods mandated by the WTO's Agreement on Technical Barriers to Trade.

### Conclusions and Recommendations

The cost of environmental damage in Pakistan is tremendous. Air pollution, and inadequate water supply and sanitation, result in tens of thousands of deaths annually. Due to these illnesses, environmental damage causes (unaccounted) annual losses to Pakistan that total at least 6 percent of GDP. By itself, this would be enough reason to encourage cleaner production initiatives. However, there is also convincing evidence that cleaner production will also have concrete economic benefits. With the increase in government regulations and voluntary standards that mandate environmental standards from exporters, Pakistan must take steps to convey the image that it is a green supplier, lest it risk falling behind countries that are acting more aggressively on this front.

Following is a brief summary of this chapter's findings:

- Government regulations issued by developing nations and green supplier initiatives on the part of foreign multinationals are of increasing concern to Pakistan. These initiatives often not only mandate that exporting firms meet certain environmental standards, they often also go down a second level, so that purely domestic firms (ones that sell inputs to exporting firms) might also be required to have cleaner production processes in place.

- These regulations often require ISO 9001 or ISO 14001 certification for the exporting firms. Pakistan does not have many firms with these sorts of certifications, and that number is not increasing fast enough.

- ISO 14001 certifications require progress towards meeting national emissions standards, but NEQS are seen as being unduly complicated and onerous; most firms in Pakistan do not feel that they will ever be able to meet the current standards.

- Common effluent treatment plants have proven cost effective in treating wastewater in certain industrial estates, but coordination problems hamper further CETP construction. Pakistan has a pollution charge system that can be used to compel polluters to pay for the construction of CETPs; however, it is currently moribund.

- CPCs have enabled firms in industrial estates to increase their number of environmental mitigations and, in some cases, to reduce the cost of production. In many cases, these CPCs are the only source of cleaner production mitigation to which firms have access.

- The recent shifting of Pakistan's environmental regulatory and policy-setting priorities has further disorganized Pakistan's already overburdened environmental regulatory apparatus. The Ministry of Climate Change is new and its situation is uncertain, while understaffed provincial EPAs are unable to compel mandatory compliance with the NEQS; hence, compliance can only be expected on a voluntary basis. This weak institutional climate also has the potential to harm Pakistan's performance on trans-boundary issues where lines of authority are not currently clear, such as the ongoing international effort to address global climate change. This uncertain climate could create instability that hampers investment in clean production.

- Due to the lack of national-level leadership on cleaner production, firms are often unaware of the intersections between export competitiveness, import-country government regulations, the industry standards of foreign multinationals, ISO certification, and NEQS compliance.

- Within Pakistan, there is currently only limited public support and NGO agitation for environmental governance. That sort of agitation had led importers and foreign multinationals to adopt their stringent environmental standards in the first place. However, there is nascent demand for environmental governance: a

**Table 7.1 Recommended Actions for Cleaner Production in Pakistan**

| Recommended action | Responsible party | Timeframe |
|---|---|---|
| **Revision of Environmental Regulations** | | |
| Develop both interim and revised permanent National Environmental Quality Standards. | New Standard Setting Committee (includes representatives of enterprises, industry associations, NGOs, and the public sector) | Short term |
| Revise and implement pollution charge system. | Government of Pakistan | Short term |
| Implement permanent National Environmental Quality Standards. | New Standard Setting Committee/ Government of Pakistan | Long term |
| **Construction of Common Effluent Treatment Plants** | | |
| Create plans for funding and construction of CETPs in industrial clusters. | Public body, industrial association, commercial venture, or public-private partnership | Short term |
| **Strengthening Cleaner Production Centers** | | |
| Extend the work and scope of cleaner production centers (CPCs) to promote long-term integration of cleaner production (CP) and environmental management systems (EMS) in firms' daily operations and management strategies, and establish additional CPCs. | CPCs, industry associations, CP working group | Short term |
| Create advisory board in CPCs to identify funding sources and develop business plans to ensure financial sustainability. | CPCs | Short term |
| Create CP working group within the Ministry of Industries and Production tasked with developing a national plan for CP and EMS, and a strategy for financing construction of CETPs. | Ministry of Industries and Production | Short term |
| Create a national cleaner production center to promote information sharing among subnational CPCs and engage in international exchanges of information with other national CPCs. | CP working group | Short term |
| **Public Disclosure and Information Dissemination** | | |
| Foster creation of informed citizenry through distribution of information regarding firms that are violating environmental regulations and data on health impacts of environmental degradation. | Pakistan Environmental Protection Agency and Provincial Environmental Protection Agencies | Short term |
| Collect, assemble, and release information to firms on foreign environmental standards, voluntary standards established by consortia and retailers, and requirements related to Pakistani products in potential export markets. | Pakistan Standards and Quality Control Authority and industry associations | Short term |
| Allow Pakistan's specific needs to be accounted for during the processes for formulating international standards in standard-setting bodies such as ISO. | Pakistan Standards and Quality Control Authority | Short term |

*Note:* CETP = combined effluent treatment plants, NGO = nongovernmental organization.

majority of Pakistanis agrees that it is important for companies to have a good environmental record.

The recommendations in table 7.1 fall into four categories: (a) revision of national environment quality standards, (b) construction of common effluent treatment plants, (c) strengthening and expansion of cleaner production centers, and (d) public disclosure and dissemination of information.

## Notes

1. IQ losses associated with BLLs > 10 µg/dL have been established long ago.

2. The high bound reflects the estimated loss in income for males and females in Salkever (1995), weighted by the rates of labor force participation of males and females in Sindh province reported by the Federal Bureau of Statistics (GoP 2010). The low and high bounds do not include the effect of IQ on the rate of labor force participation.

3. The REACH regulations make this clear at Paragraphs 55 and 65 (European Union 2006). In addition, there is an emerging REACH certification industry consisting of independent assessors who provide the testing needed to allow a company to assert that its products comply with REACH requirements.

4. For an English translation of China REACH, see the website of Chemical Inspection and Regulation Service Limited. http://www.cirsreach.com/China_Chemical _Regulation/The_Provisions_on_Environmental_Administration_of_New_Chemical _Substances_2010.html. Accessed August 23, 2011. For a summary of the new requirements, see http://www.cirs-reach.com/chinareach.html. Accessed August 23, 2011.

5. Gap Inc. Code of Vendor Conduct. http://www.itglwf.org/lang/en/documents /GapCodeofConduct.pdf. Accessed January 30, 2012.

6. Nike Inc. Code of Conduct. http://nikeinc.com/search?search_terms=code+of +conduct. Accessed January 30, 2012.

7. Joint Roadmap: Towards Zero Discharge of Hazardous Chemicals. http://www .adidas-group.com/en/sustainability/assets/statements/111118_JointRoadmap.pdf. Accessed January 31, 2012.

8. Although the original quality standard was referred to as ISO 9000, there was a shift in terminology: ISO 9000 now refers to a "family of standards," and 9001:2008 is a member of that family of standards. During the early years of the ISO quality standards, firms were said to be certified to ISO 9000, but to avoid confusion, the term "ISO 9001" is used herein in the context of organizations that have become certified, regardless of the year.

9. ISO 14001 centers on the creation of an environmental management system (EMS) to guide an organization's management of the environment inside its facilities and the immediate environment outside of its facilities. Under ISO 14001, the EMS is to be used to identify and control the environmental impact of the organization's activities, products, or services, and to implement a systematic approach to (a) setting environmental objectives and targets, (b) achieving those objectives and targets, and (c) demonstrating that they have been achieved.

10. According to Anderson, Daly, and Johnson (1999), the wording of ISO 9000 standards is such that responsibility for the quality of purchased materials rests squarely on the purchaser. "This requirement, together with emerging supplier management methods that promote long-term partnerships and strategic alliances with key suppliers, has motivated original equipment manufacturers (who are certified) to demand that their suppliers become certified."

11. Personal communication via email, with Chaudhary Laiq Ali, Environmental Consultant, Islamabad, February 5, 2012.

12. Wastewater treatment, the process of removing contaminants from wastewater, can involve physical, chemical, and biological processes. Primary treatment refers to basic processes, such as screening and passing wastewater through settling tanks,

often with a chemical agent added to promote the formation of particles that are easy to remove. Secondary treatment, which follows primary treatment, generally includes biological processes to decompose organic wastes. The key point in this context is that, in comparison to primary treatment, secondary treatment is considerably more expensive, and secondary treatment plants require operators who are more highly trained.

13. In the United States, the Clean Water Act includes "anti-backsliding" provisions: the requirement that when a wastewater discharge permit is renewed, its limits can stay the same or get stronger, but they cannot get weaker.

14. According to Hey and Waggy (1979, 128), up until 1950, the use of a natural water course in the United States as a receptor for liquid waste was widely viewed as necessary and legitimate. They reported, "[i]n 1910, only 4 percent of the population [in the United States] had its waste treated before it was discharged. Fifty percent of the urban population in 1939 still discharged their waste untreated. …the situation was not much improved by 1950." During that year, 57 percent of 3,413 surveyed factories were discharging "totally untreated waste." They further reported that in 1979, most municipal wastewater "is treated or soon will be" and industry "was still lagging behind."

15. Pakistan has numerous industrial clusters, and many others have been planned and are in various stages of implementation (Luken 2009; LUMS 2011).

16. According to Luken (2009), plans for new CETPs were shelved in two cases because firms could not agree on cost-sharing arrangements. Such problems will clearly need to be sorted out if there is to be progress in building and operating CETPs.

17. Luken (2009, 3481) reported on the Korangi plant: "A significant number of tanneries are refusing to pay the their share of the operational costs for the CETP, as evidenced by the fact that the Pakistan Tanners Association has had to report noncompliance by several tanneries to the provincial (Sindh) Environmental Protection Agency. Only nine of the 80 tanneries that need to do so have installed chromium recovery units…."

18. The CETP for Korangi tanneries in Karachi provides an example of how CETPs can function. The facility includes a 12-km-long collection and conveyance system to bring the effluents from the individual tanneries in several sectors of the Korangi Industrial Area to the CETP and to carry the wastewater after processing from the plant to the main drains leading to the sea. According to Luken (2009), the CETPs located in Kasur and Korangi that treat tannery discharges are the only CETPs in operation, and they suffer from significant operating problems.

19. The previously mentioned Shamslakha Committee developed rules for the pollution discharge system in the late 1990s; however, the Pak-EPA did not enforce the rules, due to a shift in government priorities.

20. Henningsson et al. 2001. The authors go on to argue that "[Waste Minimization Clubs] act as a way to introducing economies of scale; costs are reduced because companies share the costs of gaining information and hiring consultants. The club format creates a 'peer pressure' to encourage participants to push harder within their own firm, and to learn from the experiences of others…."

21. The website of the International Bureau of Weights and Measures defines "metrology" as "the science of measurement, embracing both experimental and theoretical determinations at any level of uncertainty in any field of science and technology." http://www.bipm.org/en/convention/wmd/2004/. Accessed October 16, 2011.

22. Website of Trade Related Technical Assistance II Programme, http://trtapakistan.org /faqs. Accessed August 29, 2011. This source also indicates the problems with fisheries and plant products noted below.

23. This paragraph is based on a presentation by Hamid Latif, summarized in Afzal (2007, 13).

24. The central government was able to enact PEPA, 1997, because, prior to 2010, the word "ecology" had been included on the Concurrent List of the Constitution. This list included items for which both the federal and provincial governments were able to enact legislation (with federal primacy in case of a conflict with a provincial law). Once the Eighteenth Amendment deleted the Concurrent List, all matters covered by the list were placed within the exclusive domain of provincial governments.

25. Article 270.AA of the Constitution (Eighteenth Amendment) Act, 2010.

26. In Punjab, for example, District Environment Officers have been appointed in most districts. However, in the other three provinces, the environment departments have set up regional offices.

27. Pakistan also has environmental tribunals (ETs), established under Section 20 of PEPA, 1997. Currently there are four ETs, one each in Lahore, Karachi, Peshawar, and Quetta. Environmental magistrates staff the ETs; the federal and provincial governments appoint these magistrates from among senior civil judges. The ETs have enabled private individuals to seek relief for their grievances against alleged polluters. For additional information, see the website of the Ministry of Law and Justice and Parliamentary Affairs: http://202.83.164.27/wps/portal/Moljhr/!ut/p/c0/04 _SB8K8xLLM9MSSzPy8xBz9CP0os_hQN68AZ3dnIwMLN09zAyOfYDNTTws TAwtzU_2CbEdFAHjnARI!/?WCM_GLOBAL_CONTEXT=/wps/wcm/connect /MoljhrCL/ministry/general/environmental+protection+tribunal. Accessed August 5, 2011.

28. Riffat and Khan (2006) found that shortfalls in implementation capacity caused shortcomings of the Pakistan EIA system; however, the empirical basis for their conclusion was unclear.

29. The Pakistani press has been active in informing the public of the weak implementation of environmental standards; for example, an Internet search of the Pakistani newspaper *The Nation* using the search term "pollution" yielded nearly 34,000 stories. http://www.nation.com.pk/pakistan-news-newspaper-daily-english-online/search .html?cx=partner-pub-2495428981136420%3A7911671418&cof=FORID%3A10& ie=UTF-8&q=pollution&sa=Search. Accessed December 24, 2011.

30. Indonesia's Program for Pollution Control, Evaluation, and Rating (PROPER) is a national-level public environmental reporting initiative. The program uses a color-coded rating, ranging from gold for excellent performance, to black for poor performance, as well as "reputational incentives." For details, see Blackman, Afsah, and Ratunanda 2004.

31. For example, China's Greenwatch program is an adaptation of PROPER.

32. Material in this paragraph and the ones that follow is from Gujadhur (2010).

## Bibliography

Aftab, Z., Ch. L. Ali., A. M. Khan., A. C. Robinson, and I. A. Irshad. 2000. *Industrial Policy and The Environment in Pakistan, NC/PAK/97/018. December 11, 2000.* Vienna: United Nations Industrial Development Organization. http://www.unido.org/fileadmin /import/userfiles/timminsk/rio10-ind-pakistan-eng.pdf.

Afzal, S. 2007. "Pak-US Standards and Conformity Assessment Workshop Proceedings." Lahore, Pakistan, May 24–25. http://publicaa.ansi.org/sites/apdl/Documents /Standards%20Activities/International%20Standardization/Regional/Europe -Middle%20East-Africa/Middle%20East/2008-06%20Pakistan%20Workshop%20 %28NIST%29/2007%20US-Pak%20SC%20workshop%20proceedings.pdf.

Ahmad, T., and S. R. Khan. 2007. "Case Study of Pakistan." In *Environmental Requirements and Market Access: Reflections from South Asia*, edited by N. Kumar and S. Chaturvedi, 264. New Delhi.

Ahmad, T., A. Mumtaz, D. Ahmad, and N. Rashid. 2009. "Lead Exposure in Children Living Around the Automobile and Battery Repair Workshops." *Biomedica* 25 (17): 128–32. http://www.thebiomedicapk.com/articles/179.pdf.

Ali, L. 2011. *Implementable Recommendations for Cleaner Production Programs in Pakistan*. Consultant report prepared for the World Bank's Non-Lending Technical Assistance for Ministry of Industries and Production, Government of Pakistan. Washington, DC: World Bank.

Ambec, S., and P. Lanoie. 2007. "When and Why Does it Pay to be Green?" Working Paper GAEL. http://www.grenoble.inra.fr/Docs/pub/A2007/gael2007-05.pdf.

Anderson, S. W., J. D. Daly, and M. F. Johnson. 1999. "Why Firms Seek ISO 9000 Certification: Regulatory Compliance or Competitive Advantage?" *Production and Operations Management* 8: 28–43.

Anjum, A., A. A. Mann, and M. A. Anjum. 2009. "Health Concerns among Workers in Weaving Industry: A Case Study of Tehsil Faialabad, Pakistan." *Journal of Agriculture and Social Science* 5: 106–08.

Azizullah, A., M. N. K. Khattak, R. Peter, and D. Häder. 2011. "Water Pollution in Pakistan and Its Impact on Public Health—A Review." *Environment International* 37 (2): 479–97. http://lecturesug3.files.wordpress.com/2013/02/water-pollution -pakistan.pdf

Bansal, P., and K. Roth. 2000. "Why Companies Go Green: A Model of Ecological Responsiveness." *Academy of Management Journal* 43 (4): 717–36.

Basu, A., and D. J. A. van Zyl. 2006. "Industrial Ecological Framework for Achieving Cleaner Production in the Mining and Minerals Industry." Special Issue of *Journal of Cleaner Production* 14 (3–4): 299–304.

Blackman, A., S. Afsah, and D. Ratunanda. 2004. "How Do Public Disclosure Pollution Control Programs Work? Evidence from Indonesia." *Human Ecology Review* 11 (3): 235–46. http://www.humanecologyreview.org/pastissues/her113 /blackmanafsahratunanda.pdf.

Bongaerts, J. C., and A. Kraemer. 1989. "Permits and Effluent Charges in the Water Pollution Control Policies of France, West Germany, and the Netherlands." *Environmental Monitoring and Assessment* 12 (2): 127–47.

Cagno, E., P. Trucco, and L. Tardini. 2005. "Cleaner Production and Profitability: Analysis of 134 Industrial Pollution Prevention (P2) Project Reports." *Journal of Cleaner Production* 13 (6): 593–605.

Christmann, P. 2004. "Multinational Companies and the Natural Environment: Determinants of Global Environmental Policy." *Academy of Management Journal* 47 (5): 747–60.

Cochrane, H. 2011. "Interview of Dr. Parvez Hassen Regarding Pakistan's Environmental Laws, March 14, 2011." *Journal of Court Innovation* 3 (1): 350–59. http://www

.pace.edu/school-of-law/sites/pace.edu.school-of-law/files/IJIEA/jciHassanInterview2
_jci_2%20jl_13-10_cropped.pdf.

Cohen, M. A., S. A. Fenn, and J. S. Naimon. 1995. "Environmental and Financial Performance: Are They Related?" Working paper, Owen Graduate School of Management, Vanderbilt University, Nashville, TN.

Colbeck, I., Z. A. Nasir, and Z. Ali. 2010. "The State of Ambient Air Quality in Pakistan: A Review." *Environmental Science and Pollution Research* 17 (1): 49–63.

Corbett, C. J. 2008. "Global Diffusion of ISO 9000 Certification through Supply Chains." *Supply Chain Analysis, International Series in Operations Research & Management Science* 119: 169–99. http://ssrn.com/abstract=913812.

de Backer, Paul. 1999. *L'impact économique et l'efficacité environnementale de la certification ISO 14001/EMAS des entreprises industrielles.* Consultant report, Paris: ADEME (French Environment and Energy Management Agency). http://www.ademe.fr /htdocs/actualite/dossier/managenement_envir/sites/documents/iso14001.pdf.

European Union. 2006. REACH Regulations. Brussels, Belgium.

Foss, I. 2002. "How Quality Can Support Development of International Trade Management." Paper presented at Q2002, the 46th EOQ Congress. September 29–October 2.

Foth, H. and A. V. Hayes. 2008. "Concept of REACH and Impact on Evaluation of Chemicals." *Human Exposure Toxicology* 27 (1): 5–21.

Ghauri, B. 2010. *Institutional Analysis of Air Quality Management in Urban Pakistan.* Consultant report, World Bank, Washington, DC.

GoP (Government of Pakistan). 2010. *Pakistan Economic Survey 2009–10.* Ministry of Finance, Islamabad.

Gujadhur, S. K. 2010. "Quality: A Prerequisite for Exports. Increasing Complexity of Technical Requirements in Export Markets." *International Trade Forum* 46 (3): 6.

Hamed, M. M., and Y. El Mahgary. 2004. "Outline of a National Strategy for Cleaner Production: The Case of Egypt." *Journal of Cleaner Production* 12 (4): 327–36.

Hart, S. L. 1995. "A Natural-Resource-Based View of the Firm." *Academy of Management Review* 20 (4): 986–1014. http://www.jstor.org/stable/258963.

Hart, S. L., and M. B. Milstein. 2003. "Creating Sustainable Value." *The Academy of Management Executive* 17 (2): 56–67.

Henningsson, S., R. M. Pratt, P. S. Phillips, and K. Hyde. 2001. "Waste Minimisation Clubs: a Cost-Efficient Policy Instrument?" *European Environment* 11: 324–39.

Hey, D. L., and W. H. Waggy. 1979. "Planning for Water Quality: 1776 to 1976." *Journal of the Water Resources Planning and Management Division* 105 (1): 121–31.

Ilyas, S. Z. 2007. "A Review of Transport and Urban Air Pollution in Pakistan." *Journal of Applied Sciences and Environmental Management* 11 (2): 113–21.

ISO (International Standards Organization). 2010. "ISO Survey of Certifications 2010," ISO. http://www.iso.org/iso/iso-survey2010.pdf.

Jiang, R. J., and P. Bansal. 2003, "Seeing the Need for ISO 14,001." *Journal of Management Studies* 40 (4): 1047–67.

Jorgensen, H. E., P. M. Pruzan-Jorgensen, M. Jungk, and A. Cramer. 2003. *Strengthening Implementation of Corporate Social Responsibility in Global Supply Chains.* Washington, DC: World Bank.

Khan, A. U. 2003. "Past, Present, and Future of NEQS Implementation in Pakistan." Sixth Sustainable Development Conference, Islamabad, Pakistan, December 11–13.

———. 2011. *Industrial Environmental Management in Pakistan*. Consultant report commissioned by the World Bank. Islamabad.

Khan, D. A., W. M. Ansari, and F. A. Khan. 2011. "Synergistic Effects of Iron Deficiency and Lead Exposure on Bloodlead Levels in Children." *World Journal of Pediatrics* 7 (2): 150–54. http://www.wjpch.com/article.asp?article_id=451.

Klassen, R. D., and C. P. McLaughlin. 1996. "The Impact of Environmental Management on Firm Performance." *Management Science* 42 (8): 1199–214.

Lanphear, B. P., R. Hornung, J. Khoury, K. Yolton, P. Baghurst, D. C. Bellinger, R. L. Canfield, K. N. Dietrich, R. Bornschein, T. Greene, S. J. Rothenberg, H. L. Needleman, L. Schnaas, G. Wasserman, J. Graziano, and R. Roberts. 2005. "Low-Level Environmental Lead Exposure and Children's Intellectual Function: An International Pooled Analysis." *Environmental Health Perspectives* 113 (7): 894–99. http://www.ncbi.nlm.nih.gov/pmc/articles/PMC1257652/.

Lahore University of Management Sciences (LUMS). 2011. A. A. Burki, K. A. Munir, M. A. Khan, M. U. Khan, A. Faheem, A. Khalid, and S. T. Hussain. *Industrial Policy, Its Spatial Aspects and Cluster Development in Pakistan*. Consultant report by the Lahore University of Management Sciences for the World Bank. Lahore, Pakistan.

Luken, R. A. 2009. "Equivocating on the Polluter-Pays Principle: The Consequences for Pakistan." *Journal of Environmental Management* 90 (11): 3479–84. http://www.sciencedirect.com/science/article/pii/S0301479709001996.

Mendelsohn, A. L., B. P. Dreyer, A. H. Fierman, C. M. Rosen, L. A. Legano, H. A. Kruger, S. W. Lim, S. Barasch, A. Loretta, and C. D. Courtlandt. 1999. "Low-Level Lead Exposure and Cognitive Development in Early Childhood." *Journal of Developmental and Behavioral Pediatrics* 20: 425–31.

Nadeem, O., and R. Hameed. 2008. "Evaluation of Environmental Impact Assessment System in Pakistan." *Environmental Impact Assessment Review* 28: 562–71.

Nehrt, C. 1996. "Timing and Intensity Effects of Environmental Investments." *Strategic Management Journal* 17: 535–47.

OECD (Organisation for Economic Co-operation and Development). 1999. *Cleaner Production Centres in Central and Eastern Europe and the New Independent States*. Paris: OECD.

Paulraj, A. 2009. "Environmental Motivations: A Classification Scheme and Its Impact on Environmental Strategies and Practices." *Business Strategy and the Environment* 18 (7): 453–68.

Porter, M., and C. van der Linde. 1995. "Green and Competitive: Ending the Stalemate." *Harvard Business Review* 73: 120–34.

Qadir, A., R. N. Malik, and S. Z. Hussain. 2008. "Spatio-Temporal Variations in Water Quality of Nullah Aik-tributary of the River Chenab, Pakistan." *Environmental Monitoring and Assessment* 140: 43–59.

Rao, P., and D. Holt. 2005. "Do Green Supply Chains Lead to Competitiveness and Economic Performance?" *International Journal of Operations and Production Management* 25 (9): 898–916.

Riffat, R., and D. Khan. 2006. "A Review and Evaluation of the Environmental Impact Assessment Process in Pakistan." *Journal of Applied Sciences and Environmental Sanitation* 1: 17–29.

Rugman, A. M., and A. Verbeke. 1998. "Corporate Strategy and International Environmental Policy." *Journal of International Business Studies* 29 (4), 819–34.

Russo, M., and P. Fouts. 1997. "A Resource-based Perspective on Corporate Environmental Performance and Profitability." *Academy of Management Journal* 40: 534–59.

Salkever, D. S. 1995. "Updated Estimates of Earnings Benefits from Reduced Exposure of Children to Environmental Lead." *Environmental Research* 70 (1): 1–6.

Small and Medium Enterprises Development Authority. n.d.

SDWF (Safe Drinking Water Foundation). 2003. *Drinking Water Quality and Health*. Safe Drinking Water Foundation. http://www.safewater.org/members/teachers/water%20 and%20 health.com.

Soomro, A. G. 2007. "PSQCA: National Standard Body." *The Reporter.* DOI: http://the -reporter.info/july-aug07/health/index.htm.

Ullah, R., R. N. Malik, and A. Qadir. 2009. "Assessment of Groundwater Contamination in an Industrial City, Sialkot, Pakistan." *African Journal of Environmental Science and Technology* 3 (12): 429–46.

United States Food and Drug Administration (U.S. FDA). 2009. Refusal Actions by FDA as Recorded by OASIS for Pakistan, March 2009. http://www.accessdata.fda .gov/scripts/importrefusals/ir_selection.cfm?DYear=2009&DMonth=3&CountryCo de=PK.

Warren, K. A., and L. Ortolano. 1999. "Pollution Prevention Incentives and Responses in Chinese Firms." *Environmental Impact Assessment Review* 19 (6): 521–40.

Wilson, M. P., and M. R. Schwarzman. 2009. "Toward a New U.S. Chemicals Policy: Rebuilding the Foundation to Advance New Science, Green Chemistry and Environment Health." *Environmental Health Perspectives* 117 (8): 1202–09.

World Bank. 2008. *Environmental Health and Child Survival, Epidemiology, Economics, Experiences*. Washington, DC: World Bank.

———. 2011. *Pakistan Transport Sector*. Washington, DC: World Bank. http://go.worldbank .org/A0D9IJ5SH0.

## CHAPTER 8

# Institutions for Sustainable Industrialization

## Introduction

The implementation of a strategy for sustainable industrialization, as proposed in this book, requires institutions that function well. Rodrik's (2004) recent work has made appealing the justification for an industrial policy through which governments proactively promote industrial growth. This argument holds that, in early stages of development, there are significant market failures due to, "…information externalities entailed in discovering the cost structure of an economy, and coordination externalities in the presence of scale economies" (Rodrik 2004, 102). These result in disincentives for entrepreneurs to search for profitable opportunities (Auerswald and Malik 2011) and retard industrial development. The way out is to follow the East Asian model, specifically that of the Republic of Korea. As described by Rodrik (1994, 39)

> …what was required was a competent, honest, and efficient bureaucracy to administer the interventions, and a clear-sighted political leadership that consistently placed high priority on economic performance.

Since an assessment of the quality of civil services is beyond the scope of this book, the present chapter focuses on institutions that would aid the formulation and implementation of a strategy for sustainable industrialization in Pakistan. The motivation for this focus is the hope that institutional strengthening can lead to an enabling environment having continuous processes for incorporating sustainability considerations into Pakistan's industrial sector. The discussion here emphasizes four dimensions of sustainability: policy coordination to ensure that

- the cost of doing business for industrial firms is kept low;
- spatial location decisions are coordinated and are based on sound economic principles;

- specialized institutions such as the Small and Medium Enterprise Development Authority (SMEDA) for small enterprise development work well; and
- environmental concerns are addressed in a manner that reflects local realities and promotes international competitiveness of firms.[1]

This chapter has the following structure: The section below discusses the role of the Ministry of Industries and Production (MoIP) as coordinator of institutions that support sustainable industrialization in Pakistan. Then, the chapter's third section focuses on the need to strengthen the National Economic Council (NEC) and the Council of Common Interests as apex institutions for coordinating spatial transformation. Section 4 focuses on the improved coordination for cost-effective delivery of skills. Section 5 also discusses the role of the Small and Medium Enterprises Development Authority in supporting industrialization. The institutional arrangements for environment management are the focus of the chapter's final section.

### MoIP as a Policy Coordinator

In its seminal 2005 report, "Towards a Prosperous Pakistan: A Strategy for Rapid Industrial Growth," the MoIP makes the best case for effective coordination at the level of the federal government. MoIP recognizes, as does this chapter, that many of the policies recommended for rapid industrial development do not fall directly under its purview. To implement the strategy, the MoIP would need to develop the capacity to coordinate with other line ministries/agencies. Table 8.1 lists the type of policies that would need such coordination, the ministries/agencies with prime responsibility for the sectoral policies, and the role of MoIP for successful coordination.

To foster sustainable industrialization, the ministry would need to develop the capacity to carry out effective dialogue with the Federal Board of Revenue, State Bank of Pakistan, Securities and Exchange Commission; with the Ministries of Finance, Energy, Railways, Communications, Ports and Shipping, and Climate Change; and, following the Eighteenth Amendment, the National Economic Council. This will require substantial specialized human resource capacity, and the cabinet mandate, to carry out the coordination role.

Another area for strengthening MoIP capacity is as service provider to the private sector for carrying out industry-specific international benchmarking exercises for competitiveness of the value chain. The MoIP would also be well positioned to carry out analysis and, based on it, developing a strategy for attracting investment from China, as well as from other relevant countries (for example, India, after the liberalization of its economic relationship with Pakistan).

Building MoIP capacity will also entail developing the ability to identify and induct (on retainer contracts or other appropriate arrangements) professionals at local universities/research institutions/private sector associations. The ministry could bring in such individuals when needed for analytical work, and to serve on specialized task forces. The recent work by a team of Lahore University of Management Sciences economists/business professors is a good example of this approach.

**Table 8.1  Strengthening MoIP Capacity for Sustainable Industrialization**

| Industrial strategy component | Ministry/line agency directly in charge | MoIP capacity needed to fulfill the role |
|---|---|---|
| Reducing macroeconomic and financial risk (including inflation, interest rates, and crowding-out issues) | Ministry of Finance, State Bank of Pakistan | • Technical capacity to present industry's perspectives on issues relating to macroeconomic stability/competitive exchange rate/access to credit<br>• Regular dialogue with the private sector |
| Energy prices and energy availability | Ministry of Water and Power, PEPCO, OGRA | Technical capacity to represent industry's energy needs and pricing issues |
| Non-discriminatory tax policy | Federal Board of Revenue | Capacity to ensure that the burden of taxation (via corporate, income, and sales tax) does not fall only on industry while other sectors escape the tax net |
| Trade policy (including regional trade) and trade facilitation | Ministry of Commerce, Federal Board of Revenue, Ministry of Foreign Affairs | • Capacity to maintain a liberalized trade regime (especially relative to the emerging large economies in the neighborhood) that is not injurious to local industry (appropriate antidumping stance)<br>• Promotion of modern customs procedures that strengthen internationally competitive supply chains |
| Efficient transportation and port handling | Ministry of Communications, Shipping and Ports, provincial governments, Ministry of Railways | Technical capacity to recommend cost-reducing public-private investment and management practices in roads, railways, ports, and shipping |
| Managing industrial waste and environment pollution | Ministry of Climate Change, Pakistan Environmental Protection Agency, and provincial environmental protection departments | Promotion of realistic environment standards and facilitation of adoption of EMS to eventual ISO 14001 certification |

*Note:* EMS = environmental management system, ISO = International Organization for Standardization, MoIP = Ministry of Industries and Production.

The MoIP is well positioned to play a significant role in Pakistan's economic restructuring as well as its approach to environmental management. The MoIP has the opportunity to play a significant role in minimizing the negative external effects of the expected increase in industrialization and urbanization by helping to move forward Pakistan's efforts in industrial environmental management. The MoIP can play this leadership role by engaging in the following activities:

• Use its position on the Pakistan Environmental Protection Council to urge reformulation of Pakistan's national-level environmental strategy
• Promote cleaner production approaches
• Ensure that industries have access to international markets by promoting compliance with internationally recognized product quality and environmental standards (for example, ISO 14001).

In addition to gaining access to international markets, excellence in industrial environmental management will allow Pakistan's firms to establish comparative advantage by promoting corporate social responsibility and high quality environmental management as part of their branding efforts.

In conclusion, the MoIP needs to enhance its capacity (or augment it as needed by collaborating with local/international universities/research centers) to play its vital role as an advocate for industry at both the federal and the provincial levels. The cabinet and—given the Eighteenth Amendment to the Constitution that empowers the provinces—the National Economic Council have to sanction this. A critical capacity is the ability to engage with the private sector to identify the crucial policy agenda (for example, exchange rate policy, credit allocation, energy pricing, tax rates, and tariff structure) to achieve a level playing field for industry and lower the costs of doing business. The capacity to dialogue with the private sector is necessary to prioritize public investment especially in times of fiscal austerity and to leverage public-private partnership in infrastructure provision.

### National Economic Council's Role in Spatial Transformation

Recent developments have made it imperative for MoIP to interact with provincial governments for successful implementation of the spatial dimension of the strategy for sustainable industrialization. Starting in 2004, provincial governments, in partnership with multilateral donors (especially the World Bank), have started to develop provincial visions for economic development. Punjab was the first to prepare its economic report, followed by Khyber Pakhtunkhwa, Sindh, Balochistan, and most recently Gilgit-Baltistan. The economic reports are comprehensive in the way national economic reports are, in terms of visions for poverty reduction, employment and income growth, and sectoral targets. Industrial growth for high productivity employment is an important objective in all of the provincial reports. It is thus important for MoIP to ensure that there is consistency between the provincial and the federal objectives and strategies regarding the spatial dimension of sustainable industrialization.

Another important recent development is the Eighteenth Amendment to the Constitution. Responding to strong demand from the provinces for greater autonomy, the concurrent list has been abolished.[2] At the same time, the seventh National Finance Award has reduced the federal share in the national pool of resources (the reduction will continue over the next several years), thus increasing the provincial share in the aggregate (to enhance equity, the share of relatively poor provinces has been increased more). This has empowered the provinces and they are now expected to take on the primary responsibility for delivering on the development objectives. These developments will further strengthen the demand for a regional balance in infrastructure provision for industry.

The regionally balanced approach to economic development in general is a welcome development in an ethnically plural society such as Pakistan's. However, this has to be weighed against the economies of scale that come from agglomeration of industrial activity in a few industrial clusters. Striking the right balance to prioritize infrastructure investment in times of fiscal tightening is a major challenge and one that the MoIP will need to take up. The right forum for debating these issues and for making decisions is the National Economic Council, chaired by the Prime Minister, with provincial chief ministers as members along with their respective economic teams. MoIP will have to set the agenda on spatial dimensions of sustainable industrialization at the NEC, in close coordination with provincial industries departments. MoIP will need to develop capacity to do this effectively.

## A Coordinated and Cost-Effective Approach to Skills Development

Pakistan's many skills-development initiatives are dispersed and poorly coordinated. The Benazir Income Support Program's Waseela-e-Rozgar program could potentially become the largest skills initiative in the country, but its relationship to other ongoing initiatives in the provinces has not been thought through. Indeed, the potentially rewarding links between Waseela-e-Rozgar and the entrepreneurship/microfinance program Waseela-e-Haq are also not well coordinated. Two useful outcomes of proper coordination will be to explore the complementarities between skills-development programs that are motivated by concerns about social protection and the one imparting skills to strengthen the competitiveness of manufacturing firms.

The design of cost-effective training programs that keep in view the location of available courses requires institutional coordination. Locating skills provision near industrial zones in the urban clusters would make it attractive for firms to move to industrial estates and thus enjoy agglomeration economies.

Funding for skills development has traditionally taken the form of direct allocations to training institutions in the public sector. Many such institutions are considered to be supply driven and not responsive to the skills needs of manufacturing firms. The Punjab government has recently started a skills-development fund that takes a different approach. It funds the trainee rather than the trainer, thereby making skills training more demand driven. It does so by making a market for private training and inviting public-sector training institutions to bid for contracts to teach courses. This innovative approach needs to be scaled up to the national level.

The Government of Pakistan (GoP) has recently set up a steering committee for the "Prime Minister's Youth Skills Development Program" with representation of major stakeholders, including those from the private sector, to propose a comprehensive strategy for a nationwide skills-development program. The areas of coordination it will examine include developing closer links with the Pakistan Business Council, reforming public provision of training, establishing employment exchanges, reforming the apprenticeship system, and improving the regulatory environment for skills training to facilitate private-sector entry. The National Vocational and Technical Training Commission is the apex body that sets standards, develops curricula, and facilitates accreditation and teacher training. Its role in the provincial skills training initiatives in these areas needs strengthening.

### Small and Medium Enterprise Development Authority

The GoP views small and medium enterprises (SMEs) as one of the major drivers of growth in Pakistan (GoP 2007, 8). Many of the SMEs in Pakistan are very small: 87 percent of SMEs in the manufacturing sector employ five or fewer people, and 98 percent of SMEs in this sector have ten or fewer employees (Kureshi et al. 2009, 64). SMEs employ about 80 percent of the non-agricultural labor force, and their share of gross domestic product (GDP) is about 40 percent. They also contribute about Rs 140 billion to exports and produce 25 percent of exported manufactured goods.[3] Given their significance, the Non-Lending Technical Assistance (NLTA) gave special attention to SMEs.

Pakistan's premier institution supporting SMEs is the SMEDA. This organization, which operates under the MoIP, is responsible for formulating and devising policies for SMEs; carrying out support and service activities for SMEs; networking with other federal, provincial, and local government entities to assist SMEs; interacting with SMEs, and evaluating their financial health and development; and garnering resources from public, private, and international bodies for the betterment of SMEs. In brief, SMEDA's mandate is to transform the potential of the SME sector into reality.

This research assessed SMEDA and determined that the SME sector is suffering from many constraints including lack of access to finance, limited access to markets, lack of infrastructure, a hostile business environment, corruption and red tape, weak management, and lack of access to skilled labor.[4] In addition, many government policies are devised from the perspective of large firms and not SMEs. The implementation of SME policies in Pakistan is fragmented and limited; it needs to be more effective in light of the SME sector's importance and contribution.

The study of SMEDA also found that the entire domain of SME policy making and development of SME's support system is becoming very disjointed and jumbled, with duplication of resources and effort, and a lack of coordination, focus, and performance accountability. For example, the MoIP had a clear leadership role in the formulation and approval of the SME policy 2007. However, after the Prime Minister and his cabinet approved the policy, the implementation of the policy was not delegated to SMEDA, and there was no set of clear goals or a business plan for at least the next five years. Adequate fiscal, human, and physical resources for policy implementation have not been set, and the policy is languishing with no implementation mechanism in place (SMEDA 2011).

This research included a survey of SMEs. The survey sample covered SMEs from manufacturing (59 percent), services (33 percent), and agriculture (8 percent). Results highlighted the many constraints on growth of SMEs in Pakistan. SMEs do not have smooth access to finance. There is a lack of proper infrastructure for SMEs to operate with, and there is lack of supply of skilled workers in Pakistan. SMEs face market constraints in the form of lack of vendors, and limited access to foreign and many local markets. SMEDA does not seem to have played its role in helping remove these constraints. Overall, its ratings in these areas have been low.

This research offered a number of recommendations to strengthen SMEs in Pakistan. In addition to restructuring SMEDA, the NLTA analytic work recommended the following actions:

- Setting comprehensive goals and targets for SMEDA's board of directors to achieve over the next five years
- Authorizing and funding SMEDA to create its own new organizational development plan in line with its institutional goals and targets, its proposed activities, and a new organizational structure as proposed by this research
- Implementing the organizational development plan of SMEDA as soon as it is ready through supplementary budgetary provisions, if necessary, and by hiring sector specialists
- The new organizational structure should also enable SMEDA to interact with the government (federal and provincial) in developing a favorable policy environment for SMEs
- Providing the budgetary support that is needed for SMEDA to be an effective body for the SMEs, and to enable it to meet the goals and targets set for it
- Creating an adequate monitoring and evaluation framework that provides SMEDA with reliable and complete data to assess the impact of its programs, as well as a better understanding of SMEs in general and the key challenges they face.

### Environmental Management

The Eighteenth Amendment to Pakistan's Constitution devolved major responsibilities for environmental management to subnational governments, which will have significant implications for environmental quality management. The typical rationale for decentralizing environmental management is as follows. Since environmental problems are typically felt locally, provinces and municipalities are often in a better position to address environmental problems, and thus would achieve superior outcomes if given the freedom to choose the most appropriate policies and instruments. In Pakistan, delegation of environmental functions from the federal government to provincial governments is comprehensive, and it has empowered provincial environmental protection agencies (EPAs) to take care of most of the environmental issues in the provinces. After the delegation of enforcement functions to the provincial governments, the Pakistan's EPA (Pak-EPA) main responsibilities became limited to assisting provincial governments in the formulation of rules and regulations under PEPA, 1997.

Because of decentralization, the sphere of operation of each provincial EPA increased considerably with the Eighteenth Amendment; however, many environmental issues cut across geographical boundaries, and systematized mechanisms for inter-sectoral coordination to tackle cross-cutting issues and harmonize common interventions are necessary for effective decentralization. Without proper coordination, decentralization often leads to substantial differences in environmental quality across regions. Decentralization efforts may fail tremendously without a reasonable level of supervision and monitoring by central governments as well as a without a good level of coordination between agencies. Even when local capacity is strong, the transfer of responsibilities may make the coordination of national policies difficult, particularly in federative systems. Coordination is required between economic and sector ministries, as well as across tiers of government.

On October 26, 2011, the Prime Minister announced the creation of the Ministry of Disaster Management at the federal level, which became the Ministry of Climate Change (MCC) in early 2012. All of the functions relating to environmental management that were under the purview of the Ministry of Environment before the Eighteenth Amendment to the Constitution were put under this new ministry. Excepted from this transfer of functions were the Pakistan Forest Institute and the National Energy Conservation Center. It is expected that the new ministry would start performing its obligations, particularly coordination in international protocols and environmental protection/management across the country. The National Disaster Management Authority (NDMA) has also been placed under the new ministry.

Pakistan might take advantage of international best practices to strengthen the new ministry. Most countries currently have an apex central environmental ministry or agency with a number of technical and action-oriented agencies that designate and implement public policies, and enforce regulations. Even in Canada, a country with strong formal mechanisms for coordination, the underlying cause of good coordination is the existence of an apex agency at the federal level. In Brazil, Mexico, and the United States, local environmental agencies were given substantial freedom to determine the way in which environmental standards are met. However, all these nations retained an apex-level body, located at the federal level, to make national environment policy and manage coordination between states and provinces. These functions are kept as central responsibilities, because failure to do so has been found to be potentially harmful to the environment and inhabitants. Specifically, the responsibilities that the central government usually maintains, regardless of the level of decentralization, include these:

- *Design and enactment of national environmental policies and standards.* This responsibility is maintained by the central government in order to provide constituents throughout the country a degree of consistency of rules and regulations, and because people whose health and livelihoods are affected by environmental policy tend to expect certain norms of environmental management, regardless of region.

- *Trans-boundary issues.* The central government better handles this function, because regional entities lack the resources and credibility to manage such matters effectively. In addition, central-level agencies represent the country at international negotiations, and in international conventions and initiatives, such as the Montreal Protocol and climate change conventions.

- *Coordination of regional agencies.* In the interest of efficiency, collaboration, and sharing of good practices, the central government level usually maintains the role of coordination of efforts among the various regional institutions. This includes monitoring and evaluating environmental programs that affect multiple regions, as well as granting permits for activities that affect the environment in more than one geographic area.

- *Research related to climate change, biodiversity, or water issues, such as glacial melting.* These issues can affect multiple states within a country, as well as multiple countries in a region, so delegation of such research would be ineffective at best.

With the recent reorganization of Pakistan's institutional climate for environmental regulation, Pakistan's environmental management agencies will need considerable technical assistance and capacity building. The newly created MCC is just beginning to explore its responsibilities. Furthermore, provincial EPAs are not currently well staffed and lack the capacity to effectively enforce environmental regulations, as evidenced by the following: The majority of SMEs participating in the survey carried out as part of this NLTA were not even aware of the existence of national environmental quality standards, and many firms had no contact at all with an EPA. In addition, provincial EPAs have limited funding for designing and implementing programs to address environmental priority problems. They also lack the ability to effectively implement existing requirements for environmental impact assessment, especially in the context of large infrastructure projects. Institutional strengthening for the MCC and provincial EPAs should be a near-term priority.

Other possible responsibilities that could be strengthened in Pakistan at the national level include the following:

- *Setting coordination incentives.* Possible coordination incentives with subnational environmental units include giving MCC the ability to co-finance investment projects at the regional level, linked to results agreements. In countries with a decentralized environmental structure, co-financing is often the most important tool national authorities have to ensure national–regional coordination. Conventional control mechanisms would serve to ensure that project funds are well spent. These mechanisms would help to bolster the federal government's ability to monitor environmental performance and could serve to finance environmental work related to cleaner production, or to strengthen the technical capacities of EPAs.

- *Establishing accountability mechanisms.* MCC could put in place a simple but effective accountability mechanism that consists of identifying a simple set of standards to measure the fulfillment of basic environmental rights, such as the right to clean air and water. Using simple language, the help of civil society organizations, and making use of national and local media, there could be broad dissemination of these standards among the population. Every year, report cards measuring the degree of fulfillment of those standards in each region or province could be produced. Furthermore, annual town hall meetings could take place to discuss the ability to comply with authorities and civil society, and to jointly find remedies and solutions.

- *Promoting public disclosure.* It is critical to have a more systematic effort for enhancing awareness of environmental issues linked to industrial activity. The publication of data in support of key environmental indicators (including health statistics or pollution load discharge in industrial clusters), and wider use of public forums for cleaner water initiatives, are ways to improve public information, and to promote transparency, accountability, and awareness. In China, Colombia, and Indonesia, among other countries, the publication of key environmental performance indicators has been critical in raising environmental awareness and placing environmental issues on the national agenda. Mechanisms to disseminate information in a manner that is easily interpretable can allow communities to play a role as informal regulators. Such mechanisms also promote accountability on the part of industries being regulated (World Bank 2005).

- *Strengthening the demand side of accountability.* Pakistan has active civil society organizations, which play important roles in implementing projects, delivering services to poor sectors of the population, and participating in policy debates. However, the capacity of civil society to participate in monitoring policy implementation and holding environmental institutions accountable is limited. International experience indicates that civil society can play an important role when citizens' organizations demand accountability from public institutions. The proposed apex environmental agency could support the development of the technical capacity of civil society organizations to promote social accountability initiatives. These organizations could independently implement these initiatives, or implement them in association with environmental agencies or with horizontal accountability institutions.

- *Reduction of vulnerability to natural disasters.* Natural disasters pose a substantial risk to transport infrastructure as well to industries; for example, earthquakes, mudslides, and flooding have the potential to cut vital rail and road links. Conversely, proper transport infrastructure is vital to disaster-relief efforts. Due to the significant impact of natural disasters on Pakistan, the government might task the new minister with policy design and implementation of nonstructural measures to reduce vulnerability to natural disasters. Creation of an office for reduction of vulnerability to natural disasters could be carried out in the short term.

A new environment unit within the Ministry of Industries and Production can play critically important leadership and coordination roles. The MoIP could seize the opportunity to take a leadership role in developing a national strategy for the diffusion of cleaner production (CP) and EMS, and for the certification of firms by ISO 14001 and other international standards. An early task for this unit is to organize a CP working group. This group would consist of representatives from EPAs, industry associations, each cleaner production center (CPC), and international aid institutions that have provided long-term support to the CPCs. The group tasks would be to create (a) a national plan for disseminating information to firms on CP, EMS, and certification to ISO 14001; and (b) an overall strategy for seeking financing to support construction of combined effluent treatment plants in industrial clusters.

Currently, the provincial EPAs suffer from (a) limited technical capacity and funding for conducting analytical work and priority setting, (b) limited funding for designing and implementing programs to address environmental priority problems, and (c) environmental impact assessment systems that are too weak to fully address potential negative environmental impacts resulting from economic growth. Pakistan's environmental management agencies need significant strengthening. Unless careful attention is given to environmental management during industrial expansion, massive environmental and social costs—in the form of human morbidity and mortality, and environmental damage from increased industrial pollution—will accompany economic gains. Few, if any, provincial environment agencies are capable of enforcing the nation's environmental regulations within the borders of their provinces. Technical capabilities are limited within key environmental agencies, including provincial EPAs. None of them has the capability to handle cross-boundary issues (which include air and water pollution, and the handling of solid waste). The 2011 Framework for Economic Growth acknowledges the role of industry in becoming a dynamic engine of economic growth and making significant contributions to meeting Pakistan's economic and human development goals. Therefore, it is imperative that institutional strengthening be undertaken to better equip agencies (at the provincial and national levels) to handle environmental issues stemming from industrial activities in the country.

In conclusion, while Pakistan has in place an institutional framework for addressing environment issues, the impact on the ground is limited. This is because of insufficient capacity in terms of skilled personnel at both federal and provincial levels, unrealistically stiff environmental standards, and inconsistencies in legislation that put provincial governments at odds with the federal government. All of these factors contribute to poor enforcement and unimpressive progress towards environmental management systems certification that is critical for environmentally sound and internationally competitive industrialization.

## Notes

1. The importance of institutions is also underscored by the recent Turkish success in diversifying its manufacturing exports by products and destination and increasing their share in GDP.

2. The concurrent list allowed both the provincial and federal governments to have development programs in the provinces; the provinces have considered the concurrent list to be the main instrument for loss of provincial autonomy to the federal government.

3. www.sbp.org.pk/bpd/Conference/Day_One/SME_in_Pakistan.ppt. Accessed May 6, 2010.

4. S. Shah carried out the analytic work on SMEs; see SMEDA (2011).

## References

Afzal, S. 2007. "Pak-US Standards and Conformity Assessment Workshop Proceedings." May 24–25, Lahore, Pakistan. http://publicaa.ansi.org/sites/apdl/Documents /Standards%20Activities/International%20Standardization/Regional/Europe -Middle%20East-Africa/Middle%20East/2008-06%20Pakistan%20Workshop%20 %28NIST%29/2007%20US-Pak%20SC%20workshop%20proceedings.pdf.

Anderson, S. W., J. D. Daly, and M. F. Johnson. 1999. "Why Firms Seek ISO 9000 Certification: Regulatory Compliance or Competitive Advantage?" *Production and Operations Management* 8 (1): 28–43.

Auerswald, P. E., and A. Malik. 2011. *Review of (LUMS) Industrial Policy: Its Spatial Aspects and Cluster Development.* Consultant report, Washington, DC: World Bank.

European Union. 2006. REACH Regulations. Brussels, Belgium.

Fujita, M., and J. F. Thisse. 2002. *Economics of Agglomeration: Cities, Industrial Location, and Regional Growth.* Cambridge, UK: Cambridge University Press.

GoP (Government of Pakistan). 2007. "National Trucking Policy." National Trade Corridor Improvement Programme, Islamabad. http://www.ntcip.gov.pk/.

Henningsson, S., R. M. Pratt, P. S. Phillips, and K. Hyde. 2001. "Waste Minimisation Clubs: a Cost-Efficient Policy Instrument?" *European Environment* 11: 324–39.

Hey, D. L., and W. H. Waggy. 1979. "Planning for Water Quality: 1776 to 1976." *Journal of the Water Resources Planning and Management Division* 105 (1): 121–31.

Kureshi, N. I., R. Mann, M. R. Khan, and M. F. Qureshi. 2009. "Quality Management Practices of SME in Developing Countries: A Survey of Manufacturing SME in Pakistan." *Journal of Quality and Technology Management* 5 (I1): 63–89.

Luken, R. A. 2009. "Equivocating on the Polluter-Pays Principle: The Consequences for Pakistan." *Journal of Environmental Management* 90 (11): 3279–484. http://www .sciencedirect.com/science/article/pii/S0301479709001996.

LUMS (Lahore University of Management Sciences). 2011. A. A. Burki, K. A. Munir, M. A. Khan, M. U. Khan, A. Faheem, A. Khalid, and S. T. Hussain. *Industrial Policy, Its Spatial Aspects and Cluster Development in Pakistan.* Consultant report by the Lahore University of Management Sciences for the World Bank. Lahore, Pakistan.

Riffat, R., and D. Khan. 2006. "A Review and Evaluation of the Environmental Impact Assessment Process in Pakistan." *Journal of Applied Sciences in Environmental Sanitation* 1: 17–29.

Rodrik, D. 1994. "Getting Interventions Right: How South Korea and Taiwan Grew Rich." NBER Working Papers 4964, National Bureau of Economic Research, Inc. Subsequently published as Rodrik, Dani. 1995. "Getting Intervention Right: How Korea and Taiwan Grew Rich." *Economic Policy* 10 (20): 53–107.

———. 2004. "Industrial Policy in the 21st Century." CEPR (Center for Economic Policy Research) Discussion Paper 4767, CEPR, Harvard University, Cambridge, MA. http://www.hks.harvard.edu/fs/drodrik/Research%20papers/UNIDOSep.pdf.

———. 2008. *One Economics, Many Recipes: Globalization, Institutions, and Economic Growth*. Princeton NJ: Princeton, University Press.

SMEDA (Small and Medium Enterprise Development Authority). 2011. *Independent Organizational Evaluation of Small and Medium Enterprise Development*, by S. Shah. Draft Report, Lahore, Pakistan.

World Bank. 2005. World Development Indicators (database). World Bank, Washington, DC. http://data.worldbank.org/data-catalog/world-development-indicators.

———. 2009. *World Development Report 2009: Reshaping Economic Geography*. Washington, DC: World Bank. http://www-wds.worldbank.org/external/default /WDSContentServer/IW3P/IB/2008/12/03/000333038_20081203234958 /Rendered/PDF/437380REVISED01BLIC1097808213760720.pdf.

## Environmental Benefits Statement

The World Bank Group is committed to reducing its environmental footprint. In support of this commitment, the Publishing and Knowledge Division leverages electronic publishing options and print-on-demand technology, which is located in regional hubs worldwide. Together, these initiatives enable print runs to be lowered and shipping distances decreased, resulting in reduced paper consumption, chemical use, greenhouse gas emissions, and waste.

The Publishing and Knowledge Division follows the recommended standards for paper use set by the Green Press Initiative. Whenever possible, books are printed on 50 percent to 100 percent postconsumer recycled paper, and at least 50 percent of the fiber in our book paper is either unbleached or bleached using Totally Chlorine Free (TCF), Processed Chlorine Free (PCF), or Enhanced Elemental Chlorine Free (EECF) processes.

More information about the Bank's environmental philosophy can be found at http://crinfo.worldbank.org/wbcrinfo/node/4.

green
press
INITIATIVE

www.ingramcontent.com/pod-product-compliance
Lightning Source LLC
Chambersburg PA
CBHW080547220326
41599CB00032B/6390